ORGANIZING FOR NATIONAL SECURITY

Edited by

Douglas T. Stuart

November 2000

*****

The views expressed in this report are those of the authors and do not necessarily reflect the official policy or position of the Department of the Army, the Department of Defense, or the U.S. Government. This report is cleared for public release; distribution is unlimited.

*****

Comments pertaining to this report are invited and should be forwarded to: Director, Strategic Studies Institute, U.S. Army War College, 122 Forbes Ave., Carlisle, PA 17013-5244. Copies of this report may be obtained from the Publications and Production Office by calling commercial (717) 245-4133, FAX (717) 245-3820, or via the Internet at rummelr@awc.carlisle.army.mil

*****

Most 1993, 1994, and all later Strategic Studies Institute (SSI) monographs are available on the SSI Homepage for electronic dissemination. SSI's Homepage address is: http://carlisle-www.army. mil/usassi/welcome.htm

*****

The Strategic Studies Institute publishes a monthly e-mail newsletter to update the national security community on the research of our analysts, recent and forthcoming publications, and upcoming conferences sponsored by the Institute. Each newsletter also provides a strategic commentary by one of our research analysts. If you are interested in receiving this newsletter, please let us know by e-mail at outreach@awc.carlisle.army.mil or by calling (717) 245-3133.

ISBN 1-58487-039-7

CONTENTS

FOREWORD

The pace and scope of change over the last decade have indeed been extraordinary. The United States has been confronted with not just the collapse of the Soviet empire but also with revolutionary scientific breakthroughs, the transformation of the global economy, and the erosion of many of the basic premises of the Westphalian system of international order. The U.S. policy community has attempted to make sense of these and other changes by recourse to bodies such as the National Defense Panel and the U.S. Commission on National Security/21st Century (USNCS/21). The USNCS/21 is currently in the third phase of its mandated activities. At the end of phase three, the members of the Commission will recommend changes in the institutions of the U.S. national security policymaking system. Its conclusions are likely to stimulate a lively, and much needed, debate.

The U.S. Army War College chose the theme of "Organizing for National Security" for its Tenth Annual Strategy Conference in order to contribute to the upcoming debate about institutional reform. This volume provides a summary of the proceedings of that conference. It includes historical, analytical, and prescriptive articles relating to the national security bureaucracy. Virtually all of the authors accept that some degree of reform is necessary for a system which can trace its roots back to the 1947 National Security Act. Not surprisingly, they differ in their opinions about which parts of the system are most in need of repair, and in their specific recommendations. Several contributors applaud the trend toward jointness in the armed services and recommend that this serve as a model for future reforms of the institutions responsible for national security policymaking.

In order for institutional reform to succeed, it will have to be guided by a coherent and compelling national strategy which must, in turn, be anchored in widely-accepted national interests. It will also have to be in accord with such constitutional principles as civilian control of the armed forces and the inviolability of the civil liberties of all Americans. This is a tall order for U.S. policymakers. Hopefully, the chapters in this volume will offer some useful insights and some encouragement.

DOUGLAS C. LOVELACE, JR.
Director
Strategic Studies Institute

CHAPTER 1

INTRODUCTION

Douglas T. Stuart

The weekend of July 25-27, 1947, was an especially hectic and stressful period for the Washington policy community. Congress was rushing to wrap up its end-of-term business before adjourning for the summer. The budget was the most contentious issue, since the Republican majority was still looking for ways to make good on its promise to cut 15 percent from the $37.5 billion that President Harry S. Truman had requested in January. These deliberations were complicated by the fact that the President had also asked Congress for supplemental funding for aid to Greece and Turkey. Legislation also had to be passed in order to terminate 175 war powers which the President still had at his disposal from World War II.

One important piece of legislation was easily dispensed with during this weekend. The so-called "unification bill," which had already been passed by the Senate, was approved in the House by a voice vote on the afternoon of July 25. Few commentators referred to the legislation by its official name—The National Security Act (NSA). The ease with which the legislation was passed belied the long process of congressional hearings and the intense struggles which preceded the final vote. The finished product was a patchwork of compromises which raised many more questions than they resolved. Commentators wondered, for example, how a new "super" Secretary of Defense, with the help of three assistants, would be able to exercise control over the military services which were theoretically under his authority. Some commentators asked how "jointness" could be achieved by the Joint Chiefs of Staff (JCS), without a strong Chairman to control their deliberations. The future of the National Security Council (NSC) was very uncertain, since President Truman viewed it as a "second"—and unnecessary—cabinet. Nor was it clear whether the new Central Intelligence Agency (CIA) would be asked to do more than simply assist the NSC in the coordination and evaluation of intelligence information provided by the separate branches of government.

Many of these questions were answered by the late 1950s. The Office of the Secretary of Defense had been expanded and given greater authority as the Department of Defense. The Joint Chiefs had acquired a Chairman, although his powers were still circumscribed. The CIA had evolved from being a support agency for the NSC into an independent and influential component of the national security system. Finally, the NSC had become established at the "top of policy hill."[1]

The national security bureaucracy which exists today differs in important respects from the system which was in place by the late 1950s. However, what is most striking about the existing system is not how much has changed, but how little. The Clinton administration came into office committed to fundamental reform of the national security bureaucracy, and some interesting changes have taken place since that time. But these changes are better understood as exercises in gardening rather than architecture.

Over the last decade many experts and political leaders have asserted that there is a self-evident need for structural reform in the national security bureaucracy, in light of the dramatic changes which have taken place since the collapse of the Soviet empire. During the spring of 1999, the U.S. Army War College selected this issue as the central focus of its Tenth Annual Strategy Conference. Entitled *Organizing for National Security in the New Century*, the conference provided an opportunity for policy analysts, government representatives, and academic experts to discuss the strengths and weaknesses of the existing arrangements for national security policy making and to propose some reforms. The organizers were careful to anchor these discussions in presentations on the institutional history of the national security bureaucracy.

The articles in this volume are based on the proceedings of the Tenth Annual Strategy Conference. This publication would not have been possible without the expert assistance and guidance of several people, including Colonel Joseph Cerami, Ms. Marianne Cowling, Ms. Victoria Kuhn, Professor Douglas Lovelace, Jr., Ms. Rita Rummel, and Dr. Earl Tilford. Special thanks must be reserved for Dr. Steven Metz, who played an indispensable role in the design of the conference and in the conceptualization of this book.

This volume will be published shortly before the election of a new U.S. president. The next president will enter the White House at a time when the United States is enjoying unprecedented power and influence throughout the world, and at a time when no nation in the world poses a direct military threat to America's survival. The new administration would be well advised to take advantage of this fortuitous situation to address fundamental problems in our national security bureaucracy. Hopefully, this book will provide some valuable guidance about what works and what does not work in the existing system.

ENDNOTES – CHAPTER 1

1. Anna Kasten Nelson, "The 'Top of Policy Hill': President Eisenhower and the National Security Council," *Diplomatic History*, No. 7, Fall 1983, pp. 307-26.

3

CHAPTER 2

PRESENT AT THE LEGISLATION:
THE 1947 NATIONAL SECURITY ACT

Douglas T. Stuart

At a time when the two most commonly asked questions about U.S. foreign policy are "Where are we going?" and "Why are we doing this?," it is only natural that people are tempted to look back nostalgically to those periods in American history when foreign policymaking shared many characteristics with the field of architecture. I have been given the enviable task of looking back to one such period, when individuals like Harry Truman, George Marshall, and James Forrestal wrestled with each other over big issues of principle and policy. This article will focus on one of the most intense debates of this period, which culminated in the passage of the 1947 National Security Act (NSA). The NSA is certainly one of the most important pieces of legislation of the 20th century. It established the post-war National Military Establishment, composed of the Departments of the Army, Navy, and (a newly created) Air Force, all under the authority of a Secretary of Defense with cabinet rank. The legislation also provided a legal identity for the Joint Chiefs of Staff and created the Central Intelligence Agency, the National Security Council, the National Security Resources Board, the Munitions Board, and the Research and Development Board.

The fact that the NSA has not received the kind of scholarly attention that it deserves is partly attributable to the inclination of most commentators to treat it as a footnote in the history of the formative period of the Cold War. When it is placed in this context, the story of the NSA tends to be overshadowed by the dramatic events of that period. This article begins from the premise that this is a misreading of

5

the history of the NSA. In fact, the 1947 Act cannot be understood unless one goes back to debates and decisions which took place during the late 1930s and early 1940s. It is of more than historical significance that these debates and decisions were both logically and chronologically prior to post-war discussions about the nature and implications of the Soviet threat. Because once it is made clear that the national security state has roots which run much deeper than the early Cold War era, we have a basis for understanding why there has been so little structural change in the national security system since the collapse of the Soviet Union.

One useful date for beginning this story is July 1937, when, in the wake of the Japanese invasion of China, President Franklin D. Roosevelt seems to have made the decision to move the nation away from a posture of "well ordered neutrality" and toward military preparedness. Over the next 4 years, the President managed a cautious campaign of half-steps, which were designed to give the United States a running start in the event that war was unavoidable.

Aside from the specific concerns that Roosevelt had about what the Japanese and Germans were saying and doing in Asia and Europe, respectively, the President was preoccupied with two broader and deeper trends in world affairs. First, as a student of geopolitics, he was increasingly concerned about the rapidly improving technologies of air power, which seemed to be on the verge of ending forever America's historic situation of relative invulnerability. Billy Mitchell had been making this argument forcefully and effectively since the early 1930s:

> What will the future hold for us? Undoubtedly an attack on the great centers of population. If a European country attacks the United States, New York, Chicago, Detroit, Pittsburgh, and Washington, D.C. will be the first targets.[1]

The President demonstrated his sensitivity to such arguments in an address to Congress on May 16, 1940, in which he noted that although the Atlantic and Pacific Oceans had served as "reasonably adequate defensive barriers" in the past, they could no longer be relied upon to protect the nation. Military preparedness, which could only be achieved by increased defense spending, had to take the place of geographic isolation as the basis for American national security.

FDR's second fundamental concern in the late 1930s had to do with the global spread of totalitarian governments. Since coming to office in the midst of the depression, Roosevelt had watched as dictatorial regimes spread across the globe. Many American commentators celebrated the dynamism and efficiencies of these authoritarian systems, while describing the U.S. system pejoratively as a "mature economy." Roosevelt and his colleagues were also acutely aware of the natural advantages that dictatorships enjoyed in foreign affairs, and in their ability to shift their nation's economies into a warfighting mode at very short notice. As early as January 1933, Roosevelt was advised by Walter Lippmann that "The situation is critical, Franklin. You may have no alternative but to assume dictatorial power."[2]

The President was too much of an optimist, too confident of his own skills as a leader, and too convinced of the inherent strengths of American democracy to entertain the notion that dictatorship was the wave of the future in the United States. He was also encouraged by the fact that America had at its disposal a community of experts who represented a relatively new field of study called public administration, which promised to employ theories of management science to create efficiencies in both the private and public sectors which would make the United States competitive with the dictatorships of the world without doing violence to our constitutional system.

As the war approached, one particular book seemed to capture both the challenges of the modern world and the potential for management science to make the United States competitive and secure. The book was *The Impact of War*, published in 1941 by E. Pendleton Herring, a Professor in Harvard's Government department who was also associated with Harvard's new Graduate School of Public Administration. It was one of the first books to use the term "national security," and it was certainly the most authoritative pre-war attempt to describe what a national security bureaucracy should look like. Herring argued that our history had not prepared us for the challenges of the modern world because it had encouraged Americans to hold a "persistent suspicion of militarism." He called for a new approach to foreign policymaking, which would include a permanent and influential place for military advisers at the top levels of government in times of both war and peace. He also recommended that the United States take advantage of new technologies of communication and transportation to enhance "centralization, standardization and regimentation" in ways that would transform our government from a "negative state" to a "positive state." Herring was confident that a more cooperative relationship could also be established between the White House and Congress, because "the pressure of circumstances closes the separation of powers." He claimed that radical reform of the foreign policymaking system was necessary because of the threats that the United States was facing in 1941. But he also stressed that the changes that he was proposing would be necessary for our country in a period of peace as well, because they would undergird a dynamic and influential foreign policy. "The Roman Phalanx," Herring reminded his readers, "was a necessary preliminary to the Pax Romana."[3]

Professor Herring's book was well received by the policy community. Reviewing the book for *The Herald Tribune*, Louis Hacker noted that:

> If Pendleton Herring's book is a sign of the times, we are at last in the process of confronting our national problems realistically. It should be said at once that it is one of the most significant analyses produced by the current emergency.[4]

Two months after Hacker reviewed *the Impact of War*, Professor Herring's thesis was overwhelmingly accepted by the American people—as a result of the attack on Pearl Harbor. The importance of Pearl Harbor is hard to exaggerate in any study of American national security. After December 7, 1941, the American people favored a new approach to foreign policymaking which gave a privileged status to the military while also creating new procedures for civilian-military collaboration.

The experiences of World War II tended to confirm both the lessons of Pearl Harbor and the wisdom of Herring's thesis. During the war there was some interesting discussion about what a post-war foreign policy system should look like, but the more important contribution of the war was the precedents that were set by the establishment of such entities as the Joint Chiefs, the Office of Strategic Services (OSS) and the State-War-Navy-Coordinating Committee (SWNCC). As a consultant to the War Department, the Navy Department and the Bureau of the Budget, Herring was one of a handful of experts who studied closely the functioning of these and other federal agencies during the war. He also chaired the Committee of Records of War Administration which published in 1946 the official administrative history of the war effort.[5]

One of the principal architects of the wartime decisionmaking apparatus was also one of the people with the strongest opinions about the need for specific post-war reforms. George Marshall's experience as Army Chief of Staff during World War II confirmed his pre-war views on the need for a complete unification of the armed services. When he attempted to raise this issue with Roosevelt and others during the war, he was routinely rebuffed on the grounds that a substantive discussion of this option while the country was at war might undermine the war effort. Marshall was not alone in arguing for the unification of the armed forces, however. One influential ally was Senator Harry Truman, who published an article in the August 26, 1944, issue of *Collier's* magazine entitled "Our Armed

9

Forces Must Be Unified." Truman concluded the article with the statement that:

> The road, as I see it, stretches straight and with no turns . . . The end, of course, must be the integration of every element of America's defense in one department under one authoritative, responsible head. Call it the War Department or the Department of National Security or what you will, just so it is one department . . . One team with all the reins in one hand . . . Under such a set-up another Pearl Harbor will not have to be feared.[6]

Truman attributed his convictions about the need for unification to his own experiences in the military during World War I, to the lessons he had learned as a member of the Senate Appropriations and Military Affairs Committees, to his chairmanship of the Special Committee to Investigate the National Defense Program and, above all, to the "Record of the Pearl Harbor Hearings."[7]

During the war, FDR's opposition made it hard for Marshall to cooperate publicly with allies like Truman, so the General had to content himself with efforts to put the need for unification on record within the military. He did so by highlighting the findings of the Joint Strategic Survey Committee (JSSC) Report (March 1944) and the Richardson Committee Report (April 1945). Both studies came out in favor of the principle of unification. Marshall had great difficulty in building upon such general statements, however. In a memo dated April 17, 1944, to Fleet Admiral Ernest King, Marshall pressed the argument that since the JSSC study had recommended that the Joint Chiefs "approve for purposes of study the principle of three services within one military organization . . ." the leadership of the War and Navy Departments should begin discussions aimed at developing plans for a "sound organization at the top . . ." to administer the new system. He also warned that Congress was beginning to look into the issue of unification, and that "If we cannot solve the question, it is going to be solved for us and probably in a manner that neither the War nor the Navy Departments would desire."[8] Marshall's pressure tactics backfired, however, because they put the Navy leadership on the defensive and convinced them to close ranks with their allies in Congress to resist unification.

It is worth noting that prior to World War II, the services spoke with one voice in their opposition to unification. This was due not only to the fact that both services wanted to preserve their independence but also to the fact that Congress was primarily interested in unification as a pretext for making deep cuts in the defense budget. A statement in 1932 by Army Chief of Staff Douglas MacArthur in opposition to one such legislative proposal is typical of the common position taken by the Army and Navy during this period;

> . . . I give it as my fixed opinion that such an amalgamation as proposed would endanger victory for the United States in case of war. . . . Pass this bill and every potential enemy of the United States will rejoice.[9]

By the second year of the war, however, most Army spokesmen agreed with Secretary of War Henry Stimson that in an age of "triphibious warfare" the services could no longer afford to think or act in isolation from each other. The Army's new position was summarized in a report to General Marshall by Brigadier General William F. Tompkins, Director of the Special Planning Division of the War Department in October 1943:

> . . . This war is, and future wars undoubtedly will be, largely a series of combined operations in each of which ground, air, and sea forces must be employed together and coordinated under one directing head . . . .[10]

Marshall and some of his colleagues in the War Department were also very sensitive to the risk that, if unification was not accomplished, it would be the Army which would take the most serious hits from budget cutters when the war ended.

While the experience of Pearl Harbor and the first stages of the war convinced the Army leadership that unity of command had to be established at the top, the Navy, with its tradition of self-reliant solutions to challenges from not just the sea, but the land and air as well, claimed that it had already solved the problem of unity of command—within its own service. This argument is best illustrated by the comments of Assistant Secretary of the Navy, Artemus Gates, during the 1944 Unification Hearings by the House Select Committee on Post-War Military Policy (Woodrum Committee). Gates argued that if "consolidation" was necessary, the government should consider "merging the whole military establishment into the existing Navy" since it already had an integrated force with sea, land, and air components.[11]

The mix of principled and particularist interests which made the debate over unification so difficult and intense also complicated post-war discussions about the reform, preservation, or elimination of other entities which had been established during the war. For example, most people believed that some type of intelligence service was going to be necessary after the war. But all of the major institutional players also understood that control of information would be an enormous source of post-war power and influence, and every agency wanted a piece of the action. The Truman administration at first attempted to resolve the inevitable turf war by coordination schemes—most notably the creation of the National Intelligence Authority (NIA) and the Central Intelligence Group (CIG).[12] In his memoirs, Dean Acheson speaks with disdain of all such formulas for coordination, noting that "A good many of us had cut our teeth and throats on this sort of nonsense."[13] In this instance, at least, Acheson's suspicions concerning inter-agency coordination proved well founded, and Truman had to accept that some form of independent entity would have to be created to centralize intelligence. Unfortunately, William Donovan and his colleagues in the OSS had made so many enemies in Washington during the war that the creation of a successor organization was extremely controversial.

The Washington policy community also recognized that after the war the government would need a new system for consultation between the civilian and military departments involved in foreign and security affairs. Here the model was the aforementioned SWNCC, even though the wartime record of this organization was quite limited.[14] Policymakers also studied British institutions and procedures for civilian-military consultation in times of war and peace. The British Committee on Imperial Defence was of special interest as a model for civil-military cooperation. It was left to Truman and his advisors, however, to decide how much power such an entity should be given, and who, or what agency, should lead it.

The Truman administration also needed to develop the institutional machinery to harness the power of science and technology in the post-war era. The Office of Scientific Research and Development(OSRD), under the dynamic leadership of Vannevar Bush, had evolved during World War II into a very influential institution, with its own budget, direct access to the President and key congressmen, and with close positive ties to the leadership of the War and Navy Departments. Encouraged by the success of the OSRD during the war, Senator Harley Kilgore and others pressed for the creation of a strong post-war agency to direct all aspects of scientific research and development. They were challenged, however, by spokesmen for various interest groups—scientists, businessmen, military leaders—who were concerned about preserving their autonomy and their access to scientific innovations.[15]

Finally, Truman and his advisers had to decide how much control the government should attempt to acquire over the post-war economy. In this regard, the lessons of World War II were a matter of dispute. Depending upon how generous one wanted to be, Roosevelt's management of the wartime economy could be described as multidirectional or directionless. One insider, who clearly leaned toward the latter interpretation, described the President's efforts as "bitched, botched, and buggered from start to finish."[16] But most people looked at America's wartime experience and concurred with the judgment of the Bureau of the Budget's post-war report on *The United States At War*: "The record is one in which the American people can take pride." Most Americans also agreed with the principal conclusion of the Bureau's study:

> The speed with which the democracies did accept the challenge and the manner in which they overwhelmed those who sought gain through war suggests that there is no need to reexamine the claims to administrative superiority of authoritarian governments.[17]

America had won the war by "resisting even the semblance of autocratic rule," by **working with** big business and by encouraging the natural competitive advantages of a democratic capitalist system. Based on these lessons, most Americans were reticent to give Washington too much control over the post-war economy.

All of these issues began to converge on President Truman in the summer of 1945, as both Congress and the media became more involved in the debates over the creation of post-war institutions. By this time, many individuals in the Navy leadership had concluded that they had already lost the battle over armed forces unification, and that the services would be combined in accordance with Marshall's and Truman's wishes. A key problem for the Navy in the management of its campaign against unification was that it did not seem to stand for anything other than resistance to innovation. This problem was solved, however, when Navy Secretary Forrestal asked his old friend Ferdinand Eberstadt to undertake a study of the whole unification issue. Eberstadt had served as Director of the Army Navy Munitions Board during the war. The experience had left him with a deep disdain for both FDR ("an apostle of confusion") and Truman.[18] On the other hand, Eberstadt had gained an appreciation of the military services, and of their ability to cooperate to accomplish common goals. Eberstadt made it clear to his staff at the outset that it was important that they retain their independence and not be perceived as merely a propaganda arm of the Navy Department. In fact, however, the Eberstadt report was a Navy product, commissioned by the Navy and staffed almost entirely by Naval officers, and Eberstadt himself was, as Forrestal had assured Admiral King, "a member of the Navy team."[19]

To put the matter simply, Eberstadt felt that the record of interservice coordination during the war was commendable, and that the wartime experience did not demonstrate the need for full unification. He also worried about the establishment of any "General Staff" arrangement, or the creation of a powerful Chief of Staff in peacetime, as potential threats to the tradition of civilian control of the military.

But Eberstadt was not brought in to be just another opponent of unification. The final report that Eberstadt presented to Forrestal in September of 1945 argued that the issue of armed forces unification was just a small part of a necessarily larger debate about post-war policy coordination. New arrangements needed to be put in place in order to facilitate civilian-military cooperation on issues of foreign policy, defense, science, and economic planning. New machinery to coordinate intelligence gathering and analysis was required. Above all, a new attitude had to be nurtured in Washington—informed by the logic of national security. If much of Eberstadt's report sounded like Herring's arguments in 1941, part of the reason was that Herring served as one of Eberstadt's primary assistants in the drafting of the report.[20]

The Navy did not like every conclusion in the Eberstadt report. In particular, they bristled at the study's support for the establishment of a separate Air Force. Eberstadt's report nonetheless gave the Navy the ammunition that it needed to recruit both public and congressional support for a system of coordinated agencies for foreign and defense policymaking as an alternative to the unification of the armed services. When the National Security Act was finally signed into law nearly 2 years later (on July 26, 1947), it bore a striking resemblance to the recommendations which were put forth by Eberstadt and his team. Rather than a single, unified military force, the legislation established a National Military Establishment (NME), with three independent services. The Navy failed to block the creation of a separate Air Force, but obtained statutory protections for land-based Naval Air and for the Marine Corps. The Joint Chiefs of Staff was transformed from a temporary wartime arrangement to a permanent component of the NME, but the Chiefs were expected to work through (and under) the newly created Office of the Secretary of Defense. The Joint Chiefs were given their own staff, of not more than 100 people, but the bill did not allow for the creation of a JCS chairman, who might have been able to bolster the negotiating position of the Chiefs in their dealings with the Secretary of Defense over issues that had the support of all three services.

The new Secretary of Defense, meanwhile, was nothing like the "super" cabinet member that some journalists described at the time. In fact, Eberstadt testified on the last day of the Senate hearings on the National Security Act that the powers delegated to the Secretary of Defense were "disturbingly general and indefinite." He noted that the proposed legislation authorized the Secretary to "administer" the entire NME, but did not give him the requisite authority to accomplish this task. He also worried that the proposed bill lacked a "definite mechanism for fostering unity and teamwork among the military services through appropriate programs of joint education and training at various stages."[21]

The NME looked nothing like the ambitious plans for armed forces unification espoused by Truman, Marshall and most of the Army leadership. Kenneth Royall, the

16

incoming Secretary of the Army, complained that the new arrangement ." . .will not save money, will not be efficient, and will not prevent interservice rivalry."[22] Supporters of the Navy, who could afford to be magnanimous in victory, offered reassuring statements about the proven ability of the services to work together in defense of the national interest. But the Navy also moved quickly to prepare for the possibility that the National Security Act was just one battle in a long war over unification. Shortly after the passage of the legislation, the office of the Chief of Naval Operations created OP 23, a study group whose mandate was to keep the Navy leadership informed of all developments relating to the issue of unification, and prepare for a new round of attacks by the Army. According to Admiral Arleigh Burke, who took over direction of OP 23 in 1948, "It was a jolt to senior naval officials" when the Army began to make a new case for unification shortly after the passage of the National Security Act.[23] It was left to the first Secretary of Defense to referee the continuing dispute between the Navy and the Army, and to help the two traditional services to make room for a very ambitious and assertive Air Force.

The NME was not the only portion of the new national security bureaucracy to be subjected to severe challenges during the period immediately following the passage of the legislation. Other institutions created by the 1947 Act were also tested, and some did not survive the shake-out. The National Security Resources Board was the most significant failure. The framers of the 1947 Act established the NSRB to insure rapid, comprehensive, and efficient mobilization of the nation's resources in the event of a new threat to national security. Eberstadt believed that, in accordance with his recommendations,

> The Statute [NSA] created no more important agency than the National Security Resources Board. It has been placed on the same level as the National Security Council and the Military Establishment—directly under and responsible to the President himself.

He described the NSRB as "a kind of economic and social general staff" which should wield during peacetime whatever powers were necessary to adequately prepare for a national emergency.[24] As previously mentioned, however, Americans came out of the war with a new confidence in unfettered capitalism and a new suspicion of government efforts to regulate the economy. And no one was more suspicious of "general staffs" with open-ended mandates than Truman. Over the next few years, the President resisted the efforts by Arthur Hill, the abrasive Chairman of the NSRB, to exploit the growing national concern about the Soviet threat to expand the influence of his agency. During the Korean War, the President used the situation of limited national emergency to shift many of the responsibilities of the NSRB to a new Office of Defense Mobilization. The NSRB was finally abolished by the Reorganization Act of 1953, and much of the responsibility for mobilization planning devolved to the separate military services.

Truman was able to draw upon the support of the Service Secretaries in his campaign to contain the NSRB because the armed forces feared any new institutional constraints on their budgeting and contracting activities. The armed services also resisted efforts to transform the Research and Development Board (RDB), which was established by the 1947 Act under the Office of the Secretary of Defense, into a regulatory agency with direct control over their laboratories and contracting activities. Vannevar Bush accepted the position of Director of the new science agency because he believed that the office could provide him with the same kind of power and influence that he had exercised during the war. This was a naive assumption, since by the time that Bush took over at RDB, the armed services had established themselves as independent (and indispensable) sponsors of basic research at the major laboratories and universities across the country. Pascal Zachary describes Bush's efforts to use the RDB to reign in the military services as "a slow-motion automobile wreck."[25]

While agencies like the NSRB and the RDB did not survive the shakeout period, other creations of the 1947 Act survived challenges during their formative years and then prospered in the Cold War atmosphere of 1950s Washington. The National Security Council demonstrated the most impressive ability to endure in a threatening post-war environment. President Truman supported in principle the creation of a successor to the wartime SWNCC for the coordination of civilian and military advice. He nonetheless worried about the possibility that the new agency would impinge upon the constitutionally-designated powers of the President. Consequently, Truman kept tight control over the NSC after its establishment, and rarely called meetings of the organization prior to the onset of the Korean War. The NSC nonetheless persisted into the Eisenhower era, and then began to take root at the "top of policy hill."[26]

Conclusion.

This brief introductory article can only tell a small part of the story of the debates which culminated in the passage of the 1947 National Security Act and the struggles which immediately followed the passage of the legislation. The Act is best understood as a major setback for both Truman and Marshall. Both men were publicly committed to the unification of the armed forces at the end of World War II, and both were frustrated by the very effective campaign of resistance to unification which was organized by the Navy and its friends in Congress. Truman and Marshall were nonetheless able to shake off this defeat, make the best of the situation, and move on to other issues. The biggest loser in all of the struggles surrounding the 1947 National Security Act was the State Department, which discovered over time that the new arrangements institutionalized the marginalization of State in ways that had been understandable during the war but were unprecedented in peacetime. State tried to resist these trends, of course. In his first memo to the President after becoming Secretary of

19

State, George Marshall opposed the creation of both the CIA and the NSC, as infringements on the constitutionally designated authority of both the President and the State Department.[27] Dean Acheson also fought a valiant rear-guard action to preserve State's influence within the policy community. His use of the Policy Planning Staff to formulate NSC-68 is a particularly interesting example of this campaign. By the time that Acheson left State, however, the momentum had clearly shifted in favor of the Pentagon-NSC nexus. One illustration of this fact is that on his first day in office as Acheson's replacement, John Foster Dulles advised Paul Nitze that the important work of the Policy Planning Staff within State would need to be shifted to the National Security Council, and that he, as Secretary of State, hoped to be able to spend 90 percent of his time with the NSC people.[28]

One of the ironies of this story is that Forrestal, who can be counted as the big winner in the struggle, was crushed by the machinery which he was personally responsible for creating.

Which leads to an obvious question: Why is it that, after having succeeded in blocking efforts to establish the Secretary of Defense as an influential player in the new National Military Establishment, Forrestal accepted Truman's offer to become the first Secretary? The answer seems to be that Forrestal saw the Secretary's power not within the National Military Establishment *per se*, but rather in the larger network of national security institutions created by the National Security Act. In a meeting held in his office just days after his appointment as Secretary of Defense, Forrestal obtained support for his plan to locate the National Security Resources Board, the National Security Council, the Joint Chiefs of Staff, the Munitions Board, the Research and Development Board, and the office of the Director of the Central Intelligence Agency "as close as possible to the Secretary of Defense" within the Pentagon. It was also suggested that the building be renamed the "National Defense Building."[29] Forrestal also assumed that the NSC would be the real driving force in the new national security system, and that the President would not be able to routinely perform his duties as *ex officio* chairman of the NSC. Under these circumstances, Forrestal believed that the President would designate the Secretary of Defense as the "presiding officer" of the NSC and that this would be his power base.[30] Just one week after the Pentagon meeting, however, Truman's assistant Clark Clifford sent the President a long memo in which he recommended that "In the absence of the President, it would seem appropriate that the Secretary of State—as ranking member—serve as Chairman [of the NSC]."[31] In fact, Truman resolved the issue by rarely convening the NSC prior to the Korean War.

I will conclude by considering Ernest May's observation that nothing in the 1947 legislation made it inevitable that the government would come to look like a wartime government, "with the military ascendant and military-security concerns dominant."[32] This is true if one looks at the institutions which were created by the legislation, but not at the debates which go back to the pre-World War II era. These debates make it clear that the United States was about to embark on a new foreign policy, based not only on new ambitions, but on new fears, which would not be mitigated by victory over the German and Japanese enemies. Nor, for that matter, by the collapse of the Soviet enemy 5 decades later.

ENDNOTES — CHAPTER 2

1. "Winged Defense," p. 16, quoted in Michael Sherry, *The Rise of American Air Power: The Creation of Armageddon*, New Haven, CT: Yale University Press, 1987, p. 30.

2. Quoted by David Kennedy, in *Freedom from Fear: The American People in Depression and War, 1929-1945*, New York: Oxford University Press, 1999, p. 111.

3. E. Pendleton Herring, *The Impact of War: Our American Democracy Under Arms*, New York: Farrar and Rhinehold, 1941, p. 243.

4. *The New York Herald Tribune*, October 19, 1941.

5. E. Pendleton Herring, *The United States at War . . .* , Prepared Under the Auspices of the Committee of Records of War Administration, Bureau of the Budget, Washington, DC: U.S. Government Printing Office, 1946.

6. "Our Armed Forces Must Be Unified," *Collier's*, August 26, 1944, reprinted in U.S. Congress, Senate, Committee on Military Affairs, 79th Congress, 1st Session, *Department of Armed Forces, Department of Military Security*, October 17-December 17, 1945, pp. 192-197.

7. *Memoirs by Harry Truman: Volume Two, Years of Trial and Hope,* New York: Doubleday, 1956, pp. 46-7.

8. *The Papers of George Catlett Marshall, Vol. 4*, Larry Brand, ed., Baltimore, MD: Johns Hopkins University Press, 1996, pp. 417-418.

9. U.S. Congress, House of Representatives, Committee on Expenditures in Executive Departments, 72nd Congress, 1st Session, Washington, DC: U.S. Government Printing Office, 1932, pp. 249-50.

10. *The Papers of George Catlett Marshall, Vol. 4*, p. 156.

11. U.S. Congress, House of Representatives, Select Committee on Post-War Military Policy, *Proposal to Establish a Single Department of Armed Forces*, 78th Congress, 2nd Session, Washington, DC: U.S. Government Printing Office, 1944, p. 226.

12. For documents and analysis, see *The CIA Under Harry Truman* Michael Warner, ed., published by the History Staff of the Center for the Study of Intelligence, Washington, DC: Central Intelligence Agency, 1994, in particular, pp. 29-33.

13. *Present at the Creation: My Years in the State Department*, New York: Norton, 1969, p. 161.

14. Created in December of 1944, SWNCC dealt mainly with the terms of surrender and planning for military occupation.

15. For a discussion of the Kilgore and Bush proposals, see Daniel Kleinman, *Politics on the Endless Frontier: Post-war Research Policy in the United States*, Durham, NC: Duke University Press, 1995, *passim*.

16. Bruce Catton, quoted by Michael Sherry, *In the Shadow of War: The United States Since the 1930's,* New Haven, CT: Yale University Press, 1995, p. 70.

17. The United States At War, p. 504.

18. See the analysis of Eberstadt's views by Jeffery Dorwart, *Eberstadt and Forrestal: A National Security Partnership, 1909-1949*, College Station, TX: Texas A&M University Press, 1991, in particular, p. 59.

19. *Ibid.*, p. 94.

20. The Eberstadt Report is reprinted in U.S. Congress, Senate, Committee on Naval Affairs, *Report to Hon. James Forrestal, Secretary of the Navy, On Unification of the War and Navy Departments and Post-war Organization for National Security*, 79th Congress, 1st Session, Washington, DC: U.S. Government Printing Office, October 22, 1945.

21. See U.S. Congress, Senate, Committee on Armed Services National Security Act of 1947, *Hearings on S. 758*, 80th Congress, 1st Session, Washington, DC: U.S. Government Printing Office, 1947, pp. 674-5.

22. Quoted in Clark Clifford and Richard Holbrooke, *Counsel to the President,* New York: Random House, 1992, p. 157

23. A Study of OP-23 and its Role in the Unification Debates of 1949 is found in *Oral History of Admiral Arleigh Burke, Vol. IV*, U.S. Naval Institute, Annapolis, MD, 1983, p. 77.

24. See the Report by F. Eberstadt to Arthur M. Hill, Washington, DC, June 4, 1948, Harry S. Truman Library, *Papers of Harry S. Truman*, President's Secretary's Files, pp. 8-9.

25. *Endless Frontier: Vannevar Bush, Engineer of the American Century*, Cambridge, MA: MIT Press, 1999, p. 336.

26. See Anna Nelson, "The `Top of Policy Hill': President Eisenhower and the National Security Council," *Orbis*, 7, Fall 1983, pp. 307-26.

27. "Memorandum by the Secretary of State to the President," February 7, 1947, *Foreign Relations of the United States, 1947, Vol. 1, National Security Policy,* Washington, DC: U.S. Government Printing Office, pp. 712-13.

28. See Leonard Mosley *Dulles: A Biography of Eleanor, Allen and John Foster Dulles and Their Family Network*, New York: Dial Press, 1978, pp. 307-308.

29. "Memorandum for the Secretary," August 2, 1947, Papers of Ralph Stohl, Box #52, Harry S. Truman Library, p. 1.

30. *Ibid.*, p. 7.

31. "Memorandum for the President," August 8, 1947, Papers of Clark M. Clifford, Box #12, Harry S. Truman Library, p. 3.

32. "The U.S. Government: A Legacy of the Cold War," In *The End of the Cold War*, Michael Hogan, ed., New York: Cambridge University Press, 1992, p. 219.

CHAPTER 3

IKE AND THE BIRTH OF THE CINCS:
THE CONTINUITY OF UNITY OF COMMAND

David Jablonsky

"The past is never dead," Gavin Stevens tells Temple Drake in William Faulkner's *Requiem for a Nun*. "It's not even past."[1] This was particularly true for Dwight Eisenhower in April 1958 when, as President of the United States, he outlined proposals to Congress for the reorganization of the Defense Department. The proposals were primarily concerned with the principle of unity of command at the highest levels. The central focus was the unified command, the multi-service combatant structure used to divide military responsibility into theaters throughout the world. The primary issue was the nature and extent of authority: By the commanders-in-chief (CINCs) of the unified commands over their component commanders and by the President and the Secretary of Defense over the CINCs.

The issue of unity of command had its origins in the interwar years, when the Joint Board of the Army and Navy prescribed the primary method of coordination between the services to be mutual cooperation, the method in effect at the time of the Japanese attack on Pearl Harbor. In that disaster, the investigating committee concluded, "the inherent and intolerable weaknesses of command by mutual cooperation were exposed."[2] As a consequence, shortly after Eisenhower joined the War Department's War Plans Division (WPD) in 1941, there was a general consensus on the need for unity of command in the field. Soon, he was involved in discussions about all aspects of unified commands and unified direction of those commands from Washington. For the next 17 years he would

25

consistently continue this involvement, whether as CINC of various unified and combined commands, as Chief of Staff of the Army, as acting Chairman of the Joint Chiefs of Staff (JCS), or as President of the United States. Throughout that period there was a consistency in his approach to unity of command that was based on an abiding belief in jointness, a belief, as he wrote in his 1958 proposals, that

> separate ground, sea, and air warfare is gone forever. If ever again we should be involved in war, we will fight it . . . with all services, as one single concentrated effort.[3]

The War Years.

There were many notable accomplishments at the U.S.-U.K. ARCADIA Conference which took place in Washington from December 23, 1941, to January 14, 1942. Chief among them was the informal emergence by February 9, 1942, of the Joint Chiefs of Staff as counterparts to the British Chiefs in the newly formed Combined Chiefs of Staff (CCS). Equally important was the British acceptance of the American approach to unified command. At the time of the ARCADIA Conference, the British had been fighting for over two years under a committee system in each theater composed of "Commanders in Chief" from the three services, none of whom was provided full authority or responsibility for the total theater operation. It was Eisenhower's job in WPD to prepare General George C. Marshall for his attempt at the second meeting to overcome the British preference for this system and to gain agreement for a unified command structure. The strength of the Allied effort in any theater, he advised in a memorandum to the Army Chief of Staff,

> would be greatly increased through single, intelligent command. The many organizations . . . cannot possibly operate at maximum effectiveness so long as cooperation alone dictates their employment, no matter how sincere a purpose may inspire the cooperative effort.[4]

The next day, Christmas 1941, Marshall introduced the question of unified command in each "natural theater," arguing the need for one commander on the ground to act as a "clearing house" for all directives and recommendations and to provide general direction to theater strategic and tactical operations.[5] The British were unconvinced. After the meeting, Marshall directed Eisenhower to prepare a letter that "would serve as a concrete suggestion" for establishing a unified command in the Pacific Theater, the only area in which the combined forces of the Allies were actually fighting.[6]

Eisenhower's draft directive for the command known as ABDA (Australia, British, Dutch, American) was designed to make the concept of unified command more palatable by demonstrating that there would be no risk to the interests of any of the powers involved. To this end, he placed numerous restrictions on the actions of the supreme commander of the new theater that were as severe as those under which Marshall Foch had labored as Allied Commander in 1918. After obtaining approval of Eisenhower's draft directive at a bedside conference with President Franklin D. Roosevelt, Marshall presented it to the American and British Chiefs. After extensive discussions, the CCS and the two heads of state agreed by early January on a directive similar to Eisenhower's draft to the ABDA Supreme Commander, General Archibald Wavell, the former CINC of British forces in India. It was a masterful achievement by Marshall who had accomplished his primary objective at ARCADIA of agreement to the principle he believed should govern all command structure. "Unity of command in ABDA area seems assured," a tired Eisenhower noted on his writing pad. "Good start!—but what an effort. Talk—talk—talk."[7]

Eisenhower's key role in discussions about unity of command was due to a number of organizational changes in Washington. Marshall was reorganizing the War Department in a manner designed to give the position of Chief of Staff broad and unequivocal powers over the entire Army. This, in turn, had the effect of placing a great amount of power in WPD, which was renamed Operations Division (OPD) on March 22, 1942. Marshall turned to that agency, as Ike noted when he became Chief of WPD, "for all the Joint and Combined work . . . , all plans and operations so far as actual theaters are concerned."[8] Equally important was the *ad hoc* emergence of the JCS as a body that reported to the President, the only civilian in the chain of command, and that issued orders and supervised theater commanders through one of its members acting as the executive agent for the Joint Chiefs. The result was that Eisenhower was constantly involved at the highest level in all matters concerned with unified and combined commands. In March, for instance, he drafted a "former Naval person" message on the command status in China for Roosevelt to dispatch to Winston Churchill.[9] And that same month, when the President proposed a division of global responsibility between the United States and the United Kingdom into three general areas, it was Eisenhower who created a study justifying the proposals that was accepted informally by both heads of state and their chiefs. Under the arrangement, operational responsibility was given to the United States for the Pacific area, to the United Kingdom for the Indian Ocean and Middle East, and jointly to both countries for Europe and the Atlantic. Although there was never any formal approval of the Eisenhower study, the Allies acted for the remainder of the war as if there had been.[10]

By the time of his global study, Eisenhower was also heavily involved as the newly promoted head of WPD in the issue of unified commands within the American forces. In the U.S.-dominated Pacific, General Douglas MacArthur would not serve under a naval officer, and the Navy was opposed to placing most of its ships under his control. As a solution, Eisenhower helped to establish two separate commands in the Pacific. On March 9, 1942, he prepared a memorandum for Marshall to the JCS outlining a detailed division of the Pacific into two theaters of operation, which was approved after a few compromises at the JCS meeting that same day. At the end of the month, the Joint Chiefs issued a directive establishing the two Pacific Commands: the Southwest Pacific Area (SWPA) under General MacArthur and the Pacific Ocean Area (POA) under Admiral Chester Nimitz. The next week, Eisenhower drafted a directive to MacArthur defining the SWPA boundaries and establishing the new command arrangements. The CCS was to exercise general jurisdiction over grand strategic policy; the JCS would exercise specific jurisdiction over all matters pertaining to theater operational strategy in SWPA, with the Army Chief of Staff acting as the executive agent: "All instructions to you will be issued by or through him."[11] As for the combined aspects of the new command, Eisenhower was careful to provide more authority to the new CINC than he had granted under the political limitations of the ABDA structure. "Commanders of all armed forces within your area," he concluded,

> will be immediately informed by their respective governments that, from a date to be notified, all orders and instructions issued by you in conformity with this directive will be considered by such commanders as emanating from their respective governments.[12]

Other command arrangements with the Navy were not always so easy to work out during the winter and spring of 1942. Eisenhower did not question Admiral Ernest King's overall commitment to jointness. "He said at one time to me," he recalled later of an encounter at the time with the irascible CNO, ". . . one of the things I continually search myself for is to see whether I am acting according to logic or merely out of blind loyalties of 40 years in the Navy."[13] Nevertheless, King proposed separate Army and Navy commands in the Caribbean, which Eisenhower advised Marshall to resist because "the Army looks upon the area as a single theater."[14] There was also a constant battle with the Navy over unity of coastal command, which Eisenhower eventually brought to a successful conclusion. It could be an exasperating process. "Fox Conner was right about allies," he wrote on his desk pad in February. "He could well have included the Navy!"[15]

Eisenhower may have been referring to his experience that same month as a permanent member, along with a naval counterpart, of the Joint Planning Committee (JPC), tasked the previous summer by the Joint Board to report on a recommendation to establish a Joint General Staff from both services as well as the position for "an officer of the Army or the Navy as Chief of the Joint General Staff." The JPC report at the end of February was signed by both men, announcing their inability to agree and the irreconcilability of their respective positions. The Admiral favored increasingly joint relations, but advised that only a combination of extended time and education could instruct officers of one service sufficiently about the other service to make any joint general staff either feasible or advisable. Eisenhower, on the other hand, favored the recommendation, emphasizing that "coordination by cooperation is ineffective," and that officers assigned to a joint staff billet would soon discover that "their exclusive responsibility to the Commander in Chief for the operations of all the armed forces should tend to free them from the purely service points of view."[16] As a result of the lack of agreement between the Army and Navy, the matter was deferred for later study; and, by the time it was raised again more than a year later, it had merged into the studies that would bring increasing focus on the larger issue of armed forces unification.

For Eisenhower, there were two important and interrelated consequences from these experiences at OPD. To begin with, Marshall recognized his growing expertise in the complex world of unified and combined commands and had him in May 1942 draw up a directive for the future American commander in a European Theater of Operations (ETO). The second consequence was that Eisenhower had become convinced that there should be no restrictions on the authority of the commander as he had written into his earlier proposal at ARCADIA for the ABDA commander.

30

The head of the ETO must have complete control over the planning and implementation of operations. "It is essential," Eisenhower insisted, ". . . that absolute unity of command should be exercised by the Theater Commander to be designated."[17]

When Eisenhower was appointed in June 1942 to carry out his own directive for the ETO, he knew from a visit to England the previous month that he could expect resistance from the British to the formation of unified commands for any Allied operation. These expectations were confirmed in August when Eisenhower was appointed as commander of the Allied North African expedition and attempted to establish control over all the services of both countries, to include direct command of the ground forces not only for the landings, but for the follow-up operations as well. The British authorities, however, provided a directive for their First Army Commander that was essentially a copy of a 1918 directive, reserving all tactical control to the British commander who could appeal to the British government if he thought his forces might be "imperiled" by allied direction.[18] Eisenhower protested that the instructions violated every concept concerning unity of command and should be rewritten

> in the form of a short statement of principles, emphasizing unity of the whole" and the purpose of both countries" to unify the Allied force and to centralize responsibility for its operation. . . .[19]

It was the new commander at his best—conciliatory, impersonal and objective, yet quietly passionate about unity of command and unified operations. In the end, the British agreed to his request, thus establishing an important new basis for Allied operations. "From the day I came over here," an elated Eisenhower wrote Marshall in October,

> I have dinned into the British the fact that you considered unity of command to exist only when the Commander of an Allied Force had the same authority . . . with respect to all

troops involved, as he had to those of his own nationality. I am now benefiting from this crusade. . . .[20]

The issue appeared again, however, when the CCS issued directives in late January 1943, stipulating that Eisenhower's three deputies would "cooperate" with each other in planning and executing the invasion of Sicily.[21] To compound the matter, the three subordinate air, land and sea commanders were all British: Air Chief Marshal Arthur Tedder, General Harold Alexander, and Admiral Andrew Cunningham. Nevertheless, Eisenhower was determined to operate his theater as a truly unified command. The British system of cooperation, he emphasized in a passionate message to Marshall, was inadequate to the demands of modern conflict. A theater CINC must be free to make decisions "under the principle of unity of command;" and in the future he would be on his guard "to prevent any important military venture depending for its control and direction upon the 'committee' system of command."[22]

Eisenhower succeeded in this goal for the Sicily operation by means of his internal administrative arrangements as well as by the force of his own personality and his focus on unity of command. He maintained close contact with his air and sea commanders, co-locating their headquarters with his own in the St. Georges Hotel in Algiers. And although he permitted Alexander to command only those ground forces actually engaged in combat, he maintained close liaison with the British general through personal visits, phone calls, messages, and the exchange of staff officers. Ultimately, the three commanders responded to Eisenhower's efforts as commander-in-chief and helped him create the organization for unified command that the Combined Chiefs had denied him in a formal directive.

By the end of the Sicilian campaign, Eisenhower had strengthened his position with a command structure that was approaching the ideal organization that he had outlined to the British Chiefs the previous August. Alexander was in charge of those land forces in Sicily engaged in actual operations, while Eisenhower retained his position of overall ground commander. And acting directly under him, Tedder and Cunningham had complete control of the theater air and sea forces. So impressed were the Combined Chiefs with the control exercised by Eisenhower under his unified structure, that they authorized him full discretion in choosing the times and places for future landings in his Mediterranean theater. In September 1943, Eisenhower summarized his views on these experiences to Lord Louis Mountbatten, recently appointed by the CCS as Supreme Commander of the Southeast Asia Theater and anxious for advice "on the pitfalls to avoid and the line you consider one should take up."[23] Mountbatten's three deputies, Eisenhower advised, would be accustomed to dealing directly with their own national ministers and would have senior subordinates of opposite nationality who would also deal directly with the authorities from their own countries. He recommended that these channels "should be interfered with as little as possible," but cautioned Mountbatten that no one else must be allowed to communicate with the Combined Chiefs. The practical result, he concluded, "was that final recommendations as to operations . . . and requests for needed resources must likewise pass through you." Drawing upon his own experiences with the Combined Chiefs, and the strengths of the personal traits that had allowed him to operate fully as a CINC without a formal charter of complete control, he concluded that:

> while the set-up may be somewhat artificial and not always so clear-cut as you might desire, your personality and good sense **must** make it work. Otherwise **Allied** action in any theater will be impossible.[24]

A few months later, after being appointed to command OVERLORD, Eisenhower once again encountered situations that were not so "clear-cut" as he attempted to resolve organizational problems concerning his new command structure under Supreme Headquarters, Allied Expeditionary Force (SHAEF). In the Mediterranean, he had commanded all the U.K. and U.S. military assets in his theater. In his new capacity, he did not initially have control of the British and American strategic bombing forces—an important point for him based on the recent experiences at Salerno. As a consequence, Eisenhower requested that, at least for several months before and after the Normandy invasion, the bombers be placed at his disposal to destroy the railroad infrastructure in France and the Low Countries and to prevent speedy German reinforcements once the location of the cross-channel assault had been revealed. Initially, the SHAEF Commander's proposal for what came to be called the "Transportation Plan" was resisted by the commanders of the two strategic bombing forces, who perceived their primary missions as the destruction of the industrial infrastructure in the German heartland. The arguments over the issue swept back and forth during February and March 1944. Eisenhower remained adamant, finally forcing a decision in his favor by being prepared "to inform the Combined Chiefs of Staff that unless the matter is settled at once I will request relief from this command."[25] Eisenhower's stance, Stephen Ambrose points out concerning the ultimate effectiveness of the Transportation Plan, "was perhaps his greatest single contribution to the success of OVERLORD."[26]

Eisenhower also drew on his Mediterranean experience when he stipulated that General Bernard Montgomery was to command only the ground forces committed to the Normandy assault. Once the Allied forces had achieved a breakout from the landing beaches, Eisenhower planned to have the British general revert to command of one army group of British and Canadian armies, while General Omar Bradley would take command of the other army group of American forces. At one point, Montgomery proposed that he continue as a ground force commander after Normandy through the fall of 1944 while retaining command of his army group—an idea that Eisenhower termed "fantastic" since it would have placed the British commander "in a position to draw at will, in support of his own ideas, upon the strength of the entire command."[27] Eisenhower was on to something. For later, when the British were unable to persuade him to change his so-called "broad-front" strategy for moving on the Rhine and the industrial heartland of Germany, they raised the idea of altering SHAEF's command structure in order to achieve their objectives for a single thrust to Berlin. At Montgomery's suggestion, the British Chiefs proposed that General Alexander, then CINC of the Mediterranean Theater, substitute for Tedder as SHAEF deputy and assume the role of a single ground commander to ease Eisenhower's task of both planning and implementing the European War. Eisenhower was adamant in his refusal, notifying General Alan Brooke, the head of the British Imperial Staff, that there could never be any question "of placing between me and my Army Group Commanders any intermediary headquarters either official or unofficial."[28]

This lack of a land commander, as Montgomery pointed out, diminished overall direction on the battlefield. But it was a price that was paid to hold together the alliance, for as Alexander had demonstrated as ground commander in the other theaters, the same pressures would apply to whoever was in charge. And those pressures, as Eisenhower well knew, could come from the very top, as demonstrated by the vehemence with which Brooke and Marshall defended the interests of their respective armies, even when those forces were under his command.

In the end, there was no other commander on either side in World War II who had more complex unified and combined command experiences than Eisenhower. Moreover, it is easy to forget from a perspective of over half-a-century how unique those experiences were. Until that conflict, no American had ever been in charge of a large unified command consisting of armies, navies, and airforces; and none had ever directed an allied command. There were, of course, unified and combined operations in other theaters of the global war. But they were less complex: in the Central Pacific because the forces were primarily naval; and in the Southwest Pacific, the Middle East, and Southwest Asia because the forces were much smaller in each theater. Finally, in the European and African theaters, the German, Italian, and Russian forces were dominated by army ground troops with no attempts to organize these forces jointly under anything approaching unified commands. And in fact, only Japan among the Axis powers attempted to unite its three services under the command of one officer.

The Post-War Years.

From the end of World War II until he assumed the Presidency of the United States in 1953, Eisenhower served in a number of positions that caused him to maintain his focus on the principle of unity of command, but in an environment that was far more complex and far less malleable than he had been accustomed to as a wartime Supreme Commander. In that position, there had been a single overriding goal. But during his tenure as Army Chief of Staff from December 1945 to February 1948, Eisenhower entered political-military conflicts as the military head of one of the services, an interested party who, despite being *primus inter pares* in prestige, was only one among equals in power. After SHAEF, it was a time of frustration for Eisenhower. Shortly after assuming his new duties, he wrote his son that the position of Army Chief "was a sorry place to light after having commanded a theater of war."[29] And more than halfway through his tenure, he confided that "since my own method worked well for me when I was a little 'Czar' in my own sector, I find it difficult to readjust to the demands of this city."[30]

Much of the frustration had to do with Eisenhower's efforts to achieve unity of command at all levels. In the field, despite a general agreement to retain the unified command system in peacetime, there were major disagreements between the Navy and the Army over which service would have command of various Pacific areas. Throughout the

36

spring and summer of 1946, the new Army Chief of Staff was constantly involved in representing General MacArthur's position to the JCS. But there were pressures for compromise, as he noted in August, in the form of "the report of the Pearl Harbor Committee, the urgent desires of the two Secretaries for an early solution to the problem, and the demands of the press and public for elimination of 'Pearl Harbor' conditions."[31] Moreover, Eisenhower had also enlarged the issue by that time to encompass a global structure to achieve "sound unified command arrangements at the earliest possible time" in "other theaters and areas in the world where in certain cases the situation is at least as acute as in the Pacific."[32] In September, he forwarded a draft global unified command plan to the JCS which outlined the roles of the Joint Chiefs, as well as of unified and component commanders. The proposal, however, also included a new plan for the Pacific that was unacceptable to the Navy. At the same time, the Navy also rejected an Air Force proposal that the Strategic Air Command (SAC), operating under one commander on a global basis, should be supported by other CINCs.

By early December, an increasingly impatient Eisenhower had worked out compromise wording on SAC authority acceptable to both services, and had made important concessions to the Navy in the Pacific, leaving MacArthur without any reference to that ocean in his title. It was a far different experience than the heady wartime days at OPD four years before, when Eisenhower had written the directive for MacArthur's command of a major Pacific theater of operations. When President Harry S. Truman approved the first Unified Command Plan on December 14, 1946, MacArthur was designated Commander in Chief, Far East (CINCFE), one of seven unified commands, and one which limited his authority in effect to the Philippines, Korea, and Japan. Most importantly, however, the document retained Eisenhower's proposals, based on recent changes to the 1935 manual, *Joint Action of the Army and Navy (JAAN)*, for the role of commanders in the global unified plan. Unified commands would consist of two or more components, each component to be commanded by an officer authorized to communicate directly with his appropriate service headquarters concerning administration, logistics, and training. The commander of the unified command would operate with a joint staff composed of appropriate members of the service components under his command. Finally, the JCS would exercise strategic direction, as it had in wartime, assigning forces to the unified commands as well as stipulating the missions and tasks for those commands. The JCS would also continue the wartime practice of designating a service chief to act as an executive agent for the Joint Chiefs to oversee the operation of each unified command.[33]

All in all, the first Unified Command Plan was a tremendous accomplishment for the new Army Chief of Staff—the result of conciliation, principled compromise, and the ability to move beyond service parochialism to a global vision. Typically, Eisenhower played down the Service infighting and his pivotal role when he reminded a Congressional Committee the following May that his wartime experience

> was that of a unified single commander, having all services under my command. . . .
>
> The team that I saw developed in that area, in my conviction, was the only kind of team that could have won the European war. I think that lesson is so clearly understood by all of us that there is no one of the services that objects or would tolerate any other solution except the single command in a single theater of war. We have believed that so much that we have attempted to carry that into our peacetime practices in attempting to set up a single commander in the Western Pacific, the Central Pacific, in the Caribbean, and so on. No matter from what service he comes, he commands the operations, the defenses and strategic concerns in those areas.[34]

The presence of the Army Chief at the congressional hearing was also a reflection of the larger issue of defense unification that had been festering since early in the war. For Eisenhower, the successful wartime experience in the field under unity of command made a compelling argument for unification at the highest level of the armed forces with clear and accountable authority down to the unified commanders in the field. "I am convinced," he testified in November 1945,

> that unless we have unity of direction in Washington, through the years of peace that be ahead, we may enter another emergency, in a time to come, as we did in Pearl Harbor.[35]

To this end, he favored the War Department proposal to unify all services under a single, cabinet-level head, a Secretary of National Defense, who would in turn be served by a single Chief of Staff of the Armed Forces. The Navy, on the other hand, proposed to maintain a coordinate, not a unified organization, with a committee system to adjust activities of the War and Navy departments and to integrate military policy and programs with overall domestic and international requirements.

Both services outlined their proposals before a Senate committee in October 1945. The War Department plan, as presented by General J. Lawton Collins, was confusing and inconsistent, particularly in the peculiar dual relationship of the service chiefs as subordinates to the Chief of Staff of the Armed Forces in the departmental hierarchy, but as equal members of the advisory Joint Chiefs of Staff. In addition, the solid command line used by Collins on his chart clearly showed the theater commanders directly under the Chief of Staff of the Armed Forces, thus implying that he alone would direct operations by the CINCs in the field. Collins was at great pains to emphasize that the single Chief of Staff would not have a large staff and that the individual service chiefs would continue to act for the Joint Chiefs as executive agents to carry out the JCS directives with the operational staffs of their own services. But 2 weeks later, before the same committee, Eisenhower rejected the solid command line on the organizational chart.

The Chief of Staff of the Armed Forces, he recommended, should be removed from the chain of command between the Secretary on the one hand and the service chiefs and theater commanders on the other, and be depicted in the advisory organizational box of the JCS as the chief advisor to the civilian head. Eisenhower was sure that this had been the original intent since "by drawing him as he appears on the chart, it looks like he is the fabulous man on horseback that we are always talking about."[36]

On December 19, 1945, President Truman sent a unification message to Congress that clearly favored the single department proposed in the Collins Plan. Nevertheless, Secretary of the Navy James Forrestal was optimistic as the new year began, since the new Army Chief of Staff and his naval counterpart, Admiral Chester Nimitz, had already begun negotiations that appeared likely to settle what the Secretary termed the unification lawsuit. "Eisenhower is a good practical Dutchman and so is Nimitz," Forrestal observed, "and between them I believe we will make progress."[37] Another year would pass, however, before both chiefs and both service secretaries could arrive at a draft proposal for unification, and even then it required presidential decisions on several intractable issues. Eisenhower was committed throughout the process to establishing overall unity of command exercised by a civilian secretary. "I personally do not care what the language of the bill is," he testified to Congress that spring.

> I want to get started with a man to whom we can all go, a civilian who comes down here and tells you people. . . . "Here is the picture of national security of the country; here is what we think we need. . . ." That is important to me.[38]

The compromise unification proposal was dispatched to Congress early in 1947 and emerged with some modifications after prolonged hearings and deliberations on July 26 as the National Security Act. The new law created a coordinated defense establishment more in keeping with the Navy model—an organization which Eisenhower aptly characterized as "little more than a weak confederation of sovereign military units."[39] The compromise was most noticeable in the powers provided to the Secretary of Defense, who instead of presiding over one single executive branch department, was to head a National Military Establishment consisting of three executive departments, one for each service and administered by cabinet-level secretaries. The services, which now included an Air Force, retained their essential autonomy as well as the roles and missions that had emerged from the war—a status explicitly acknowledged in the Act's provision "for their authoritative coordination and unified direction under civilian control but not to merge them." Equally important, the Act established the JCS as a permanent organization served by a joint staff limited to 100 officers divided with equal numbers from each of the military departments. The Joint Chiefs were provided with statutory authorization to continue their wartime roles: To act as the principal military advisors to the President and the Secretary of Defense; to prepare strategic plans and provide for the strategic direction of the armed forces; and "to establish unified commands in strategic areas when such unified commands are in the interest of national security."[40]

Despite his support for the unification compromise, Eisenhower revealed some key reservations in his occasionally unguarded testimony to the House and Senate committees in the spring of 1947. The idea that the JCS would continue as a collaborative, coordinated body obviously bothered him when he acknowledged under persistent questioning that

> there is weakness in any council running a war. . . . In war, you must have a decision. A bum decision is better than none. And the trouble is that when you get three, you finally get none.[41]

One solution was a single Chief of Staff, which he admitted was his personal preference, but too disruptive an issue. "Time may bring it about, and it may show that this is the better system."[42] In the meantime, it was necessary to establish a truly joint culture. It was a basic fact, he pointed out, that

> when you have kept services apart and you wait until men are 50 before they begin to meet and know much about each other, it is pretty difficult to develop the kind of team play that applies on one of the Knute Rockne football teams.[43]

A year later, Eisenhower returned to the theme in his farewell memorandum to Secretary of Defense Forrestal. "Someday it will be possible," he wrote,

> to give to selected officers of the several services 'combined arms' commissions that will transcend in prestige and in public regard anything they could hold of comparable rank in one of the individual services.[44]

The memorandum was also a reminder of the need for an evolutionary approach to the provisions of the National Security Act.

> There should be no hesitancy in using the 'trial and error' method so long as these proceed from minor innovation toward larger and more radical objectives in final result.[45]

The two men were able to act on this advice when, less than a year later, Forrestal asked Eisenhower to serve as his adviser and informal Chairman of the JCS. From December 1948 to July 1949, Eisenhower divided his time between his duties as President of Columbia University and his responsibilities as Chairman in increasingly tense sessions with the Joint Chiefs. He later recalled that, as Chairman, "I was an umpire between disputing services; sometimes a hatchet man on what Fox Conner used to call Fool Schemes."[46] A major motivation for Forrestal was to use Eisenhower effectively as a senior military adviser interacting with the JCS in order to obtain an amendment to the National Security Act that would provide a permanent Chairman for that body. "With Ike here for 60 days," he confided in his diary, "I think we can get the pattern set and prove its workability by pragmatic experience."[47] At first, however, Eisenhower was more inclined to focus on a self-imposed majority rule procedure for the JCS, whereby if the Joint Chiefs failed three times to reach unanimity on a given issue, the majority view would prevail. But after his initial experiences of attempting to adjudicate bitter interservice parochial disputes, he changed his mind. "The JCS need a chairman at the very least—and by that I mean a fourth member who can divorce himself from his service background."[48]

By that time, Eisenhower was heavily involved in all aspects of proposed changes to the 1947 Act. The Chairman, he suggested, should "take precedence" over all others, but be a non-voting member of the JCS, a move that would "tend to allay suspicions that the man was going to be an arbitrary boss."[49] Nor should there be any fixed ceiling for the Joint Staff. In addition, he was particularly concerned that the right of service secretaries to appeal directly to the President and the Director of the Budget be eliminated. It was a matter, after all, of the centralizing spirit of the law and how that was to be conveyed in the proposed amendments.

> I think that the language should carry the clear intent of Congress to place the **maximum** amount of authority in the hands of the Secretary of Defense with restrictions imposed in only a few vital areas where obviously Congress should dictate the type of organization desired. My impression of the law as now written is that it sets up an official upon whom is placed great responsibility and then a deliberate shackle was imposed upon him to the extent that his effectiveness is curtailed.[50]

On August 10, President Truman signed PL 216, the National Security Amendments of 1949, which transformed the National Military Establishment into the executive Department of Defense. The amendments, reflecting some congressional modifications, remained essentially concerned with the two issues for which Eisenhower had provided input: The extent to which the Secretary of

Defense's formal authority was to be increased and the scope of the authority of the Chairman position that was to be added to the JCS. In terms of the Secretary, the qualifying "general" was removed from the original description of his "direction, authority, and control." Equally important, the service secretaries lost considerable power with their removal from the National Security Council and their loss of cabinet status, although they still retained statutory obligation to "separately" administer what were now military departments. As for the recommendation that the Chairman "head" the JCS and act as the principal adviser to the President and the Secretary of Defense, Congress agreed that he would preside over the Joint Chiefs as a non-voting member. The JCS, however, not the chairman, would be the principal advisers and in this capacity would be aided by a Joint Staff increased to 210. In addition, although the service secretaries and military chiefs were no longer permitted to deal directly with the President or the Budget Director as Eisenhower had recommended, they were allowed, after informing the Secretary, to take to Congress, "any recommendations relating to the Department of Defense." Finally, the new law specifically prohibited any of the major combat functions of the military departments from being "transferred, reassigned, abolished or consolidated."[51]

This last prohibition reflected the continued sensitivity to service roles and missions, an issue deliberately not addressed in detail in 1947. This issue had ostensibly been settled by the so-called Key West Agreement, hammered out by Forrestal and the JCS in April 1948, 2 months after Eisenhower quit as Army Chief. Equally important, it was a reflection of trends set in train by the Key West Agreement that would increase the tensions between the authority of service component commanders and that of unified commanders. To begin with, the overwhelming interest of the chiefs at that conference was to protect the integrity of their service activities in operational commands involving more than one service. Moreover, the agreement provided that the JCS continue the well established practice of designating one of its members as executive agent for each unified command. All this was compounded by the 1949 Act, which not only explicitly forbade the Secretary to interfere with the combat functions of the forces being assigned to unified commands, but increased the power of the service chiefs even as it diminished that of the service secretaries. The chiefs, of course, were still individually responsible to their secretaries. But collectively the Joint Chiefs were the principal military advisers of the Secretary of Defense; and since they were the only service departmental representatives provided a statutory role in the departmental policy process, they became, as they had in World War II, the spokesmen for their services.

These trends culminated in 1951 with the publication of the *Joint Action Armed Forces (JAAF)* manual, the first joint document to supercede the 1935 *JAAN*. In the first post-war change to the old document, which Eisenhower had cited in establishing the first Unified Command Plan, the CINCs were explicitly given command over service components, as the organizational norm. In the new document, that command was couched in terms of exception and even then in terms that were solicitous of the services.

> Unless authorized to do so by the appointing authority, the commander of a unified command does not exercise direct command of any of the Service components or of a subordinate force. In exercising command, he shall take cognizance of the prerogatives and responsibilities of his Service component commanders. . . .[52]

By 1951, Eisenhower had assumed duties as the first Supreme Allied Commander Europe (SACEUR), a position as much political as military, which within a few months he was referring to as "this dismaying and unattractive assignment. . . ."[53] Part of his frustration had to do with conflicting parochial national interests—whether it was the British insistence that one of their admirals be CINC of either the Atlantic or Mediterranean Command, or French suspicions of any attempts to rearm the Germans. The German issue was particularly frustrating because it involved Eisenhower in discussions about centralized command in a European Defense Force in which he believed, but which was doomed to failure precisely because of the degree of national integration down the chain of command that he found so attractive. In fact, much of Eisenhower's frustration was focused on the Joint Chiefs who complicated his efforts to build a unified structure by indulging in service rivalries in their dealings with the North Atlantic Treaty Organization (NATO), by refusing to share intelligence as well as atomic weapons and secrets, and by resisting efforts to transfer operational control of U.S. units to NATO. These types of problems were symbolized by IRONBARK, the JCS war plan that had as a basic assumption that NATO forces could delay but not prevent the onslaught of communist forces across Europe. This assumption was at odds with the political-military NATO strategy that required a vigorous defense along the Rhine, for which the Europeans were struggling to provide manpower and resources. Eisenhower recognized the need for the JCS to prepare emergency war plans on a global basis. "However, with respect to my area," he reminded them,

> the fact that the U.S. has taken the lead in establishing a unified command structure, and has, with other nations, agreed to place its forces under that command, makes it mandatory that U.S. emergency plans recognize clearly my authority as the Supreme Allied Commander Europe. . . . I consider, therefore, that it must be made absolutely clear that the directive of the President, placing all U.S. forces in Europe under my operational command for the accomplishment of my mission, has no qualifications or limitations. . . .[54]

The Presidency.

Eisenhower's earlier experiences concerning unity of command virtually assured that defense reorganization would be an immediate priority for him when he assumed the office of President in January 1953. It was still, as he had believed since agreeing to the 1947 compromise, a matter of organizational evolution. "Valuable lessons have been learned through six years of trial by experience." Moreover, there were what he termed "changing conditions" in the domestic and international arena. To begin with, America would have to continue to live through years that were "neither of total war nor total peace," in which large standing forces would have to be used efficiently and effectively in unified commands around the world to reassure allies, to deter aggression, and, if deterrence failed, to fight and win. Efficiency was the key to maintaining freedom and economic solvency, both of which he believed were vital components of national security. At the same time, Eisenhower still had concerns about the lack of full centralized civilian control, which had not been alleviated by the 1949 Act or the experiences in the intervening years. In fact, even as the status of the service secretaries had declined in the wake of that Act, the JCS had returned to its dominant position of World War II in the Korean conflict, directing combat operations and dealing directly with the President concerning implementation of United Nations (U.N.) directives. As a consequence, the new President believed there was a need to reduce the role and political power of the JCS, which had already begun to deadlock on reduced budgetary allocations as the Korean War came to an end.[55]

To resolve these issues, Eisenhower appointed the Rockefeller Committee in early February to develop specific recommendations for Department of Defense (DoD) reorganization. The April 11 Committee Report continued the general tenor of the criticism concerning the JCS, concluding that in order for the Joint Chiefs "to rise above the particular views of their respective services," they must be moved out of all command channels and serve only as a planning and advisory staff.[56] This conclusion, however, presented the committee with a dilemma. One group believed that the only way the Joint Chiefs would transcend

47

service interests was to end their relationships with the services. They recommended a hierarchical, general staff model that would terminate the "dual-hat" role of the JCS. Acting solely in a "staff" capacity for the Secretary, the Joint Chiefs would turn naturally from "parochial" to "national" advice. Another group opposed a complete separation between operational and planning responsibilities. The compromise was to strengthen the position of the Chairman in order to bring about a reorientation of the JCS and its subordinate staff structure, in which the JCS staff role for the Secretary would be emphasized and the role of the chiefs as service representatives would be de-emphasized, but not ended.[57]

Eisenhower incorporated this compromise proposal, as well as other committee recommendations, into his April 30 message forwarding the reorganization plan to Congress. He was careful to point out that the JCS, as provided in the 1947 National Security Act, "are not a command body, but are the principal military advisers to the President, the National Security Council, and the Secretary of Defense."[58] In their dual-hat capacity, however, the JCS could not plan effectively on joint matters while fulfilling their responsibilities to the secretaries for the efficiency of their services and their readiness for war. One way to further the strategic planning and military advisory capabilities of the "clearly overworked" chiefs, the solicitous President concluded, was to make the Chairman solely responsible for managing the work of the Joint Staff and its Director, to include the provision that the service of officers on that staff would be subject to the Chairman's approval.

Eisenhower was equally solicitous on the related issue of clarifying lines of civilian authority, which he assured Congress could be attained without any legislative change. It was simply a matter of altering by executive order that part of the Key West Agreement that had legalized the Joint Chiefs executive agent system for each unified command. This practice, the President emphasized, had led to "considerable confusion and misunderstanding" with respect to the relationships of the JCS to the Secretary of Defense and of the individual service chiefs to their service secretaries. As a consequence, he intended to direct the Secretary of Defense to revise the Key West Agreement and to designate a military department as executive agent for each unified command. "Under this new arrangement," he concluded, "the channel of responsibility and authority to a commander of a unified command will unmistakably be from the President to the Secretary of Defense to the designated civilian Secretary of a military department." At the same time, however, Eisenhower also included almost verbatim what the Rockefeller Committee termed "an important proviso" as part of its internal compromise—a compromise in this case that continued the ambiguity in the chain of command.

> It will be understood, however, that for the strategic direction and operational control of forces and for the conduct of combat operations, the military chief of the designated military department will be authorized by the Secretary of Defense to receive and transmit reports and orders and to act for that department in its executive agency capacity. This arrangement will make it always possible to deal promptly with emergency or wartime situations.

In October 1953, the Secretary of Defense issued the executive order revision of the Key West Agreement derived from the President's April 30 message. The actual legislation concerning the reorganization plan had already passed at the end of June. In the hearings on that legislation, there were some traditional concerns that the changes concerning the Chairman could lead to a man on horseback. But after "clarifying the matter" for legislative leaders, Eisenhower was generally able to quiet these concerns.[59] In addition, there was a general tendency on the part of most congressmen and witnesses in the hearings to defer to the new leader who had justified his reorganization request as "a former soldier who has experienced modern war at first hand, and now as President and Commander in Chief of the Armed Forces and the United States."[60]

Admiral Leahy, for instance, testified that the changes proposed in the plan would create a system greatly different from the World War II experience. But since the United States had been so successful in that conflict, the committee chairman asked, why should the changes in the reorganization plan be approved? "President Eisenhower wants it," the Admiral replied; "that is all." Was that the only reason, the chairman continued. "That is the only reason I can see," Leahy explained.

> .... He has been a grand soldier and he has been in it all his life. When people ask me whether I object to this or not, I say, "How can I object to it if the President approves it?" He has more experience in wars than I have had. He is recognized as an expert. So if he wants it why not let him have it? That is my answer to it.[61]

This kind of deference had long since disappeared by Eisenhower's second term. There were new tensions within the military establishment brought about by the rising cost of fielding modern forces for war in an environment of fixed budgets. All this was intensified by the October 1957 Soviet launch of Sputnik, which led to renewed public debate concerning DoD organizational structure and to alarming predictions from independent studies and committees. Eisenhower had already formed several advisory groups on the subject, primarily to reinforce his ideas on unity of command. "Military organization was a subject I had long lived with," he recalled later in classic understatement; "... I had definite ideas of the corrective measures that needed to be taken."[62] On January 9, 1958, he presented his State of the Union address to Congress and listed DoD reorganization as the top priority of the eight tasks he set out for his administration. He would send specific recommendations to Congress by separate message, he concluded, to enthusiastic applause.

That message on April 3 represented the culmination of Eisenhower's thoughts and experiences concerning unity of command since the early days of World War II. That conflict had proved that warfare could no longer be waged effectively under separate service efforts. But in the debates and eventual compromise that marked the 1947 reorganization, "the lessons were lost, tradition won. . . ."[63] In 1949 and 1953, there were reforms leading to increased centralization and authority for the Secretary of Defense—all necessary given the new technologies and the Cold War requirements for readiness and deterrence. The process had been slowed, however, by concerted resistance from the separate services and their friends in Congress. The service leaders, Eisenhower emphasized, were honest in their forceful presentations of their views on the importance of their programs in the overall national effort.

> But service responsibilities and activities must always be only the branches, not the central trunk of the national security tree. . . . We must cling no longer to statutory authority. We must free ourselves of emotional attachments to service systems of an era that is no more.

The central theme of Eisenhower's April proposals, as it had been in his 1945 Congressional testimony, was that unity of command must run in a symbiotic thread from the highest level down into the theater commands.

> The need for greater unity today is most acute at two points—in the office of the Secretary of Defense and in the major operational commands responsible for actual combat in the event of war.

In terms of the operational level, the President specifically addressed the organizational deficiencies of the unified commands that limited the CINCs authority over the component commands, their influence over resources, and their ability to promote greater unity of effort within their commands. The solution was to build upon the World War II experience and organize forces into "truly unified" commands as the "cutting edge" of the entire defense organization.

Because I have often seen the evils of diluted command, I emphasize that each unified commander must have unquestioned authority over all units of his command.

The key to reform in the field was clear command lines from the President to the CINCs in order to avoid confusion of authority and defusion of responsibilities. The existing chain of command from the 1953 reorganization, Eisenhower explained, had expanded from the service secretaries to the point that "ultimately the chief of an individual service issues in the name of the Secretary of Defense orders to a unified commander." That this was "staff" taking over responsibilities of the "line" was self-evident, since the role of the Joint Chiefs, he reminded the Congress, should be only to furnish professional advice and staff assistance to the Secretary of Defense. To this end, he had directed the Secretary to discontinue the use of military departments as executive agents for unified commands. "I consider this chain of command cumbersome and unreliable in time of peace and not usable in time of war," Eisenhower emphasized. "Clearly, Secretaries of military departments and chiefs of individual services should be removed from the command channel."

The result was an operational chain of command "running from the Commander in Chief and Secretary of Defense directly to unified commands." At the same time, Eisenhower planned to maintain the support channel to the CINCs through the military departments which, relieved by his directive of responsibility for military operations, could concentrate on the administration, training, and logistics of their service forces assigned by the Secretary to the unified commands. But for this support channel to work, provisions in the current law must be eliminated, such as the one prescribing "separate administration" by the service secretaries of their departments which inflicted "needless and injurious restraints on the authority of the Secretary of Defense." And chief among such provisions, as Eisenhower examined the command linkage to the CINCs, was the specter of service functions that always hovered on the fringes of such considerations. The 1949 law had contained the first explicit statutory limitations on executive alterations of combatant functions—an ironic outcome of the efforts that year to clarify and strengthen the Defense Secretary's power. Now in the spring of 1958, Eisenhower proposed in the strongest terms that these restrictions be amended in order "to remove any possible obstacles to the full unity of our commands and the full command over them by unified commanders!" This recommendation, he added, did not contemplate any repeal of laws prescribing the composition of the services, nor would it have such an effect.

All these changes would also require the JCS to change. In order for that body to assist the Secretary of Defense in his exercise of direction over the unified commands, Eisenhower asked Congress to raise or remove the statutory limit of 210 officers on the Joint Staff, and to authorize the Chairman to assign duties to that staff and to appoint its Director. As for the service chiefs, the President was as solicitous as he had been in 1953 of their dual-hat "burdens." He proposed, therefore, that the law be changed to emphasize that each chief was authorized to delegate much of his service responsibilities to his vice chief, thus allowing him to make the JCS role the primary duty. Finally, Eisenhower served notice to Congress that he was changing the Joint Staff committee system, which he perceived as a vestigial organization from 1942 when the staff reflected the informal nature of the JCS. "Had I allowed my interservice and inter-allied staff to be similarly organized in the theaters I commanded during World War II," he explained, "the delays and resulting indecisiveness would have been unacceptable to my superiors." The new system would center on an integrated operations division with joint directorates designed to make it easier for the Joint Staff, as it assumed the duties heretofore performed by the service staffs, to work with similar structures in the unified commands.

In considering the reorganization proposal, the Armed Service committees in both Houses agreed with the necessity to organize the operational commands into "truly unified" military structures tailored for a rapidly changing world. But they expressed concerns about the methods to achieve that objective, particularly concerning the request to grant the Secretary of Defense greater authority to determine the service roles and missions. In a similar manner, both committees were concerned about any increase in the authority of the Chairman and the size of the Joint Staff, and were generally not persuaded by administration arguments that delegation of service duties to the vice chiefs would not sever the ties of the chiefs to their individual services. Nor were the committees fully convinced that the words "separately administered," as currently applied to the military departments, posed a threat to the Secretary, or for that matter, that there was any challenge that could mitigate his authority over the CINCs. Even the popular General Omar Bradley could not escape unscathed at one point in his continued insistence that the Defense Secretary did not have adequate authority. "Can you suggest to the committee," the exasperated House chairman asked, "any English word that carries more authority than 'direction, authority and control'?"[64]

The House and Senate committee hearings on various modifications of the proposed legislation lasted from May to July. Eisenhower was extremely active throughout the period, meeting with key legislative leaders and writing influential persons to marshal pressure on Congress. "So strong were my convictions on the need for this reform...."[65] The result was a compromise bill that clearly favored the administration. The legislation granted the President's request for authority concerning service combatant functions, but also provided that Congress would have 70 days to reject by simple majority any transfer or abolition of such functions. Eisenhower considered that the latter provision "made a small hole in the doughnut," since in an emergency he was also authorized to transfer major combatant functions without consulting Congress.[66]

There was a similar pattern of compromise with the authorization of the Chairman to vote in the JCS and to manage the Joint Staff. The Chairman was permitted to select that staff, but only "in consultation" with the JCS, and to manage it, but only "on behalf" of that collaborative body. Moreover, the legislation specifically authorized the Chiefs to retain their right to assign duties to the Joint Staff. And there was no way for the President to gloss over what he termed "legalized insubordination" in the final legislation that authorized the service secretaries and the military chiefs to go directly to Congress with "any recommendations relating to the Department of Defense that they might deem proper." Still, Eisenhower consoled himself with President Ulysses S. Grant's reaction to similar circumstances: "I cannot make the Comptroller General change his mind, but I can get a new Comptroller General."[67]

Balanced against these compromises were the authorizations for the Chairman to vote in JCS deliberations; for the service chiefs to delegate service duties to their Vice Chiefs; and for the Joint Staff to increase its size to 400 officers. Moreover, in terms of the military departments, the words "separately administered" were replaced with the specification that each department would be "separately organized" under its secretary with all services functioning under the "direction, authority and control of the Secretary of Defense." More important for Eisenhower, the 1958 law authorized him, acting through the Secretary of Defense and with the advice of the JCS, to establish unified commands, to assign their missions, and to determine their force structure. In turn, the CINCs of those commands were made responsible to the President and the Secretary of Defense for implementing assigned missions. To this end, the law delegated the CINCs full "operational command" over assigned forces that could only be transferred with presidential approval. At the same time, the responsibility for the administration, training and support of these component forces was maintained in the respective military departments. Finally, by separate executive action, the Secretary of Defense discontinued the system of executive agents for the unified commands. Henceforth, the chain of command was to begin with the President and run through the Secretary of Defense to the CINCs.

The Evolutionary Process.

When he signed the Defense Reorganization Bill into law on August 6, 1958, Eisenhower praised it as a remarkable achievement. His positive reaction was understandable since the new legislation represented a major move from the coordinate philosophy that had triumphed in 1947 toward his ideal of centralized civilian authority. That authority extended on the one hand in a direct operational line to the CINCs and on the other, in an administrative and support line to those commanders through the military departments. In theory, those two lines would be brought together for the Secretary within the JCS advisory system. The effort would be led by the Chairman, gradually approaching the Chief of Staff of the Armed Forces status outlined so long ago in Eisenhower's interpretation of the Collins Plan. Under this system, the service chiefs would bring their superior expertise on service force capabilities and programs to the joint arena, and at the same time would emerge from the JCS deliberations with a broader perspective on national defense that would be used as they exercised their individual service responsibilities. Moreover, the new law granted more sweeping authority to the CINCs than Eisenhower had exercised over all the American forces assigned to OVERLORD. "In my own experience in the European theater," he acknowledged,

> I had found little difficulty with a loose theater organization partly because of the spirit of cooperation existing in wartime and partly because I was the administrative commander of by far the largest single component force in Europe, the United States Army, which included the Air Force.[68]

The changes, however, were deceptive. To begin with, the military departments and services exercised residual *de facto* power and influence out of all proportion to their new statutorily assigned duties. The Office of the Secretary of Defense was still not organized for full and effective integration of service capabilities into the forces required for the missions of the Unified Commands. Nor were the Joint Chiefs, the principal staff contact for the CINCs, able to make meaningful programmatic inputs. As a consequence, the unified commanders had to plan for their missions with resources provided by the services through a process defended by the services. The result was that the CINCs had limited power to influence the capability of assigned forces, leaving the services and thus the components with the primary influence on both the structure and the readiness of the forces for which the CINCs were responsible. This continued strength and independence of the component commands would in many aspects insure that despite Eisenhower's termination of the executive agent arrangement, the practice would persist outside the formal DoD directive.

This failure to adequately implement Eisenhower's concept of unified command resulted over the next several decades in operational deficiencies that became increasingly evident during the Vietnam War, the seizure of the *Pueblo*, the Iranian hostage rescue attempt, and the incursion into Grenada. The 1983 Grenada operation, in particular, caused Congress to focus its efforts on ensuring that the CINCs had sufficient authority both to maintain unity of command during operations and to prepare effectively for assigned missions. To that end, it would also be necessary to make the Chairman of the JCS responsible for developing joint doctrine and joint training policies. That same year, former Secretary of Defense James Schlesinger summarized the problem before the Senate Committee on Armed Services.

> In all of our military institutions, the time-honored principle of "unity of command" is inculcated. Yet at the national level it is

formerly resisted and flagrantly violated. Unity of command is endorsed if and only if it applies at the service level. The inevitable consequence is both the duplication of effort and the ultimate ambiguity of command.[69]

These types of continuing problems leading up to the Goldwater-Nichols Act of 1986 were something Eisenhower would have understood from his 17-year involvement with the problems of unity of command at the national and theater levels. At the August 1958 signing of the Reorganization Act, he reminded his associates "that the law was just another step toward what the majority of experienced military men knew was necessary."[70] But Eisenhower's underlying philosophy was expressed in his 1949 testimony concerning the first changes to the National Security Act.

> We are expecting perfection too quickly. It is just exactly, gentlemen, as when we were waging a great war in Europe.... We get a set-back, deliberately risked to get ahead with this war.... These set-backs are an inescapable part of all group activity....[71]

ENDNOTES – CHAPTER 3

1. William Faulkner, *Requiem For A Nun*, New York: Random House, 1951, p. 92.

2. U.S. Congress, Joint Committee on the Investigation of the Pearl Harbor Attack, Washington, DC: U.S. Government Printing Office, 1946, p. 245. See also U.S. Joint Army and Navy Board. *Joint Action of the Army and the Navy (JAAN)*, Washington, DC: U.S. Government Printing Office, 1935, p. 5.

3. The Department of Defense. *Documents on Establishment and Organization, 1944-1978* (hereinafter *DoD Documents*), Alice C. Cole, Alfred Goldberg, Samuel A. Tucker, Rudolf A. Winnacker, eds., Washington, DC: OSD Historical Office, 1978, p. 175.

4. Alfred D. Chandler, Jr., ed., *The Papers of Dwight David Eisenhower. The War Years* (hereinafter *EP*), Vols. I-V, Baltimore: The Johns Hopkins University Press, 1970, Vol. I, No. 22, p. 24.

5. *Ibid.*, No. 23, p. 25.

6. *Ibid.*, p. 26.

7. *Ibid.*, No. 32, p. 35. For Eisenhower's draft ABDA directive, see *Ibid.*, No. 24, pp. 28-31. On the final instructions, see *Ibid.*, No. 49, and Louis Morton, *Strategy and Command: The First Two Years*, Washington, DC: Office of the Chief of Military History, 1962, pp. 606-610.

8. *EP*, Vol. I, No. 119, p. 101. Ike became Director of WPD on February 16, 1942. On War Department reorganization, see *Ibid.*, No. 167, pp. 161-163; Dwight D. Eisenhower, *Crusade in Europe*, Garden City, NY: Doubleday & company, Inc., 1948, pp. 31-49; Ray S. Cline, *Washington Command Post: The Operations Division*, Washington, DC: Office of the Chief of Military History, 1951, pp. 90-142; Stephen E. Ambrose, *The Supreme Commander: The War Years of General Dwight D. Eisenhower*, Garden City, NY: Doubleday & Company, Inc. 1970, p. 29; and Dwight D. Eisenhower, *At Ease: Stories I Tell to Friends*, Garden City, NY: Doubleday & Company, 1967, p. 248, in which he looks back on "the frantic, tumultuous months I spent in the War Department in the Planning Section and later as Chief of Operations. . . ."

9. Eisenhower drafted a March 19, 1942, memorandum from Secretary of War Stimson to the President with an attached message for FDR to send to Churchill on the command status of General Stilwell in China. *EP*, Vol. I, No. 201, pp. 194-195. The message was sent on March 20 as Eisenhower had drafted it; and Churchill later reprinted in his World War II memoirs. Winston S. Churchill, *The Second World War*. Vol. IV. *The Hinge of Fate*, Boston: Houghton Mifflin Company, 1950, pp. 169-170.

10. For Eisenhower's March 8, 1942, memorandum to Marshall recommending that his study be proposed to the President "to implement his verbal instructions of March 7," see *EP*, Vol. I, No. 178, pp. 174-176. Marshall's primary revision of Eisenhower's study was to change the term "area" to "theater." *Ibid.*, No. 1, p. 176. See also Maurice Matloff and Edwin M. Snell, *Strategic Planning for Coalition Warfare, 1941-1942*, Washington, DC: U.S. Army Center of Military History, 1958, pp. 165-167.

11. *EP*, Vol. I, No. 222, p. 223. For Eisenhower's March 9, 1942, memorandum on the division of the Pacific for Marshall's dispatch to the JCS, see *Ibid.*, No. 180, pp. 176-177. For the March 30, 1942, JCS Directive, see Morton, pp. 244-256, 614-618.

12. *EP*, Vol. I, No. 222, p. 223.

13. U.S. Congress. House. Committee on Expenditures in the Executive Departments. Hearings on H.R. 2319. *National Security Act of 1947.* 80th Congress, 1st Session (hereinafter *Hearings*, H.R. 2319), Washington, DC: U.S. Government Printing Office, 1947, p. 302. For a similar recollection, see Eisenhower, *At Ease*, p. 252.

14. *EP*, Vol. I, No. 204, p. 197.

15. *Ibid.*, No. 199, pp. 100-101.

16. Lawrence J. Legere, Jr., "Unification of the Armed Forces," Ph.D. dissertation, Harvard University, 1951, p. 200; and *EP*, Vol. I, No. 165, note 3, pp. 159-160.

17. *EP*, Vol. I, No. 293, p. 295. See also Chandler, "Introduction," *EP*, VOL. I, p. xxi.

18. *Ibid.*, No. 541, p. 603. On Eisenhower's May visit to England, see his May 30, 1942, "Memorandum for Record" on BOLERO, *Ibid.*, No. 318, pp. 318-326. On Eisenhower's idea for TORCH organization, see his memorandum to General Ismay on August 6, the day he was appointed TORCH commander. *Ibid.*, No. 411, pp. 444-447.

19. *Ibid.*, No. 541, p. 603.

20. *Ibid.*, No. 559, p. 627. "You will carry out any orders issued by him," the final directive informed the British commander concerning Eisenhower. *Ibid.*, No. 541, note 1, p. 604.

21. *Ibid.*, No. 811, note 2, p. 946.

22. *Ibid.*, No. 811, p. 944.

23. *Ibid.*, Vol. III, No. 1256, note 1, p. 1424.

24. Original emphasis. *Ibid.*, pp. 1421, 1423.

25. *Ibid.*, No. 1601, p. 1785.

26. Ambrose, p. 367.

27. Eisenhower, *Crusade in Europe*, pp. 284-288.

28. *EP*, VOL. IV, No. 2284. See also Stephen Ambrose, "Eisenhower as Commander: Single Thrust Versus Broad Front," *Ibid.*, Vol. V, pp.

46-48; Chandler, "Introduction," *Ibid.*, p. xxvi; and Louis Galambos, ed., *Ibid.*, *Columbia University*, Vols. X-XI, Baltimore: The Johns Hopkins University Press, 1984, Vol. X, No. 321, p. 420, in which Eisenhower writes in 1949 to Montgomery's wartime chief of staff:

> I feel that I learned many, many things during the war and if I had to do the whole thing over again there are many arrangements I would alter and revise. I would never, however, in such a command as we had in Europe appoint a so-called ground "Commander in Chief."

29. Louis Galambos, ed., *Ibid.*, *Chief of Staff.*, Vols. VI-IX, Baltimore: The Johns Hopkins University Press, 1978, Vol. VII, No. 552, p. 637.

30. *Ibid.*, Vol. VIII, No. 1465, p. 1683.

31. *Ibid.*, No. 1074, p. 1258.

32. *Ibid.*, No. 1108, p. 1297.

33. *Ibid.*, p. 1299. In his September 14, 1946, proposal to the JCS, Eisenhower quoted from Chapter 2, paragraph 12, of the 1935 *JAAN* as amended in 1945 to reflect the wartime command structure. See Change 17, June 26, 1945, *JAAN*, pp. 5-6. See also Ronald H. Cole, Walter S. Poole, James F. Schnabel, Robert J. Watson, Willard J. Webb, *The History of the Unified Command Plan 1946-1993,* Washington, DC: Joint History Office, Office of the Joint Chiefs of Staff, February 1995, p. 13.

34. Hearings, HR 2319, p. 288.

35. U.S. Congress. Senate Committee on Military Affairs, *Hearings on S. 84 and S. 1482*, 79th Congress, 1st Session, Washington, DC: U.S. Government Printing Office, 1945, p.362.

36. *Ibid.*, p. 366, On Collins, see *Ibid.*, pp. 155-180.

37. Jeffery M. Dorwart, *Eberstadt and Forrestal. A National Security Partnership, 1909-1949*, College Station: Texas A&M University Press, 1991, p. 131. For Truman's December 19, 1945, message to Congress, see *DoD Documents*, pp. 7-16.

38. Hearings, HR 2319, p. 326. Forrestal reported that Eisenhower believed "the broad principle of a Secretary of Common Defense should

be accepted with the details to be worked out afterwards." Walter Millis, ed., *The Forrestal Diaries*, New York: The Viking Press, 1951, p. 205.

39. *DoD Documents*, p. 177.

40. For the quotations and provisions of the 1947 National Security Act, see *Ibid.*, pp. 35-50.

41. U.S. Congress, Senate, Committee on Armed Services, Hearings on S.758, *A Bill to Promote the National Security by Providing for a National Defense Establishment.* 80th Congress, 1st Session, Washington, DC: U.S. Government Printing Office, 1947, pp. 113-115.

42. *Ibid.*, p. 99. For Forrestal's adverse reaction to Eisenhower's testimony, see *Forrestal Diaries*, pp. 269-270.

43. Hearings, HR 2319, p. 99.

44. Eisenhower added: "The thought injects itself, however, that when this does become possible, *it may no longer be necessary*, because of the perfection of cooperation." Original emphasis. *EP,* VOL. IX, No. 2055, p. 2251.

45. *Ibid.*, p. 2243. Eisenhower also addressed this theme in his official farewell report:

> Fortunately, the Act does not bind the National Military Establishment to a detailed and blueprinted program . . . , leaving the development of organization and administrative practices to time and experience.

Dwight D. Eisenhower, *Final Report of the Chief of Staff United States Army*, Washington, DC: U.S. Government Printing Office, 1948, p. 20.

46. Eisenhower, *At Ease*, p. 352.

47. Forrestal Diaries, p. 540.

48. *EP,* Vol. X, No. 313, note 5, p. 399.

49. *Ibid.*, No. 327, 433 and NO. 288, p. 358.

50. Original emphasis. *Ibid.*, No. 288, p. 359.

51. For the quotations and provisions of the 1949 amendments, see *DoD Documents*, pp. 84-106.

52. Departments of the Army, Navy, and Air Force. *Joint Action Armed Forces (JAAF) (Army-FM 110-5; Air Force AFM 1-1)*, Washington, DC: U.S. Government Printing Office, September 19, 1951, p. 30.

53. *The Papers of Dwight David Eisenhower. NATO and the Campaign of 1952*, Vols. XII-XIII, Louis Galambos, ed., Baltimore: The Johns Hopkins University Press, 1984, Vol. XII, No. 58, p. 91.

54. *Ibid.*, No. 405, p. 592.

55. All quotations in *DoD Documents*, pp. 150-151. See also Dwight David Eisenhower, *The White House Years, Mandate for Change, 1953-1956*, Garden City, NY: Doubleday & Company, Inc., 1963, pp. 445-447 and 449-450; and John C. Ries, *The Management of Defense: Organization and Control of the U.S. Armed Services*, Baltimore: The Johns Hopkins Press, 1964, p. 152.

56. *DoD Documents*, p. 131.

57. Ries, pp. 152-154; and *DoD Documents*, pp. 131-136.

58. All quotations and provisions of the April 30, 1953, message to Congress are contained in *DoD Documents*, pp. 149-157.

59. Eisenhower, *Mandate for Change*, p. 448. Unlike earlier reorganizations, the 1953 plan was submitted under a special congressional device established in the 1949 Act, which allowed presidential reorganization proposals after a 60-day period without a disapproving resolution from either House of Congress to become law. Eisenhower's Reorganization Plan No. 6 took effect on June 3, 1953. *DoD Documents*, pp. 157-159. The October 1, 1953, revision of the Key West Agreement was incorporated into *DoD Directive 5100.1* dated March 15, 1954. *Ibid.*, pp. 293-305.

60. *Ibid.*, p. 149.

61. U.S. Congress, House, Committee on Government Operations, Hearings on H. J. Res. 264, (*Reorganization Plan No. 6 of 1953 [Department of Defense]*), 83rd Congress, 1st Session, Washington, DC: U.S. Government Printing Office, 1953, pp. 211 and 224-225.

62. Dwight D. Eisenhower, *The White House Years: Waging Peace, 1956-1961*, Garden City, NY: Doubleday, 1965, p. 244.

63. For the quotations and provisions hereafter from the April 3 message, see *DoD Documents*, pp. 175-186.

64. U.S. Congress, House, Committee on Armed Services, *Reorganization of the Department of Defense*. Hearings pursuant to HR 11001, HR 11002, HR 11003, HR 11958, and HR 12541, 85th Congress, 2nd Session, Washington, DC: U.S. Government Printing Office, 1958, p. 6474.

65. Eisenhower, *Waging Peace*, p. 251.

66. *Ibid.*, p. 252.

67. *Ibid.* For the provisions of the final law, see *DoD Documents*, pp. 188-230.

68. Eisenhower, *Waging Peace*, p. 247.

69. U.S. Congress, Senate, Committee on Armed Services, Hearings, *Organization, Structure and Decisionmaking Procedures of the Department of Defense,* 98th Congress, 1st Session, Washington, DC: U.S. Government Printing Office, 1984, Part 5, p. 187. See also James R. Locher III, "Taking Stock of Goldwater-Nichols," *Joint Force Quarterly*, No. 13, Autumn 1996, p. 15; and U.S. Congress, Senate, Committee on Armed Services, *Defense Organization and the Need for Change*, 99th Congress, 1st Session, Washington, DC: U.S. Government Printing Office, 1985, pp. 3-4, 84, 87, 162, 168, 303 & 309-310.

70. *Ibid.*, p. 253.

71. U.S. Congress, House, Committee on Armed Services, Hearings, *The National Defense Program—Unification and Strategy*, 81st Congress, 1st Session, Washington, DC: U.S. Government Printing Office, 1949, pp. 563-564. In September 1948, in response to written questions posed by Ferdinand Eberstadt, the creator of the coordinate organization that emerged in 1947, Eisenhower wrote:

I believe that the 1947 Act represents a distinct advance. I believe changes will prove necessary, but I believe that all of them should be evolutionary rather than revolutionary.

EP, Vol. X, No. 165, p. 207.

CHAPTER 4

THE DoD REORGANIZATION ACT OF 1986: IMPROVING THE DEPARTMENT THROUGH CENTRALIZATION AND INTEGRATION

Douglas C. Lovelace, Jr.

Reorganizing the military establishment of the United States has been a subject of considerable congressional interest throughout much of this century. As early as 1921, Congress began considering proposals to combine or unify the military departments under a single executive agency. Between 1921 and 1945, for example, Congress considered some 50 proposals to reorganize the U.S. armed forces. Due largely to opposition from the Departments of War and Navy, however, none of these initiatives resulted in legislation.[1]

The experiences of World War II made it clear that, for the U.S. armed forces, future warfare would increasingly be characterized by unified operations,[2] and that a centrally coordinated process for providing U.S. military capabilities was needed. In a message to Congress (December 1945), President Harry S. Truman stated that "There is enough evidence now at hand to demonstrate beyond question the need for a unified department." He urged Congress to ". . . adopt legislation combining the War and Navy departments into one single Department of National Defense."[3] President Truman's message led to the National Security Act (NSA) of 1947 which created the "National Military Establishment" and initiated a trend toward unification of the U.S. armed forces that would continue throughout the remainder of the century.[4]

The type of unification advanced by legislation and considered in this chapter has not eliminated the separate services or merged the military departments into one.[5] As used herein, unification refers to the centralized direction of the U.S. armed forces and the concomitant subordination of the military departments and services to a centralized control structure. This contrasts with a separatist approach by which each military department would be a relatively autonomous organization—coordinating, and perhaps synchronizing, its activities with the other departments, but retaining essential decisionmaking autonomy in most areas.

The National Security Act of 1947 marked the beginning of a process of unification which continues today. Congress contributed to the evolutionary process by passing the 1949 and 1958 amendments. In 1986, Congress passed seminal legislation that significantly reorganized the Department of Defense (DoD), moving it further toward a unified structure. In the Goldwater-Nichols Department of Defense Reorganization Act of 1986 (GNA), Congress sought to strengthen civilian control of DoD, improve military advice to civilian leadership, clarify the authority and responsibilities of the combatant commanders, improve strategy formulation and contingency planning, and provide for more efficient use of defense resources. Over a decade old, the Act has been substantially implemented in most respects. The GNA is the most comprehensive defense reorganization package enacted since the 1947 National Security Act. Designed to accelerate the unification of the U.S. armed forces by fundamentally altering the manner in which they were raised, trained, commanded, and employed, the GNA has affected virtually all major elements of DoD. Many consider the GNA instrumental in the success of U.S. forces during OPERATION DESERT STORM. Some believe that the question confronting DoD now is what initiatives are required to progress the department beyond the framework established by GNA? Still others believe that the process and pattern of reform which led to passage of the Act should be replicated to achieve a commensurate degree of unification among the various national agencies involved in formulating and implementing national security strategy. The purpose of this chapter is to analyze the GNA in order to provide a historical context for the contemporary debate about what steps should be taken to improve further the functioning of the DoD within the overarching national security structure.

UNIFICATION EFFORTS AND CONCERNS

How best to balance the unified and separatist approaches to DoD organization has been a challenge that has confronted Congress over the past half-century. Since 1947, Congress has gravitated slowly toward the unification pole of these contrasting views of armed forces organization, but the attraction of the separatist philosophy remains significant. Since the end of World War II, almost every Secretary of Defense has supported increased centralization of authority. The military departments, on the other hand, have generally attempted to retain their autonomy.

In attempts to craft the most effective balance between these opposing forces, Congress has recognized that increased unification of the U.S. armed forces erodes congressional control over the military. Consequently, Congress has sought to limit this erosion by not over-centralizing authority within the executive branch.[6] The interaction of these dynamics has resulted in an evolutionary unification process that continues as implementation of the GNA nears completion.

The National Security Act of 1947 was the first, albeit relatively ineffective, piece of unification legislation. Although the act created the position of Secretary of Defense, it gave the Secretary no real authority over the secretaries of the Army, Navy, or Air Force. Congress perceived both the benefits and the dangers associated with unification, and decided not to enact more radical legislation for fear of yielding much of its control over the military to the executive branch.[7] By 1949, however, the executive branch was pressing for legislation to achieve greater unification. Commenting on the National Security Act, President Truman, in a March 1949 message to Congress, stated:

> This act has provided a practical and workable basis for beginning the unification of the military services and for coordinating military policy with foreign and economic policy . . . The past 18 months have dispelled any doubt that unification of the armed forces can yield great advantages to the nation . . . [but] the act fails to provide for a fully responsible official with authority adequate to meet his responsibility, whom the president and the Congress can hold accountable.[8]

The 1949 Amendment to the National Security Act represented an important, but limited, step in further unifying the U.S. military establishment. Congress established DoD as an executive department and made the Secretary of Defense responsible for its general direction. Congress also redesignated the executive departments of the Army, Navy, and Air Force as military departments, which reduced them in stature, but the legislation also instructed that they continue to be "separately administered."[9]

The congressional intent stated in Section 2 of the Amendment was:

> . . . to provide three military departments, **separately administered**, . . . to provide for their authoritative coordination and unified direction under civilian control of the **Secretary of Defense** but not to merge them . . . and for their integration into an efficient team of land, naval, and air forces **but not to establish a single Chief of Staff over the armed forces nor an armed forces general staff (but this is not to be interpreted as applying to the Joint Chiefs of Staff or Joint Staff)** [emphasis in original].[10]

An important feature of the 1949 Amendment was that, while clearly avoiding the actual merging of the military departments and the creation of a "single Chief of Staff," the amendment provided for a Chairman of the Joint Chiefs of Staff (CJCS). The Joint Chiefs of Staff (JCS) was given legal identity by the 1947 NSA, with a mandate to serve as the principal military advisory agency to the President, NSC, and the Secretary of Defense.[11] The 1949 amendment to the NSA created the position of CJCS, but significantly circumscribed his authority. He was not to exercise command over the military services nor the Joint Chiefs, and, in fact, he was not even a voting member of the JCS.[12]

With the 1949 Amendment to the National Security Act, Congress took a further step toward unifying the armed forces but stopped short of merging the military departments. Not surprisingly, unification pressures continued. By 1958, the benefits of unified strategic direction of the armed forces were more apparent, but Congress still feared the creation of too much centralized authority over the military. With the DoD Reorganization Act of 1958, which amended the NSA, Congress nonetheless gave the Secretary of Defense real authority over the U.S. military establishment, including the power to reorganize DoD. The amendment modified the requirement that the military departments be "separately administered" to say that they must be "separately organized."[13] The 1958 Act,

> further subordinated the military departments to the central authority of the Secretary of Defense, established the chain of command from the President, through the Secretary of Defense and the Joint Chiefs of Staff, to the unified and specified commands, and provided for the central direction and control of research and development.[14]

During the next 25 years, there was little congressional action to unify the U.S. armed forces, but the Secretary of Defense used his increased authority to take limited steps toward further unification.[15] In the early 1980s, however, several events helped shape a congressional consensus that DoD required significant reform.

THE ROAD TO REFORM

The Iran Hostage Rescue Attempt.

On November 4, 1979, Iranian militants stormed the U.S. Embassy in Tehran, seizing 53 American hostages. The attack on the embassy should not have come as a complete surprise. Almost 9 months earlier, a similar incident occurred but was resolved diplomatically.[16] Although a contingency plan for the evacuation of U.S. personnel existed,[17] it is unclear if the JCS, in response to the first attack on the embassy, advised the Secretary of Defense or the President that the contingency plan should be made ready for potential execution. In any event, over 5 months elapsed after the second seizure and the taking of American hostages before the United States mounted a military response.

The U.S. national leadership was confronted with a situation for which it seemed unprepared. Direct White House supervision, excessive devotion to secrecy and compartmentalization, and a general circumvention of the established crisis action planning process characterized operational planning for the rescue mission.[18] The plan that resulted was "joint"[19] in that it provided for forces from all services but, at the same time, it was not a unified operation in that it did not provide for unified command, unified action, or joint training of the forces.[20] Acting on the advice of the JCS that the high-risk mission had a better than average chance of succeeding, President Jimmy Carter directed that the operation be executed.[21]

OPERATION EAGLE CLAW, designed to quickly and dramatically rescue the hostages, ended in catastrophe. American planning, equipment, tactics, and leadership proved inadequate.[22] Eight people on the mission were killed, expensive U.S. equipment and classified information were abandoned, and not a single hostage was rescued.[23] The entire world wondered if the United States had indeed become a military "paper tiger."

In the months following the failed rescue attempt, a stunned American public endured the daily media reminders of the continued plight of the hostages and America's inability to do anything about it.[24] It is not surprising that the Iran hostage rescue experience aroused congressional suspicions about the way in which the U.S. armed forces were commanded, organized, trained, and employed.[25] Those suspicions were confirmed by subsequent events.

Beirut.

During the fall of 1983, congressional concern over the command, organization, and employment of U.S. armed forces again peaked following another military disaster. The previous year, some 1,200 U.S. Marines joined French and Italian contingents in a multinational force. Their mission was to preserve peace in and around Beirut, Lebanon, facilitate the restoration of the sovereignty and authority of Lebanon's government, and help bring peace to the war-torn country. The Marines occupied positions in the vicinity of Beirut International Airport (BIA).

In April 1983, a massive explosion destroyed the U.S. Embassy in Beirut, killing 17 U.S. citizens and over 40 others. Fighting between indigenous factions intensified throughout the spring and summer. From March through October 1983, the Marines suffered a number of casualties (4 dead and 15 wounded) from the various factions involved in Lebanon's civil war.[26] Events culminated on October 23, 1983, when a suicide bomber attacked the Marines' headquarters building, killing 241 U.S. military personnel and wounding over 100 others.[27] Shortly thereafter, President Reagan withdrew the remaining U.S. forces.[28]

Congressional reaction was swift. A delegation from the Investigations Subcommittee of the House of Representatives Committee on Armed Services arrived in Beirut by December 12, 1983. Their report to the Committee Chairman (December 19, 1983) criticized several military

71

aspects of the incident. Transcending the tactical level, the more notable criticisms included an ambiguous chain of command, lack of proper oversight by higher levels of command, lack of adequate intelligence support, reporting by military sources of incomplete or inaccurate information,[29] the failure of civilian leadership to heed the advice of senior military leaders concerning the overall risks of the operation, and the inability of the military to anticipate and protect against such an attack.[30]

With the memories of the Iran hostage rescue attempt still vivid, the Beirut tragedy suggested that the deficiencies of the U.S. armed forces that contributed to the debacle in Iran had not been corrected, but somehow had worsened. Those sentiments began to prevail, and even a successful military operation would not arrest the congressional movement toward sweeping reform of DoD.

Grenada.

President Ronald Reagan came into office with the task of restoring U.S. prestige, in part by improving the credibility of its military capabilities. The U.S. experience in Lebanon did not further that objective. Some believed, however, that the successful use of military force, for a just cause, could restore the confidence of the American people in their military and government.[31] Cuban activities on the island of Grenada necessitated a military operation that was large enough to be credible, but not so large as to present significant risk of a substantial number of U.S. casualties.[32]

On October 25, 1983, 2 days after the Beirut bombing, the invasion of Grenada, OPERATION URGENT FURY, began.[33] The mission was to secure and evacuate about 1,000 U.S. citizens, defeat the Grenadian and Cuban forces present, and stabilize the situation so that a democratic government could be restored.[34]

Taken as a whole, OPERATION URGENT FURY was a success; the students were freed unharmed, the government of Prime Minister Maurice Bishop was ousted, Cuban troops were removed, and democracy was restored. Still, critics reported many problems with the operation.[35] These included a lack of accurate, up to date maps, imperfect intelligence support, and U.S. casualties resulting from accidents and fratricide.[36] There were interoperability problems among the services, particularly in the area of communications.[37] And although some forces acted bravely, U.S. Army units reportedly performed sluggishly, used inappropriate tactics, and suffered from breakdowns in discipline.[38] While the validity of such claims has been debated, the fact remains that the overall success of the operation failed to preclude congressional criticism, and the Reagan administration again found itself on the defensive.[39]

Congressional Reaction.

The military setbacks of the late 1970s and early 1980s provided the historical context that shaped the widespread congressional perception in 1983 that the U.S. military was in need of reform. As early as June of that year, members of Congress were calling for changes within DoD. Senators John Tower and Henry (Scoop) Jackson, then Chairman and Ranking Minority member of the Senate Committee on Armed services, respectively, directed the committee staff to conduct a study of the organization and decisionmaking procedures of DoD. For the next 18 months, the study took the form of hearings, interviews, and research. In January 1985, Senators Barry Goldwater and Sam Nunn directed that a more formal and vigorous study be undertaken.[40]

The Locher Report.

The resulting staff study yielded a report entitled *Defense Organization: The Need for Change,* informally known as the Locher Report (October 1985, Study Director:

James R. Locher). The report indicated the consensus that was building in Congress that DoD required reorganization. The essence of the report was reflected in the testimony of former Secretary of Defense, James R. Schlesinger:

> ... in the absence of structural reform I fear that we shall obtain less than is attainable from our expenditures and from our forces. Sound structure will permit the release of energies and of imagination now unduly constrained by the existing arrangements. Without such reform, I fear that the United States will obtain neither the best military advice, nor the effective execution of military plans, nor the provision of military capabilities commensurate with the fiscal resources provided, nor the most advantageous deterrence and defense posture available to the nation.[41]

The report addressed a wide range of issues affecting the performance of the DoD, including its four major organizational elements: the Office of the Secretary of Defense (OSD), the Organization of the Joint Chiefs of Staff (OJCS), the unified and specified combatant commands, and the military departments. The report also addressed two key decisionmaking processes: the Planning, Programming, and Budgeting System (PPBS) and the acquisition process.[42] Additionally, congressional review and oversight of defense policies and programs and civilian control of the military received scrutiny.

The report went beyond the mere cataloging of deficiencies and issues. It offered numerous recommendations for overhauling DoD, its decisionmaking processes, and its organization. The more significant recommendations included:

- establishing three new Under Secretary of Defense positions—for nuclear deterrence, North Atlantic Treaty Organization (NATO) defense, and regional defense and force projection;

- creating the position of Assistant Secretary of Defense (Strategic Planning);

- disestablishing the JCS and replacing it with a Joint Military Advisory Council consisting of a chairman and a four-star officer from each service who is on his last tour of duty;

- authorizing the chairman of the Joint Military Advisory Council to provide military advice in his own right and designating him as the principal military advisor to the Secretary of Defense;

- authorizing the chairman of the Joint Military Advisory Council to develop and administer a personnel management system for officers assigned to joint duty;

- removing the service component commanders within the unified combatant commands from the operational chain of command; and

- fully integrating the Secretariats' and the service headquarters' staffs.

Although Congress did not directly act on any of the report's fairly radical recommendations, the report effectively illuminated numerous deficiencies within DoD.[43] Moreover, the report affirmed the congressional perception of the need for change within DoD and helped shape the debates that would occur over the next year.

Presidential Reaction.

In June 1985, out of concern that Congress, if left to its own devices, might impose ill-advised, or at least unwanted changes upon DoD, President Reagan established the Blue Ribbon Commission on Defense Management, informally known as the Packard Commission (after its chairman, David Packard). Establishing the commission also served to stanch any public perception that the executive branch was not willing or able to reform one of its departments. The President charged the commission to:

. . . conduct a defense management study of important dimension, including: the budget process, the procurement system, legislative oversight, and the organizational and operational arrangements, both formal and informal, among the Office of the Secretary of Defense, the Organization of the Joint Chiefs of Staff, the Unified and Specified Command systems, the military departments, and Congress.[44]

In February 1986, the commission provided the President with an interim report containing several recommendations. The President officially endorsed the preliminary recommendations in April 1986, and designated many for "quick and decisive implementation."[45] The commission published its findings in June 1986. They were generally consistent with the conclusions of the Locher Report released some 8 months earlier.[46] However, the commission's key recommendations were considerably less radical:

- defense planning should begin with a comprehensive statement of national security objectives and priorities;

- the president should issue provisional 5-year budget levels to the Secretary of Defense;

- the CJCS should prepare a military strategy and options for operational concepts;

- the CJCS, with the advice of the JCS and the combatant commanders, should prepare broad military options, framing explicit trade-offs among the armed forces, and submit recommendations to the Secretary of Defense;

- the CJCS, with the assistance of the JCS and the Director of Central Intelligence, should provide net assessments of U.S. and allied armed forces relative to those of potential adversaries. The assessments should be used to evaluate risks inherent in the options developed;

- the president should select a particular option and specify an associated budget level upon which DoD would base its 5-year defense plan and 2-year budget;

- the CJCS should be designated as the principal uniformed military advisor to the president, the NSC, and the Secretary of Defense, representing his own views as well as those of the corporate JCS;

- the Joint Staff and the OJCS should be placed under the exclusive direction of the chairman;

- the Secretary of Defense should direct that commands to and reports from the unified and specified commands be channeled through the chairman;

- the position of vice chairman of the JCS should be created;

- broader authority should be assigned to the unified commanders to structure subordinate commands, joint task forces, and support activities;

- the Unified Command Plan should be revised;

- the Secretary of Defense should be provided with the flexibility to establish the shortest possible chains of command to deployed contingency forces; and

- the Secretary of Defense should establish a single unified command to integrate global air, land, and sea transportation.[47]

During early spring 1986, while both houses of Congress considered defense reform bills, influential congressmen such as Senator Barry Goldwater conferred with members of the Packard Commission. As a result of these discussions, Congress began to embrace the Packard Commission's recommendations over the more revolutionary changes recommended in the Locher Report.[48]

CONGRESSIONAL ACTION

Throughout the first half of 1986, discussions continued regarding the need to reorganize DoD. On one side of the debate was the U.S. Congress, convinced that reform was necessary. On the other side were the Secretary of Defense and the services.[49] Interestingly, the president sided with Congress.[50] With the executive branch seemingly divided over the issue of defense reorganization and against the background of the Iran hostage rescue attempt, the Beirut bombing, and the incursion into Grenada, Senators Barry Goldwater and Sam Nunn and Representative Bill Nichols were able to build exceptionally strong bipartisan support for reform.

During the spring and summer, each house passed its version of the reform bill by an overwhelming majority.[51] With the Congress united in support of defense reorganization, the joint conference to resolve inter-committee issues went quickly and smoothly.[52] The conference report was published on September 12, 1986, and this substantial piece of legislation sailed through the Senate and the House of Representatives on September 16 and 17, respectively. By October 1, 1986, the GNA was law.

Congressional Intent.

Traditional congressional concern over the migration of control of the military from the legislative to the executive branch has, in some respects, retarded the evolution toward unification. Congress recognizes the value of separately organized military departments competing to meet the requirements of the combatant CINCs by offering alternative program recommendations. Congress also worries that too much centralization of authority might inhibit its discretionary authority over defense matters. At the same time, however, Congress recognizes the need for more unified direction of the U.S. armed forces. The provisions of the 1986 GNA reflect these countervailing concerns.

The scope of the legislation clearly evidenced congressional dissatisfaction with the lack of unified direction of, and action by, the U.S. armed forces. Congress believed the problems derived from dysfunctional relationships among the Secretary of Defense, service secretaries, CJCS, JCS, CINCs and service components, and the service chiefs. In passing the GNA, Congress intended:

1. to reorganize DoD and strengthen civilian authority within the Department;

2. to improve the military advice provided to the resident, the NSC, and the Secretary of Defense;

3. to place clear responsibility on the commanders the unified and specified combatant commands for the accomplishment of missions assigned to those commands;

4. to ensure that the authority of the commanders of the unified and specified combatant commands is fully commensurate with the responsibility of those commanders for the accomplishment of missions assigned to their commands;

5. to increase attention to the formulation of strategy and to contingency planning;

6. to provide for more efficient use of defense resources;

7. to improve joint officer management policies; and

8. to otherwise enhance the effectiveness of military operations and improve the management and administration of DoD.[53]

Each provision of the Act addressed one or more of these elements of congressional intent. An in-depth analysis of every provision of the Act is beyond the scope of this essay. However, an assessment of the more significant provisions provides a sufficient basis for determining the extent to which the Act has served its purpose. A summary of the Act's major provisions follows.

Strengthening Civilian Authority.

Congress formulated several provisions of the Act to strengthen directly the authority of the Secretary of Defense. The two most significant provisions increased the secretary's influence over program planning conducted by DoD components and the contingency planning conducted by the CINCs. Other provisions indirectly enhanced the secretary's control. The more significant of these relate to improving the advice the secretary receives from the uniformed military, thus enhancing his ability to command.

Defense Planning Guidance.

First, to increase the secretary's authority and control over programs developed by DoD components, the Act provided that

> the Secretary of Defense, with the advice and assistance of the Chairman of the Joint Chiefs of Staff, shall provide annually to the heads of Department of Defense components written policy guidance for the preparation and review of the program recommendations and budget proposals of their respective components. Such guidance shall include guidance on—
> a. national security objectives and policies;
> b. the priorities of military missions; and
> c. the resource levels projected to be available for the period of time for which such recommendations and proposals are to be effective.[54]

The authority provided by this section clearly empowered the secretary to establish the criteria upon which the military departments and other DoD components must base their programs.[55] The secretary uses the *Defense Planning Guidance (DPG)*, a classified document, as his tool for providing the program planning guidance required by the Act.

The *DPG* initiates the first phase of the DoD PPBS.[56] The PPBS is the biennial process by which DoD plans for the force capabilities that will be needed from 2 to 8 years in the future. It facilitates the development of programs to attain those capabilities and translates those programs into budget submissions. By asserting himself at an early stage in the program planning process, the secretary has enhanced his influence over the programs which are ultimately submitted for approval.

Contingency Planning Guidance.

The GNA also increased the Secretary of Defense's authority and responsibility in the area of contingency planning.[57] The Act provides that

> the Secretary of Defense, with the approval of the president and after consultation with the Chairman of the Joint Chiefs of Staff, shall provide annually to the Chairman written policy guidance for the preparation and review of contingency plans.[58]

The tool used by the secretary to implement this provision of the Act is the *Contingency Planning Guidance (CPG)*.

The *CPG* is a concise, classified document that the secretary uses to inform the chairman of general and specific strategic areas of concern to the civilian leadership, for which contingency planning should be conducted. The chairman then uses this guidance to fulfill his responsibility to "[provide] for the preparation and review of contingency plans . . .," also as required by the GNA.[59] The *CPG* also informs the chairman of the general requirements of the secretary, or his representatives, to review contingency plans during their development as well as upon completion. This element of the GNA has been implemented quite effectively.[60]

Through the *CPG*, the Secretary of Defense has inserted himself, and his selected representatives, squarely into the contingency planning process. He has done so in a manner that gives primacy to the policies of civilian leadership, appropriately defers the actual development of contingency plans to the uniformed military leadership, and, by

81

involving himself early, maintains effective civilian control throughout the planning process. This is precisely what Congress intended in the GNA.[61]

Improving Military Advice.

Several significant provisions of the GNA sought to improve the military advice given to the president, the Secretary of Defense, and the NSC. The sponsors of the Act believed the JCS was incapable of providing concise, timely, and useful advice to the National Command Authorities (NCA).[62] Testifying before the Senate Armed services Committee, former Secretary of Defense James R. Schlesinger bore out this conclusion:

> The existing structure [of the JCS], if it does not preclude the best military advice, provides a substantial, though not insurmountable, barrier to such advice . . . [T]he recommendations . . . must pass through a screen designed to protect the institutional interest of each . . . service. . . . [N]o service ox may be gored. . . .
>
> The unavoidable outcome is . . . log-rolling, back-scratching, marriage agreements, and the like. . . . The proffered advice is generally irrelevant, normally unread, and almost always disregarded.[63]

Not only did the JCS system inhibit innovative thought, it also was not an efficient decisionmaking system. For example, General David Jones, a former CJCS, described to Congress how the JCS had spent an entire afternoon arguing over which service should provide the attache to the U.S. Embassy in Cairo.[64]

To eliminate these shortcomings, Congress assigned increased responsibility to the CJCS. In the GNA, it transferred the duties and functions previously the responsibility of the corporate JCS to the chairman, designated the chairman as the "head" of the JCS and the principal military advisor to the NCA and NSC, and directly subordinated the Joint Staff to the chairman.[65] The Act further provided that the chairman, subject to the direction of the president, may participate in NSC meetings.[66] Additionally, the Act permitted the Secretary of Defense to assign overall supervision of certain defense agencies and field activities to the chairman.[67] The Act also created the position of the vice chairman of the JCS to assist the chairman in discharging his new duties.[68]

However, Congress tempered the measures taken to increase the chairman's authority with others that circumscribed it. Notably, the Act vested the chairman with no command authority. The chain of command prescribed by the Act runs from the president, to the Secretary of Defense, to the CINCs.[69] Also, the other members of the JCS retained their responsibilities as military advisors to the NCA and NSC. The Act provided further that, should a member of the JCS disagree with the advice the chairman intended to give to the NCA or the NSC, the member may submit his dissenting view, which the chairman must offer at the same time he presents his own.[70] The Act also provided that each member of the JCS, after informing the Secretary of Defense, may make independent recommendations to Congress.[71] Finally, the Act provided that the chairman shall, as he considers appropriate, consult the other members of the JCS and convene regular meetings.[72] While the Act enlarged the chairman's responsibilities and authority, it clearly did not intend for him to become too powerful, nor for the JCS to become an inert organization.

The lessons of the Persian Gulf War provide evidence that the GNA strengthened civilian control over the armed forces.[73] In the official DoD report on the war, the Secretary of Defense noted that the conflict was the first test of the Act in a major war. He complimented the chairman, the vice chairman, and the other members of the JCS for the "excellent military advice" they provided. He reported that the Act's strengthening of the position of the chairman enabled the chairman to bring to bear his strategic insight and exceptional leadership to ensure the CINC was provided with all he needed to successfully prosecute the war.[74]

Expanding the Authority and Responsibility of the CINCs.

In addition to improving civilian control of the armed forces, the GNA also provided more authority to the CINCs. This was done in order to reduce further the influence of service parochialism and better focus DoD strategic planning on the needs of the unified and specified combatant commanders.[75] Congress crafted several provisions of the Act with this goal in mind. The Act reemphasized and clarified the responsibilities of the CINCs for accomplishing assigned missions as well as for ensuring their commands' preparedness to do so.[76] It also described, in detail, command authority, specifying that a CINC has authority to:

- direct subordinate commands in all aspects of military operations, joint training, and logistics;

- prescribe the chain of command to the commands and forces within the command;

- organize the command and forces within the command;

- employ forces within the command as he considers necessary to accomplish the command's missions;

- assign command functions to subordinate commanders;

- coordinate and approve administrative support, and disciplinary activities necessary to carry out missions assigned to the command;

- select and suspend subordinate commanders and staff officers; and

- convene courts martial.[77]

The Act also provided that the Secretary of Defense shall periodically review the authority of the CINCs and ensure that their authority is commensurate with their responsibilities. The Act gave the CINCs the responsibility to report promptly to the secretary any instances in which they feel their authority to be inadequate.[78] Additionally, Congress considered terms like "full operational command," traditionally used to describe the authority of the CINCs, to be inappropriate for describing their new authority.[79] The Act gave rise to a new term, "combatant command," that DoD has formally adopted.[80]

The Act further reinforced the CINCs' authority by directing the secretaries of the military departments to assign all forces under their jurisdiction to the CINCs,[81] except for those forces needed to carry out the twelve service functions.[82] Although the Act specified a single, clear chain of command from the president to the Secretary of Defense to the CINCs,[83] it notably did not provide for an administrative chain of command from the president to the Secretary of Defense to the military departments. Thus, while the Act allowed each military department to retain unspecified authority and control over a portion of their forces, the bulk of the U.S. armed forces were placed under the authority of the CINCs.

Recognizing the geographic dispersion of the CINCs and the broad spans of control inherent in the offices of the president and the Secretary of Defense, Congress included provisions in the Act that allow the chairman to assist the NCA in overseeing the CINCs. Specifically, the president may direct that all communications between himself or the secretary and the CINCs go through the chairman. The president may also direct that the chairman assist him in the performance of his command functions. The Secretary of Defense may assign the chairman responsibilities for assisting in overseeing the combatant commands; however, such assignment confers no command authority.[84]

85

Although the chairman is vested with no command authority, his role in making the chain of command function effectively is pivotal. In addition to making him the principal military advisor to the NCA, the Act designated him as the spokesman for the CINCs, especially for the requirements of their commands, and made him responsible for informing other elements of DoD of the CINCs' requirements. This provision of the Act not only increased the chairman's real authority, but also enhanced the ability of the CINCs' to influence the NCA.[85]

Another provision of the Act indirectly, but substantially, increased the authority of the CINCs. It made the secretaries of the military departments responsible for "fulfill[ing] (to the maximum extent practicable) the current and future operational requirements of the [CINCs]. . . ."[86] In short, the CINCs were made responsible for identifying requirements for military capabilities, the chairman was made responsible for synthesizing the requirements, and the services were tasked to fulfill the requirements. Thus, the services were not to interpret, on their own, the CINCs' requirements and base service programs on the capabilities the services determined to be most important to the CINCs. Via the GNA, Congress sought to clearly establish the primacy of the CINCs over the service Chiefs with respect to the determination of required military capabilities.

Improving Strategy Formulation and Contingency Planning.

Through the GNA, Congress also sought to improve strategy formulation at both the NCA and CJCS levels. At the NCA level, the Act required the president to "transmit to Congress each year a comprehensive report on the national security strategy of the United States."[87] The national security strategy report is to be submitted at the same time the president's budget is submitted. It is to contain,

. . . the national security strategy of the United States [including] a comprehensive description and discussion of the following:

1. The worldwide interests, goals, and objectives of the United States that are vital to the national security of the United States.

2. The foreign policy, worldwide commitments, and national defense capabilities of the United States necessary to deter aggression and to the national security strategy of the United States.

3. The proposed short-term and long-term uses of the political, economic, military, and other elements of the national power of the United States to protect or promote the interests and achieve the goals and objectives referred to in paragraph (1).

4. The adequacy of the capabilities of the United States to carry out the national security strategy of the United States, including an evaluation of the balance among the elements of the national power of the United States to support the implementation of the national security strategy.

5. Such other information as may be necessary to help inform Congress on matters relating to the national security strategy of the United States.[88]

In adopting the language of this section of the Act, Congress intended for the president to describe comprehensively the short and long-term national security strategies and to provide assessments of the risks associated with implementing the strategies. Congress could use the national security strategy reports to make better informed decisions regarding funding to support the various elements of national power.

Congress recognized the need to address the specifics of strategy at the military strategic planning level as well. The GNA assigned the chairman of the Joint Chiefs of Staff specific strategic and contingency planning responsibilities. With respect to strategic planning, he is to assist the NCA in providing for the strategic direction of the armed forces and is to prepare strategic plans which conform to resource guidance provided by the Secretary of Defense.[89]

To assist the NCA in providing strategic direction, the chairman prepares a national military strategy.[90] Additionally, the chairman provides for the preparation and review of contingency plans which conform to NCA policy guidance.[91] The chairman uses his Joint Strategic Capabilities Plan (JSCP) to translate the policies set forth in the secretary's *Contingency Planning Guidance* into specific planning tasks for the CINCs. In response to the JSCP, the CINCs develop operation plans and submit them to the chairman for approval.[92]

In addition to providing for the preparation and review of contingency plans, the chairman is also required by the GNA to prepare strategic plans.[93] A strategic plan, global in scope, is meant to guide the development and integration of the regional and functional plans developed by the separate CINCs.[94] While the current planning processes enable the CINCs to develop sound regional plans, the chairman, due to his global responsibilities and perspective, is best situated to reconcile, rationalize, and orchestrate the CINCs' plans. The chairman's efforts in this regard must be more than merely compiling the CINCs' plans.[95] He is expected to proactively set forth, in a global context, the priority of the specific objectives for the planning period, the national strategic concepts for attaining the objectives, the national resources that will be applied, and guidance about how their application will be tailored to best serve the established priorities. By performing this strategy formulation role, the chairman can ensure that contingency planning better adheres to policy guidance and is in a better position to provide strategic advice to the NCA.

Providing for More Efficient Use of Defense Resources.

To complement the chairman's increased strategic planning responsibilities, Congress designed several provisions of the GNA to enable the chairman to promote the efficient use of defense resources. When combined, these provisions describe an integrated process for determining required military capabilities and ensuring their efficient provision. The process focuses on the identification, synthesis, and satisfaction of requirements identified by the CINCs. The chairman's role in the process is to solicit the CINCs' requirements, provide national level analyses of these requirements, assess the extent to which the proposed programs of the services efficiently satisfy the CINCs' requirements, and advise the NCA accordingly. Tools which the chairman can use to fulfill these responsibilities include the CINCs' Integrated Priority Lists, the Joint Requirements Oversight Council, the chairman's authority to evaluate the preparedness of the combatant commands,[96] and the chairman's Current Readiness System.

Three additional provisions of the Act also enable the chairman to facilitate the efficient use of defense resources: his responsibility to develop doctrine for the joint employment of the armed forces, his triennial responsibility to appraise the roles and functions assigned to the services, and his biennial responsibility to review the missions, responsibilities, and force structure of the combatant commands.[97]

Improving Joint Officer Management.

One of the more significant provisions of the GNA addressed

> policies, procedures, and practices for the effective management of officers of the . . . active duty list who are particularly trained in, and oriented toward, joint matters....[98]

These officers were to become skilled in "the integrated employment of land, sea, and air forces, including matters relating to national military strategy, strategic planning and contingency planning, and command and control of combat operations under unified command."[99] Through joint officer management measures, Congress intended to improve the quality of the Joint Staff as well as the quality of the CINCs' staffs.

To facilitate the development of "Joint Specialty Officers" (JSOs), Congress prescribed minimum requirements for the number of joint duty positions that must be filled by qualified JSOs, their education and tour of duty length, and promotion requirements for officers who have served or are serving in joint assignments. Implementation of these provisions has presented a daunting challenge to DoD.[100]

Title IV's salient provisions include a requirement for the Secretary of Defense to publish a list of the joint duty positions within DoD and to ensure that at least half are filled by JSOs or JSO nominees. Furthermore, he is to designate at least 1,000 critical joint duty assignment positions that could be held only by fully qualified JSOs.[101] Title IV of the GNA also provides that an officer may not be selected as a JSO until he/she attends a joint professional military education school and, subsequently, completes a full tour of duty in a joint duty assignment.[102]

Title IV also requires the Secretary of Defense to establish a "Capstone Course" for newly appointed general and flag officers that prepares them to work with the other services. The Act requires each officer selected for promotion to one-star rank to attend this course, unless: The officer's immediately preceding assignment was joint; there are no joint requirements for his/her field of expertise; or it would otherwise be in the best interest of the officer's service that he/she not attend.[103]

CONCLUSIONS

Since passage of the NSA in 1947, Congress has sought progressively to unify effort within DoD, improve the quality and fidelity of the military advice provided to the national command authorities and the NSC, and strengthen civilian control over the U.S. Armed forces. The last significant congressional action to these ends was passage of the 1986 GNA. DoD's implementation of the GNA has contributed to the evolution toward unified armed forces. The Office of the Secretary of Defense, the chairman and other members of the JCS, the Joint Staff, the combatant commands, and the services are arriving at a balanced relationship in which civilian authority is supreme.

The DoD has substantially implemented the Act and now is in a position to progress beyond its provisions. But DoD's continued evolution depends on the institutional progress of other agencies of the government involved in national security strategy formulation and implementation. The most important question for the future is how a unified Department of Defense can achieve synergy with the other agencies of national government that also "provide for the common defense and promote the general welfare." Perhaps an approach analogous to the passage of the GNA is appropriate.

ENDNOTES – CHAPTER 4

1. U.S. Congress, Senate, *Defense Organization: The Need for Change*, Staff Report to the Committee on Armed services of the United States Senate, 99th Congress, 1st Session, Washington, DC: U.S. Government Printing Office, 1985, p. 49.

2. Unified operations are those that take place within the unified combatant commands which are composed of forces from two or more military departments. Unified operations is the generic term used to describe the wide scope of actions that take place under the direction of the CINCs of the unified combatant commands. Office of the Chairman of the Joint Chiefs of Staff, *Joint Pub 1-02, Department of Defense*

Dictionary of Military and Associated Terms, Washington, DC: U.S. Government Printing Office, March 23, 1994, p. 400.

3.Office of the Secretary of Defense Historical Office, *The Department of Defense; Documents on Establishment and Organization, 1944-1978*, edited by Alice C. Cole, *et al.*, Washington, DC: U.S. Government Printing Office, 1979, p. 7.

4. *Defense Organization: The Need for Change*, pp. 49-53.

5. Although some of the early proponents of unification advocated such a radical reorganization, that option has not been seriously considered since at least 1949. Lawrence J. Korb, "Service Unification: Arena of Fears, Hopes, and Ironies," *Naval Institute Proceedings, Naval Review*, 1976, p. 176.

6. Generally, the belief is that to the extent that unified armed forces would speak with one voice, Congress would be less able to uncover and debate divergent views on critical defense issues. That, in turn, would inhibit congressional ability to reasonably oversee the armed forces.

7. *Defense Organization: The Need for Change*, p. 50.

8. *The Department of Defense; Documents on Establishment and Organization, 1944-1978*, pp.77-80.

9. *Defense Organization: The Need for Change*, p. 52. The 1949 Amendment also removed the Secretaries of the Military services from the NSC. *The Department of Defense; Documents on Establishment and Organization, 1944-1978*, pp. 84-86.

10. *Ibid.*, p. 86.

11. The President and the Secretary of Defense make up the NCA. *Joint Pub 1-02*, p. 253.

12. *The Department of Defense; Documents on Establishment and Organization, 1944-1978*, pp. 94-95.

13. *Defense Organization: The Need for Change*, p. 52-53.

14. *The Department of Defense; Documents on Establishment and Organization, 1944-1978*, pp. 161-162.

15. *Ibid.*, pp. 239-241. The fundamental underlying rationale for the continued movement toward unification was the belief that independent military departments and services resulted in

unnecessary duplication and waste. Centralized direction and control, on the other hand, promised better rationalization of the acquisition and application of forces, leading to increased effectiveness and efficiency.

16. Paul B. Ryan, *The Iranian Rescue Mission, Why it Failed*, Annapolis, MD: Naval Institute Press, 1985, p. 6.

17. *Ibid.*, p. 20.

18. *Ibid.*, 16-43. Gregory P. Gass, *Command and Control: the Achilles Heel of the Iran Hostage Rescue Mission*, Alexandria, VA: Defense Technical Information Center, February 13, 1992, p. 11.

19. "Joint" connotes activities, operations, and organizations in which elements of more than one Service of the same nation participate. *Joint Pub 1-02*, p. 200.

20. Gass, pp. 11-18.

21. Ryan, pp. 12-16, 28-30, 125.

22. Gass, pp. 1-26.

23. Ryan, pp. 1-2.

24. Howard Husock, *Seige Mentality: ABC, the White House and the Iran Hostage Crisis*, Cambridge, MA: Harvard University, Kennedy School of Government Case Program, 1988, pp. 1-22. Ryan, pp. 97-99. Ryan, pp. 95-97.

25. *Ibid.*, p. 105. The release of the hostages on January 20, 1981, within minutes of President Reagan's inauguration, did not assuage congressional concern.

26. U.S. Department of Defense Commission on Beirut International Airport Terrorist Attack, *Report of the DoD Commission on Beirut International Airport Terrorist Act*, Washington, DC: U.S. Government Printing Office, October 23, 1983, pp. 1-34.

27. *Ibid.*, pp. 29-34.

28. On February 7, 1984, President Reagan announced the redeployment of the Marines, and on March 30, 1984 he reported to Congress that the United States was no longer involved in the multinational force in Lebanon. Gary M. Stern and Morton Halperin, *The U.S. Constitution and the Power to Go to War*, Westport, CT: Greenwood Press, 1984, p. 68.

29. U.S. Congress, House of Representatives, *Adequacy of U.S. Marine Corps Security in Beirut. Summary of Findings and Conclusions of the Investigations Subcommittee of the Committee on Armed services*, 98th Congress, Washington, DC: U.S. Government Printing Office, 1983. pp.1-3.

30. *Ibid.*, pp. 25-70.

31. In an address to the nation on October 27, 1983, President Reagan suggested a direct relationship between the Beirut bombing and the invasion of Grenada. "When Threatened, We Stand Shoulder to Shoulder," *The Washington Post*, October 28, 1983, p. A14.

32. Reynolds A. Burrowes, *Revolution and Rescue in Grenada*, Westport, CT: Greenwood Press, 1988, pp. 71-75; "Secrets From the Reagan Years," *Newsweek*, October 30, 1995, p. 6.

33. Although planning for the Grenada invasion was underway by October 14, the president did not give his approval for the operation until October 24. William C. Gilmore, *The Grenada Intervention: Analysis and Documentation*, New York: Facts on File, 1984, pp. 31-24.

34. Burrowes, pp. 79-80.

35. In an April 1984 report to the Congressional Military Reform Caucus, William S. Lind, of the Military Reform Institute, made the following observation:

> The United States required seven battalions of troops, plus elements of two other battalions, to defeat fewer than 700 Cubans and a Grenadian army that hardly fought at all. Only about 200 of the Cubans were troops; the remainder were construction workers with some militia training. The overwhelmingly superior U.S. forces took 3 days to defeat the Cuban defense and about another 5 days to secure the entire island. By way of contrast, the British defeated more than 11,000 Argentines with just eight infantry battalions in the Falklands.

In addition to criticizing the disappointing performance of special operations and U.S. Army units, Lind cited deficient military planning and the insistence of the JCS that all four services be involved ("just as in the Iran hostage rescue mission"). William S. Lind, *Report to the Congressional Military Reform Caucus, Subject: The Grenada Operation*, Washington, DC: Military Reform Institute, 1984, pp. 2-5.

36. Fred Hiatt, "Many U.S. Casualties Caused by Accidents," *Washington Post*, November 1, 1983, p. 1.

37. Mark Adkin, *Urgent Fury, The Battle for Grenada*, Lexington, MA: Lexington Books, 1989, pp. 221-230, 333-342.

38. Lind, pp. 2-5.

39. Burrowes, pp. 82-83.

40. *Defense Organization: The Need for Change*, p. 13.

41. *Ibid.*, p. III.

42. The acquisition process is the process by which requirements for military capabilities are converted into defense acquisition programs which yield fielded capabilities.

43. *Defense Organization: The Need for Change*, pp. 1-12.

44. David Packard, *A Quest for Excellence, Final Report to the President by the Blue Ribbon Commission on Defense Management*, Washington, DC: U.S. Government Printing Office, June 1986, p. 1.

45. David Packard, letter, June 30, 1986, transmitting to President Reagan the *Final Report of the President's Blue Ribbon Commission on Defense Management.*

46. Packard, pp. xvii-xviii.

47. *Ibid.*, pp. xvii-xxx. In the interest of brevity and since they are not central to an assessment of the 1986 Department of Defense Reorganization Act, the specific recommendations concerning acquisition reform and government-industry accountability are not provided in this study.

48. Michael Ganley, "Reorganization Bill Almost Certain to Reach the President's Desk This Year," *Armed Forces Journal International*, April 1986, p. 16.

49. Then Secretary of Defense Casper Weinberger believed that congressionally mandated reorganization of the DoD was unnecessary and that any increase in the influence of the CJCS would be at the expense of the Secretary of Defense. Assistant Secretary of the Air Force Tidal McCoy believed that DoD was already too centralized and that the service secretaries needed more, not less, autonomy. Secretary of the Navy John Lehman claimed that the executive branch had been

worshipping "at the altar of the false idols of centralization and unification" for the past 30 years. Bryan Howard Ward, *United States Defense Reorganizations: Contending Explanations*, Ann Arbor, MI: UMI Dissertation services, 1995, pp. 324-327.

50. Although prior to establishing the Packard Commission in mid-1985, President Reagan considered defense reorganization an issue to be handled by the Secretary of Defense. His formation of the Commission and rapid approval of its recommendations evinced his belief that reform was necessary. Ward, pp. 324-327.

51. On May 7, 1986, the Senate approved its version of the reorganization bill by a vote of 95 to 0. On August 5, 1986, the House approved its version by a vote of 406 to 4. It seemed that in the entire Congress, only four members did not support the type of reform under consideration. The United States Congress, *Congressional Record, Proceedings and Debates of the 99th Congress, 2nd Session*, Washington, DC: U.S. Government Printing Office, September 17, 1986, pp. H7005-H7008. *Congressional Record, Proceedings and Debates of the 99th Congress, 2nd Session*, Washington, DC: U.S. Government Printing Office, September 16, 1986, p. S12652.

52. The conference met formally on August 13 and September 11, 1986. While over 100 amendments were considered, there were only three substantive areas that required resolution and were easily resolved. Senator Goldwater characterized the conference as the most cordial and cooperative in his memory. *Congressional Record, Proceedings and Debates of the 99th Congress, 2nd Session*, Washington, DC: U.S. Government Printing Office, September 17, 1986, p. H7005. *Congressional Record, Proceedings and Debates of the 99th Congress, 2nd Session*, Washington, DC: U.S. Government Printing Office, September 16, 1986, pp. S12652-S12653.

53. *Goldwater-Nichols Department of Defense Reorganization Act of 1986*, Conference Report (99-824), p. 3.

54. *Ibid.*, p. 5.

55. Prior to passage of the GNA, the Secretary of Defense promulgated a similar document, the *Defense Guidance (DG)*. The DPG which resulted from the GNA has proven to be a more authoritative document. For a description of the discontinued *DG*, see *Department of Defense Instruction 7045.7*, p. 2-1.

56. Office of the Secretary of Defense, *Department of Defense Directive 7045.14, Subject: The Planning, Programming, and Budgeting System (PPBS)*, Change 1, July 28, 1990, p. 3.

57. Contingency planning is the deliberate and crisis oriented operation planning conducted by the CINCs. Unlike DoD's program planning that addresses the mid-range planning period, contingency planning is for potential near-term operations that may be conducted during the next 2 years. Contingency planning considers the best ways to use existing military capabilities while program planning helps develop future capabilities.

58. *Goldwater-Nichols Department of Defense Reorganization Act of 1986*, Conference Report (99-824), p. 5.

59. *Ibid.*, p. 17.

60. U.S. General Accounting Office, *Defense Reorganization, Compliance with Legislative Mandate for Contingency Planning*, GAO/NSIAD-91-312, Gaithersburg, MD, September, 1991.

61. *Goldwater-Nichols Department of Defense Reorganization Act of 1986*, Conference Report (99-824), p. 5.

62. *Defense Organization: the Need for Change, p. 158.* The President and the Secretary of Defense make up the NCA. *Joint Pub 1-02*, p. 253.

63. *Defense Organization: The Need for Change, p. 159.*

64. *Congressional Record—Senate*, October 3, 1985, p. S 12535.

65. *Ibid.*; *Goldwater-Nichols Department of Defense Reorganization Act of 1986*, Conference Report (99-824), p. 17, 15, and 19, 94, respectively.

66. *Ibid.*, p. 21.

67. *Ibid.*, p. 30. Office of the Secretary of Defense, *Department of Defense Directive 5100.1, Functions of the Department of Defense and its major Components*, September 25, 1987, p. 6.

68. *Goldwater-Nichols Department of Defense Reorganization Act of 1986*, Conference Report (99-824), p. 18.

69. *Ibid.*, p. 23.

70. *Ibid.*, p. 15.

71. *Ibid.*, p. 16.

72. *Ibid.*, pp. 15-16.

73. Office of the Secretary of Defense, *Conduct of the Persian Gulf War*, Interim Report to Congress, Washington, DC: U.S. Government Printing Office, July 1991, pp. 26-1, 26-2.

74. Office of the Secretary of Defense, *Conduct of the Persian Gulf War*, Final Report to Congress, Washington, DC: U.S. Government Printing Office, 1992, p. xxv.

75. A unified command is a command with broad continuing missions under a single commander and composed of forces from two or more military departments. A specified command is a command that has broad continuing missions and is normally composed of forces from a single military department. Office of the Joint Chiefs of Staff, *Joint Pub 0-2, Unified Action of the Armed Forces (UNAAF)*, Washington, DC: Joint Staff, February 24, 1995, p. xv. Although, presently, no specified commands exist, their creation remains provided for in Title 10, United States Code and the UNAAF recognizes their viability.

76. *Goldwater-Nichols Department of Defense Reorganization Act of 1986*, Conference Report (99-824), p. 24. During the Joint conference, a Senate amendment was introduced that would have had the Act specify the basic CINC responsibilities such as security of the command, mission accomplishment, and directing coordination among subordinates. The conferees determined the general responsibilities of the CINCs would be better promulgated by administrative regulation, and they have been via the Unified Command Plan.

77. *Goldwater-Nichols Department of Defense Reorganization Act of 1986*, Conference Report (99-824), pp. 24-25.

78. *Ibid.*, p. 25.

79. *Ibid.*, p. 121.

80. *Joint Pub 0-2*, pp. III-5.

81. *Goldwater-Nichols Department of Defense Reorganization Act of 1986*, Conference Report (99-824), p. 23.

82. *Ibid.*, pp. 46,56,68. The twelve functions are: recruiting, organizing, supplying, equipping, training, servicing, mobilizing,

demobilizing, administering, maintaining, construction, outfitting and repair of military equipment, and construction, maintenance, and repair of real property.

83. *Ibid.*, p. 23.

84. *Ibid.*, pp. 23-24.

85. *Ibid.*, p. 24. For example, the chairman is responsible for soliciting, evaluating, integrating, and establishing priorities for the CINCs' requirements and advising the Secretary of Defense accordingly.

86. *Ibid.*, pp. 47, 56, 69.

87. *Goldwater-Nichols Department of Defense Reorganization Act of 1986,* Conference Report (99-824), p. 88.

88. *Ibid.*, pp. 88-89.

89. *Goldwater-Nichols Department of Defense Reorganization Act of 1986,* Conference Report (99-824), p. 19.

90. Office of the Chairman of the Joint Chiefs of Staff, Memorandum of Policy No. 7, (1st Revision—March 17, 1993), *Joint Strategic Planning System*, Washington, DC: Joint Staff, pp. I-2.

91. *Goldwater-Nichols Department of Defense Reorganization Act of 1986,* Conference Report (99-824), p. 17.

92. Office of the Chairman of the Joint Chiefs of Staff, *User's Guide for JOPES (Joint Operation Planning and Execution System)*, Washington, DC: Joint Staff, May 1, 1995, pp. 10-13.

93. *Goldwater-Nichols Department of Defense Reorganization Act of 1986,* Conference Report (99-824), p. 17.

94. Recalling the Packard Commission's charge that the NCA requires better integration of the efforts of the CINCs, it seems logical that the chairman should provide this integration, in part, through the development of overarching strategic plans harmonized with the 6-year defense planning periods. For a more complete discussion of the need for a national military strategic plan, see Douglas C. Lovelace, Jr., and Thomas-Durell Young, *U.S. Department of Defense Strategic Planning: The Missing Nexus*, Carlisle Barracks, PA: U.S. Army War College, Strategic Studies Institute, September 1995, pp. 14-32.

95. For an explanation of why the Joint Strategic Capabilities Plan is not, as its title might imply, a strategic plan as defined by the GNA, see Lovelace and Young, pp. 16-17.

96. *Goldwater-Nichols Department of Defense Reorganization Act of 1986*, Conference Report (99-824), p. 21.

97. *Ibid.*, pp. 18, 22.

98. *Goldwater-Nichols Department of Defense Reorganization Act of 1986*, Conference Report (99-824), p. 36.

99. Kathleen Van Trees Medlock, *A Critical Analysis of the Impact of the Department of Defense Reorganization Act on American Officership*, dissertation, George Mason University, Fairfax, VA, 1993, p. 61 (quoting U.S. Congress, House, Committee on Armed services, *Reorganization of the Department of Defense*, 99th Congress, 2d Session, February 19-March 12, 1986, H.A.S.C. No. 99-53).

100. Even before the Act became law, DoD began work on the recommendations of the Packard Commission, many of which were reflected in the Act. Nonetheless, 2 years elapsed after passage of the Act before provisions of Title IV began to take root. Casper Weinberger, *Annual Report to the Congress for FY 88/89 Budget*, Washington, DC: Office of the Secretary of Defense, January 12, 1987, p. 114.

101. *Goldwater-Nichols Department of Defense Reorganization Act of 1986*, Conference Report (99-824), pp. 37-41.

102. *Goldwater-Nichols Department of Defense Reorganization Act of 1986*, Conference Report (99-824), p. 37.

103. *Goldwater-Nichols Department of Defense Reorganization Act of 1986*, Conference Report (99-824), p. 38.

CHAPTER 5

INSTITUTIONALIZING DEFENSE REFORM: THE POLITICS OF TRANSFORMATION IN THE ROOT, MCNAMARA, AND COHEN ERAS

Joseph R. Cerami

In November 1997, Secretary of Defense William Cohen released a "Defense Reform Initiative Report." He announced several areas for public management reform in the Department of Defense (DoD), in support of ongoing executive branch reinvention programs. This chapter looks at the Root reforms of the early 20th century and the McNamara reforms of the 1960s, and then offers some comments about the prospects for success for the ongoing 1997 Defense Reform Initiative. The theoretical literature on reinvention and transformation will also be used to analyze and evaluate Secretary Cohen's reform efforts, and to address several key questions relating to defense reform: What is the role of senior leadership today? What combination of knowledge, skills, abilities, and experience are required for senior leaders in DoD? Are the environmental conditions within DoD right for reform? What will be the catalyst for change in our current era of globalization? Are current business models useful guides to defense reform? Can executive-legislative conflict be turned into cooperation and compromise in order to improve defense management?

The Root Reforms.

Several themes stand out in the history of military reform in the United States. These include executive leadership, budget control and integration, executive-legislative-bureaucratic conflict, "scientific and business-like" public management, and civil-military relations.[1] Studies of Progressive Era reform efforts highlight the internal struggles for executive control between the civilian Secretary and the Army general-in-chief. These civil-military struggles were complicated by the autonomy of the Army bureaus, such as the ordnance and commissary organizations, that allied themselves with congressional committee members. The decentralized bureau system was flawed from a managerial efficiency and effectiveness perspective—but powerful politically. The catalyst for change was failure, especially in Army logistics and administration, during the Spanish American War.[2] Initiating change required a dedicated group of individuals, typically described as Neo-Hamiltonians.[3] The most influential of these Progressive reformers, was Elihu Root, who was named Secretary of War in 1898. While not a military expert, Root had demonstrated impressive skills as a public manager while serving as governor for the territories of Puerto Rico and the Philippines. Root also had exceptional skills as a lawyer and negotiator. Significantly, Root had experience in "dealing with legislative committees and drafting legislation"[4] and spent several years shepherding his reforms through Congress and the legislative process.[5]

Secretary Root sought to improve the Army's internal structure, including strengthening the top leadership and modernizing the staff and planning functions. His ideas on military organization were taken from the writings of Emory Upton and the Prussian general staff system.[6] Root was able to implement his administrative and organizational reforms by personally drafting the legislation that made reform possible. Elting Morison described his 1903 General Staff bill as

> the most enlightened piece of legislation dealing with military organization ever passed in this country . . . [which] was almost exclusively the work of Elihu Root.[7]

Most importantly, the legislation codified the American tradition of civilian supremacy of the military, which remains a foundation of the American system of government.[8] In effect, Root based his reforms on a broad-based synthesis of Progressive Era government reform theory, Taylor's scientific management, Upton's military writings, the Prussian general staff model, and traditional American democratic values.

Even a very brief survey of Root's record as Secretary of War is sufficient to demonstrate the scope and significance of the military reforms that he was able to accomplish. It is also sufficient to generate three important questions: Is the Prussian General Staff model still a useful point of reference for DoD reform? Are any of the conditions that made it possible for Root to accomplish his reforms in the early twentieth century in place today? Is Root the appropriate model for a modern Secretary of Defense engaged in reform and innovation?

The McNamara Reforms.

The era of the McNamara DoD reforms also stands out as a significant period of change in defense management. By the time that Robert McNamara came to the Office of Secretary of Defense, the post World War II growth of government agencies had created significant pressure for the creation of a new system to rationally allocate federal resources. Furthermore, information technology and computers had significantly enhanced the government's capability for quantitative data analysis. These are some of the factors that convinced McNamara that it was both necessary and possible to introduce a new Planning-Programming-Budgeting System (PPBS) within the Department of Defense.

The political conditions also seemed to be in place by the time that the Kennedy administration took office in 1961. The National Security Act of 1947 had placed the Army, Navy, and Air Force within a new National Military

Establishment (NME) under the titular control of a new Secretary of Defense.[9] Unfortunately, the NME system precipitated intense rivalry between the services that took time and effort to overcome. Congress enacted additional legislation a decade later to try to resolve some of the initial difficulties in establishing the new defense organization. The DoD Reorganization Act of 1958 clarified the Secretary of Defense's authority over the services in the areas of budgeting, force structure, and research and development.[10] Reform to integrate planning, programming, and budgeting was now possible.

Armed with this new legislative authority, it remained for McNamara and his staff to implement Planning, Programming, and Budgeting System (PPBS) reforms in DoD. Their goal was to develop a process to coordinate strategy and plans, force requirements and programs, and resources and budgets. The intent was to centralize decisionmaking and design explicit criteria for major systems acquisitions.[11] In keeping with the PPB concept, they sought an analytical approach to assessing costs and needs and developing alternatives to present to the Secretary of Defense. They would develop multiyear programs through the Five-Year Defense Plans. In their view, an analytical, largely civilian staff would be free of the influence of military parochialism and thus be independent both intellectually and careerwise.[12]

Prior to PPB, under performance budgeting approaches, budgets and military strategy were not related. McNamara set out to fix the problems of the existing system, which to that point had simply set DoD ceilings for each of the armed services.[13] PPB was designed to reverse the traditional informational and decision flows within DoD. In the past, estimates were sent upward in the organization to gain approval in light of existing resources. By contrast, as Allen Schick has observed, PPB established a "top policy" approach in which the "critical decisional process—that of deciding on purposes and plans—has a downward and disaggregative flow."[14] Schick also correctly predicted that

104

this would in turn require the centralization of policy making, and subsequent DoD reforms did aim to centralize key budgeting and planning functions.

DoD operations research analysts Alain Enthoven and Wayne Smith have provided an insiders' history of the McNamara PPB reforms. In their book *How Much Is Enough?*, Enthoven and Smith chronicle the roles that they played in support of McNamara's efforts to shape the defense program in a centralized, top down fashion.[15] The authors proposed that their systems analysis organization, working directly for the Secretary of Defense, would provide the analytical staff that would make the relevant data available for making major program and spending decisions within DoD.[16] Enthoven and Smith's focus was on developing a sophisticated approach to budgetary integration that went well beyond the simple control or bookkeeping function. In the Whiz Kids' view, the process would optimize the national interest and minimize the tradition of service budget compromises. To their credit, their vision for linking planning, programming, and budgeting is still in effect today within the Defense Department.[17]

Enthoven and Smith also write about the myriad problems that the McNamara team faced, and the many mistakes that they made, starting in 1961.[18] In summary, they argue that: There was no centralized leadership over the services; no centralized planning; no coordination of research and development programs; no quantitative data analysis; no analysis staff in DoD; and no adequate cost accounting standards.

The Failings of PPB.

It is significant to point out that President Lyndon Johnson's attempt to extend the PPB system in all federal agencies failed. Hal Rainey notes that Johnson's efforts failed to meet the conditions for successful organizational change. That is, the initiative lacked "sustained support from higher levels, participative planning, and flexible implementation."[19] Rainey adds that "the reason for the failure of PPBS was not necessarily that it was a bad idea. It was a well-intentioned innovation advocated by many experts in public administration."[20]

Schick echoes Rainey's assessment in a 1973 article in *Public Administration Review*. He takes note of the 1971 Office of Management and Budget memorandum that led to the "Demise of Federal PPB."[21] He writes of the primary purpose of PPB to recast the budgetary role in the bureaucracy, that is, to transform the budget into an instrument for deciding the purposes and programs of government. Cost-effectiveness and analysis were to serve as change agents. Schick concludes that PPB failed because it could not penetrate budget routines. Trying to force the DoD system on other government agencies, without integrating planning and analysis at the top of the agencies, led to failure.

Schick, Rainey, and Henry Mintzberg, all agree that PPB was introduced across the board without adequate preparation within the organizations.[22] The implementing directives were insensitive to bureaucratic traditions, institutional loyalty, and personal relationships. The reforms also suffered from inadequate support, leadership, and resources. A third problem area was in the realm of policy analysis itself. Good analysts and data were in short supply.

Schick also borrows from political scientists Charles Lindblom and Aaron Wildavsky to point out deeper problems. In their assessment, Lindblom and Wildavsky claim that PPB attempted to ride roughshod over American political values.[23] They highlight the bargaining-incremental, "muddling through," model in American public administration.[24] In effect, budgets traditionally have been instruments of conflict suppression. PPB served to escalate conflict. After all, PPB sought to develop consistent program objectives, build an understanding of program purposes, terminate low-yield programs, expand a range of program alternatives, and unveil the costs and benefits of all federal programs. All of these initiatives took the comfort level out of the traditional incremental approach and fueled the fires of bureaucratic and interservice competition.

Another part of the problem with PPB was in the education and background of its pioneers. They were first and foremost economists and systems analysts. "They knew little about public administration or about the tardiness of budgeting for the vast changes they undertook."[25] This lack of knowledge of public administration in general, and the fields of public management, organization theory and development, all help to account for the ham-handed, top-down manner by which McNamara's innovations were implemented within the bureaucracy. McNamara's problems would have been even more serious if he had attempted to make changes across the cabinet and diverse agencies rather than within DoD.[26]

Another problematic aspect of PPB relates to the role of Congress.

> PPB was conceived almost exclusively from an executive perspective, as if Congress does not exist and that all it takes to make a budget is to review agency requests within an administrative setting. Moreover, PPB was engineered in a way that enabled the Bureau of the Budget to bypass Congress. The appropriation accounts were not restructured nor were significant alterations made in the budget submissions to Congress. The special PPB plans and analyses were destined for executive use and were not incorporated into the flow of data to Congress.[27]

These problems were further compounded by the executive branch's reluctance to show its program analysis to Congress because of traditional fears of legislative micromanagement.

The struggle between the White House and Congress continues today in the Gore reinvention efforts. A recent article highlights the conflict between Gore's executive branch "Performance-Based Organization" initiatives and Congress's "Government Performance and Results Act of 1993." The author writes that "The NPR (National Performance Review) is an instrument in the larger struggle between the Clinton administration and some elements in Congress over the role and organization of the federal government."[28]

Comparing Root and McNamara.

A comparison of the Root and McNamara reform efforts leads to several insights, which are relevant to the post-Cold War situation. Root called for reform within the overarching context of the Progressive Era. In that period, public administrators searched for principles of scientific management to find ways to improve government effectiveness and efficiency. Root remained within the mainstream of institutional reformers in the Neo-Hamiltonian mold. The German general staff system provided the benchmark for comparison. Root's ideas, as guided by the emerging public management theory, were for centralization and streamlining under the executive branch. James Hewes, in *From Root to McNamara* writes that:

> The principal issue in the development of the organization and administration of the War Department/Department of the Army from 1900 to 1963 was executive control . . . . Tight control had existed . . . within the headquarters of each of a series of autonomous bureaus, which largely governed themselves under the detailed scrutiny of Congress. The question was whether tight authority should be imposed on the bureaus at the level of the Secretary of War.[29]

The McNamara era was an extension of executive control by further centralizing defense management under the Secretary of Defense at the expense of the armed services. McNamara's guiding theory was not derived from public administration, nor was he an experienced

108

government manager like Root. His emphasis on systems analysis and economics was derived directly from his education in a management school and executive level experience in the hierarchical world of the automobile industry. McNamara's corporate experience did not prepare him adequately for the inside game of Washington politics. There is no evidence that he approached Root's ability to work through Congress to institute reforms. While Root achieved a legislative mandate for his management innovations, McNamara's reforms were done internally, largely within the executive branch, and often in the face of a hostile Congress.

Clearly, during their tenure, McNamara's analysts saw Congress as the enemy. Enthoven and Smith, in their chapter on "Unfinished Business" call for more balanced and informed congressional debate and involvement in military issues.[30]Their writing is filled with anecdotes pointing to an "unholy" alliance between Congress and senior military officers. Their discussion does not reflect Root's sophisticated political approach. As Secretary of War he faced similar congressional opposition. But Root, unlike McNamara, was able to work out a successful legislative strategy to neutralize his political and military opponents and legitimize his reform effort. Both men wanted to achieve similar goals, but Root's understanding of political realities caused him to build an alliance with Congress, not criticize them openly for their lack of information and balance.

DoD Reform in the Cohen Era: Transformation and Reinvention.

The tendency to regard Congress as the enemy and to view government as another form of business organization continues to this day. During the 1990s, calls for DoD reform rely heavily on the latest business practices. The literature in public management and change includes ideas regarding transformation and reinvention. Rainey summarizes the literature and identifies a number of conditions for effective transformation. These include creating conditions in four major areas: (1) need; (2) leadership; (3) participation; and (4) implementation.[31] Rainey notes that there must be a widespread belief in the need for change. This belief must be coupled with clear, sustained leadership and support from top executives. At the same time, there must be broad participation throughout the organization in diagnosing problems and planning change. Also, there must be flexible, incremental implementation with experimentation, feedback, and adaptation. All must build on prior success to institutionalize change.

Within the business management community, Kotter is viewed as an expert on transformation, leadership, and change. In a 1995 article, he lists the following "Eight Steps to Transforming Your Organization."[32]

1. **Establishing a Sense of Urgency**: Examining market and competitive realities. Identifying and discussing crises, potential crises, or major opportunities.

2. **Forming a Powerful Guiding Coalition**: Assembling a group with enough power to lead the change effort. Encouraging the group to work together as a team.

3. **Creating a Vision**: Creating a vision to help direct the change effort. Developing strategies for achieving that vision.

4. **Communicating the Vision**: Using every vehicle possible to communicate the new vision and strategies. Teaching new behaviors by the example of the guiding coalition.

5. **Empowering Others to Act on the Vision**: Getting rid of obstacles to change. Changing systems or structures that seriously undermine the vision. Encouraging risk taking and nontraditional ideas, activities, and actions.

6. **Planning for and Creating Short-Term Wins**: Planning for visible performance improvements. Creating

those improvements. Recognizing and rewarding employees involved in the improvements.

7. **Consolidating Improvements and Producing Still More Change:** Using increased credibility to change systems, structures, and policies that don't fit the vision. Hiring, promoting, and developing employees who can implement the vision. Reinvigorating the process with new projects, themes, and change agents.

8. **Institutionalizing New Approaches**: Articulating the connections between the new behaviors and corporate success. Developing the means to ensure leadership development and success.

Public management reforms regarding transformation are linked to the literature on reinvention. "The Gore Report on Reinventing Government" is in step with the 1990s notions of organizational change and reform. The document is filled with references to fostering "historic change—in the way government works."[33] The NPR includes a list of principles for reform:[34]

We will invent a government that puts people first, by:

- Cutting unnecessary spending
- Serving its customers
- Empowering its employees
- Helping communities solve their own problems
- Fostering excellence

Here's how. We will:

- Create a clear sense of mission
- Steer more, row less
- Delegate authority and responsibility

- Replace regulation with incentives

- Develop budgets based on outcomes

- Expose federal operations to competition

- Search for market, not administrative, solutions

- Measure our success by customer satisfaction

The NPR is thus filled with management concepts similar to those in the reinvention and transformation literature. In keeping with the principles of transformation, the NPR includes the stages of agenda setting and implementation. Agenda setting occurred during Gore's initial 6-month review of the federal government, citing his leadership in an effort that included teams of federal employees.[35] Specific reform programs, "success stories," are highlighted throughout the report.

The NPR has its share of critics in the writings of public administration scholars and others.[36] In its defense, the report points out that it is aimed at improving **how** government works, and not **what** it does.[37] So it is open to the charge that it is primarily concerned with improving the effectiveness and efficiencies of government. It can also be criticized for focusing on cutback management. In fact, Chapter 4 is entitled "Cutting Back to Basics" and calls for cutting programs, eliminating duplication, collecting more, and reengineering to cut costs. However, that represents only part of the total package. To evaluate the NPR in light of the transformation literature, we can compare how Gore's proposals fit within Rainey's condition and Kotter's transformation model.

The NPR's opening paragraph makes a case for the widespread belief in the need for change:

Public confidence in the federal government has never been lower. The average American believes we waste 48 cents of every tax dollar. Five of every six want "fundamental change" in

Washington. Only 20 percent of Americans trust the federal government to do the right thing most of the time—down from 76 percent 30 years ago.[38]

Throughout the introductory chapter the report establishes the widespread perception of the need for government change. It cites polls of the American people, and criticism from federal workers, state and local politicians and administrators, and Congress. The fact that the Vice President has his name on the report and the President is quoted throughout lends credibility to Rainey's second condition, that is, that clear and sustained leadership of the government's top executives is fundamental. The final condition, of flexible and incremental implementation, is also validated. The Preface of the NPR calls for creating Reinvention Teams and Laboratories, which serve to institutionalize new approaches.[39]

The rhetoric in the report is meant to signal a clear sense of urgency. The report notes that the

> movement to reinvent government . . . is driven . . . by absolute necessity. . . . Government is broken, and it is time to fix it.[40]

Gore repeatedly cites the impatience of taxpayers as a rationale for making reinvention urgent. The report also addresses the importance of a guiding coalition. It mentions the broad support for bureaucratic reform in Congress and all levels of government. The NPR vision includes developing a government that works better and costs less through revolutionary change. This is captured in President Clinton's citation in the Introduction:

> Our goal is to make the entire federal government both less expensive and more efficient, and to change the culture of our national bureaucracy away from complacency and entitlement toward initiative and empowerment. We intend to redesign, to reinvent, and to reinvigorate the entire national government.[41]

This goal has been reinforced through the Vice President's personal commitment and travel to build support for reinventing government. Another key transformation principle is empowerment, which is covered in two dimensions. First, Chapter 3 of the report emphasizes empowering federal employees to get results through decentralizing the bureaucracy, developing an entrepreneurial spirit, and cutting "red-tape." A second dimension calls for empowering state and local governments.[42]

To illustrate the idea of creating short-term wins, the NPR cites several examples. These include one success story from the DoD:

> The military: the most conservative, hierarchical and traditional branch of the government and the bureaucracy least likely to behave like a cutting-edge private company, right? Wrong. One of Washington's most promising reinvention stories comes from the Air Combat Command.[43]

The report also conforms to the transformation model in seeking instruments that can consolidate improvements. It notes the significance of the Government Performance and Results Act of 1993 and highlights its requirement for agencies' 5-year strategic plans and performance budgeting.[44] Performance budgeting is being extended throughout federal agencies. Thus, through legislation, and its efforts to build support within the cabinet, the NPR seeks to institutionalize the reinvention initiatives. The strategic plans and prodding of the Office of Management and Budget (OMB) all contribute to a long-term process in keeping with transformation principles. The NPR notes that transforming major corporations can take 6 to 8 years, and it is reasonable to expect that the federal government will take longer.[45]

Appendix A of the NPR lists more specific "major recommendations, by agency."[46] For DoD, it lists two significant areas and 12 others for improvements. The two areas of significance include early Clinton Administration strategy and force structure requirements—the Bottom-Up Review (BUR)—and acquisition reform. Of the 12 recommendations, most fall in the category of efficiency and effectiveness enhancements, such as more privatization, productivity enhancements, incentives, organizational restructuring, etc. It is interesting to note that nine of the fourteen items are listed as "cbe" (cannot be estimated due to data limitation or uncertainties about implementation time lines) for changes in spending and receipts.[47]

There is little to note regarding significant changes to the basic PPBS processes of the McNamara era. The BUR set the military force structure in 1993 with its requirement for conducting two major theater wars modeled after the Persian Gulf War scenario. This has remained relatively unchanged during the Clinton Administration. Acquisition reform remains a perennial reform issue for DoD, with continual calls for eliminating $600 toilet seats, bolts, hammers, etc., as well as reducing the perceived waste, fraud, and abuse of defense contractors and pork-barrel politics.

All in all, the 1993 NPR does follow the principles of transformational management when it discusses change in the management practices of the federal government. However, when it comes to the specifics of the Defense Department program, the Gore Report called for relatively little new in transforming DoD in terms of the key aspects of planning, programming, budgeting, or execution. The NPR was not the final word for 1990s DoD reform, however.

Defense Reform Initiatives.

William S. Cohen, the Secretary of Defense for the second Clinton Administration has made reinvention one of his major areas of emphasis. Both his November 1997 "Defense Reform Initiative" and the 1998 "Annual Report to the President and Congress" returned to the idea of reforming defense management. For the federal government in the Clinton Administration, the Gore Report

115

set the agenda, and Cohen signed on to the reinvention concept. In Cohen's opening paragraph in the Defense Reform Initiative he writes:

> Having inherited the defense structure that won the Cold War and Desert Storm, the Clinton Administration intends to leave as its legacy a defense strategy, a military, and a Defense Department that have been transformed to meet the new challenges of a new century.[48]

In the same vein, the final section of the introduction is titled "Transforming Our Military."[49] This section stresses using advanced information and other new technologies to transform warfighting and develop new ways of organizing and employing military forces. To carry out the new defense strategy and operational concepts, Cohen calls for "fundamental reform in how the Defense Department conducts business."[50] DoD has jumped on the transformation bandwagon and the Secretary's introduction is filled with ideas similar to Kotter and Gore. Cohen uses the metaphor of DoD going on a diet. In his view, DoD put on "excess pounds, built up during the long winter of the Cold War."[51] He suggests that: "Losing weight successfully requires not a one-time diet, but a permanent change in lifestyle."

The final section of this chapter will look in more depth at what the permanent lifestyle change entails. Clearly, Cohen stresses the theme of more business-like public management. Again, his introduction highlights this point:

> DoD has labored under support systems and business practices that are at least a generation out of step with modern corporate America. DoD support systems and practices that were once state-of-the-art are now antiquated compared with the systems and practices in place in the corporate world, while other systems were developed in their own defense-unique culture and have never corresponded with the best business practices of the private sector. This cannot and will not continue. This Defense Reform Initiative reflects the insights of numerous business leaders who have restructured and downsized their

116

corporations and not only survived but thrived in a rapidly changing marketplace.

Taken within the context of the innovation and transformation literature, the Cohen initiatives are focused narrowly. Mostly the reforms center on what are called in Chapter 1: Best Business Practices. Chapter 1 calls for a "Revolution in the Business Affairs of the Department of Defense [which] includes adopting and adapting the best business practices of the private sector to the business of defense."[52] Included in Best Business Practices are paper free logistics and acquisition systems; using purchase cards; electronic catalogues; reengineering the systems used for shipping household goods; etc. These electronic, Internet, and paper free practices for administration, finance, and logistics no doubt make sense in the information age. These proposals seem worthwhile for improving how DoD does its support business. They are not geared to transforming the nature of what DoD does with respect to either roles and missions or strategy, force structure or budgetary requirements.

The same is true of Chapter 2: Changing the Organization. Again, there is no attempt to address or reform what DoD does. Instead the chapter focuses on organizational changes that fall squarely into the category of cutback management. While some of these reforms may be overdue for trimming the aforementioned Cold War fat, there is no accompanying analysis linking organizational cuts to changes in DoD functions, roles or missions. The chapter generally points out

> three central principles guiding the changes: Department headquarters should be flexible enough to deal with future challenges; the Office of the Secretary of Defense (OSD) should focus on corporate-level tasks; and operational management tasks should be pushed to the lowest appropriate level. As a result, all headquarters structures should be thinned, flattened, and streamlined. . . .[53]

The highlights of the reorganization stress the level of cuts expected:

- OSD reduced 33 percent from FY 1996 over the next 18 months;

- Defense Agencies personnel reduced 21 percent over five years;

- Personnel in DoD Field Activities reduced 36 percent over 2 years;

- Joint Staff personnel reduced 29 percent by FY 2003;

- All other headquarters reduced 10 percent by FY 2003;

- Headquarters of Combatant Commands reduced 7 percent by FY 2003;

- Reduce Presidentially Appointed, Senate-confirmed OSD positions by 9 percent;

- Eliminate the entire category of Defense Support Activities;

- Reduce number of non-intelligence Defense Agencies by 8 percent;

- Reduce the number of DoD Field Activities by 22 percent.

Overall, these cuts are expected to result in a total 33 percent reduction in OSD personnel.[54] As opposed to the transformational notion of flexible, incremental implementation, Cohen has opted to "jump-start the reform process."[55] This is to be aided by a set of principles, an agenda of organizational changes in a series of initiatives. The guiding philosophy is that DoD will be positioned to face future challenges by empowering subordinate activities, weeding out redundancy, and strengthening OSD to prepare for the longer-term for strategy, program, and financial planning.

Another transformation principle addressed in the report is that of institutionalizing the new approach. Cohen proposes a Defense Management Council (hereafter, DMC) at the undersecretary (vice chiefs of service staff) level.[56] The DMC will work for the Deputy Secretary of Defense and be responsible for reform initiation, implementation, and oversight. The DMC is thus expected to promote integration and general savings and improve performance throughout DoD in the years ahead. Yet the DMC remains at the top of the centralized DoD pyramid. There are no proposals for decentralization, or involving all layers of the organization, as the New Public Management favors.

The report also targets the Joint Chiefs of Staff (hereafter, JCS) organization. Under the 1986 Goldwater-Nichols Act the position of the Chairman and the JCS staff were strengthened at the expense of the individual armed services. While applauding the soundness of the legislation, the JCS and the subordinate regional Combatant Commands are also marked for reductions.[57]

Another business-like practice Cohen highlights is privatization or contracting out. Chapter 3 focuses on "Streamlining Through Competition." Here he proposes relying on the "competitive powers of the marketplace to help us become more efficient."[58] The Initiative emphasizes its roots in OMB Circular A-76 from the Eisenhower Administration. The circular, proposed in 1955, published in 1966, updated in 1979 and 1983, and revised in 1996 sets the rules for public-private competitions. Cohen cites A-76 cost comparisons from 1978-1994, which resulted in more that 2,000 competitions, with an average annual savings of $1,478 million, and a 31 percent savings overall.[59] The potential of future cost savings sets an example for the positive possibilities of these competitions and reinforces the transformation notion for "creating" short-term wins.

A final initiative in Cohen's report calls for two additional rounds of Base Realignment and Closings (BRAC). Chapter 4 points to "Eliminating Unneeded Infrastructure" and compares the relative drawdown of the defense budget (-40 percent), military personnel (-36 percent), and domestic base structure (-21 percent). Cohen calls for two additional rounds of BRAC in 2001 and 2005 to correct this imbalance.[60] In fact, in Bill S.1814, "Defense Reform Act of 1998," the Senate has written one section regarding "Congressional Disapproval" of base closures or realignment (without meeting several onerous conditions).[61] The politics of defense reform, while an executive branch initiative, must include congressional backing and account for conditions of divided government as well as traditional, executive-legislative branch tensions.

The 1998 Secretary of Defense's "Annual Report to the President and the Congress" echoes the Defense Reform Initiative's calls for reform. It includes four major principles: reengineer, consolidate, compete, and eliminate. In a section titled, Strategic Planning: DoD, the Report notes six critical corporate-level goals consistent with the Government Performance and Results Act:[62]

- Goal 1. Shape the international environment through DoD engagement programs and activities.

- Goal 2. Shape the international environment and respond to the full spectrum of crises by providing appropriately sized, positioned, and mobile forces.

- Goal 3. Prepare now for an uncertain future by pursuing a focused modernization effort that maintains U.S. qualitative superiority in key warfighting capabilities.

- Goal 4. Prepare now for an uncertain future by exploiting the Revolution in Military Affairs to transform U.S. forces for the future.

- Goal 5. Maintain highly ready joint forces to perform the full spectrum of military activities.

- Goal 6. Fundamentally reengineer the Department and achieve a 21st century infrastructure by reducing costs while maintaining required military capabilities across all DoD mission areas.

A skeptic might say that in addition to a Defense Department that is reengineered to work better and cost less, the report urges the organization to do more. Simultaneously, the Department is expected to maintain current capabilities, while shaping the international environment and preparing for the uncertain future. Whether it can perform those diverse tasks as well as reform its management structure remains an open question.

Conclusions: Kotter's Cautions and Advice on Leading Transformations.

Kotter's research provides several lessons on why many of the more than 100 transformation efforts failed. His most general lesson is that the change process goes through a series of phases and takes a considerable period of time. He cautions against skipping steps. A second general lesson is that a critical error can have a devastating impact. One could argue that Cohen's initiatives to "jump start" transformation may signal a lack of patience for the long haul. The much criticized Clinton Administration's amendment to the earlier BRAC legislation, to maintain existing depots in the electorially important states of Texas and California, may represent critical errors.[63] Kotter cites eight major errors that can cause transformation to fail.[64]Ongoing DoD reform shows evidence of each, but long-term cures may be possible for the future health of DoD.

Error #1: Not Establishing a Great Enough Sense of Urgency.

According to Kotter, this step is essential to motivate the organization to change. It requires a "hard look" at the organization's competitive situation, market position, technological trends and financial performance. In 1997, the Congress called on DoD to conduct a Quadrennial Defense Review (QDR) with a follow-on "outside" review by an expert National Defense Panel (NDP).

The error: the QDR focused on reinforcing the call for a Revolution in Business Practices. Otherwise, in terms of force structure, missions, budgets, and weapons acquisitions it remained well within the parameters of the *status quo*. In relative terms the NDP report, titled "Transforming Defense," is more change-oriented and transformational. The NDP criticized DoD for maintaining the strategic requirement for conducting two major regional contingencies.[65] The panel proposed shifting resources into experimentation, research, and development of new technologies. It also called for developing new operational concepts, relooking missions (especially peacekeeping and humanitarian operations), and canceling major weapons system acquisition plans. In keeping with the earlier discussion on the problems of PPBS, the panel also recommended that DoD "rethink the Planning, Programming, and Budgeting System (PPBS) to make it less burdensome and more receptive to innovation and change."[66]

DoD's conservative approach on current strategy, force structure, and weapons requirements may not establish the needed sense of urgency. At the same time the pointed cuts in the Defense organizations will also hurt the motivation to transform. Setting future goals to the year 2003 for sizeable personnel and organizational cuts gives the appearance of cutback management as opposed to transformation.

A cure: Kotter recommends hiring and promoting "real" leaders into senior-level jobs. Certainly it will require exceptional executive leadership to manage transformation and day-to-day work simultaneously. Naturally a high priority for the Secretary of Defense will be to hire both senior civilian and military leaders who are ambidextrous—who will help guide a long-term transformation, while managing short-term operational and administrative responsibilities.

Error #2: Not Creating a Powerful Enough Guiding Coalition.

Kotter notes that an effective guiding team must have strong line leadership. That is why the Secretary himself must spearhead the reform movement. The lesson is that the Secretary must be directly involved in leading the reform movement internally, along with the Deputy Secretary of Defense, the Defense Management Council, and other key stakeholders. External coalitions will be most important. The Secretary should seek to maintain key allies in the White House, while building bridges to Congress.

A cure: the Secretary should look to the Progressive Era, Root Reforms for a model of congressional relations, and avoid McNamara's sole reliance on presidential support. Given the current public lack of interest in defense issues, the Secretary will be forced to work inside the Washington beltway to build a powerful coalition inside the Pentagon, the White House, and Congress. DoD reports should continue to show how initiatives are in synch with the Government Performance and Results Act.

Error #3: Lacking a Vision.

The DoD vision must avoid becoming shop-worn and maintain a clear direction for reform. If the Secretary continues a conservative approach, then the reform efforts could get lost in the myriad of daily details in the conduct of the business of defense.

A cure: the vision should be refreshed periodically through high-level meetings of civilian and military defense officials. Periodic updates of the vision will help to keep transformation on the agenda. The NDP's more aggressive proposals for transforming defense in a context wider than the QDR should be evaluated. More forward looking changes regarding transformation and experimentation will help sustain the momentum for reform.

Error #4: Undercommunicating the Vision by a Factor of Ten.

Kotter writes "Without credible communication, and a lot of it, the hearts and minds of the troops are never captured."[67] As noted in the previous section, periodically updating the vision, through a process that includes many members of the organization, at all levels, can help the communication process. Kotter notes also that this is "particularly challenging if the short-term sacrifices include job losses."[68]

A cure: to help Kotter suggests including new growth possibilities and fair treatment during downsizing. Given trends towards globalization, new threats, and new technologies there should be many ways to refocus, if not grow portions of the defense organization. Providing incentives to shift agency assets and individuals into new security areas should help to reinforce the transformation vision. To emphasize fair treatment during organizational and personnel downsizing, resources will have to be allocated to provide education, transition, and severance packages to individuals forced to leave government service.

Error #5: Not Removing Obstacles to the New Vision.

Removing obstacles to transformation in DoD, such as bureaucratic inertia, service parochialism, and conservative culture is sure to be a significant problem. Rainey notes that one of the benefits of Gore's NPR is that it "revealed many of the obstacles to reform."[69] In the case of DoD these obstacles will be further complicated due to the anxieties future downsizing will create.

A cure: Kotter suggests examining the organizational structure itself, along with the personnel selection compensation and appraisal systems. No doubt it will require a holistic evaluation of the total management system to remove obstacles. The Defense Management Council's charter gives it oversight responsibilities. The Secretary should have them directly address the problem of "obstacles" by analyzing potential threats to transformation and developing solutions to overcome them. Given the assumptions and planning for downsizing, traditional interservice rivalries, and organizational complexity, it is safe to assume that managing obstacles to transformation should be a full-time concern of the DMC.

Error #6: Not Systematically Planning for and Creating Short-Term Wins.

Kotter calls for actively creating short-term wins within 12 to 24 months. Gore's innovation awards program (Hammer Awards) represents one method for doing this. Other visible symbols and incentives should be created. The Senate Armed Services Committee has used legislation and oversight to redirect one of the Combatant Commands to spearhead joint service experimentation.[70] These congressional initiatives are in keeping with the stated DoD goals and the NDP's call for "A Transformation Strategy."[71]

A cure: The Secretary should find ways to emphasize his support of these congressional initiatives and incentives. Supporting transformation will also help to build the coalition on Capitol Hill and among those influential members of the defense community that are encouraging experimentation with new technologies, organizational structures, and weapons systems. For instance, the Secretary can help insure that the new experimentation roles and missions are fully supported. He can set personnel policies to insure that the best and brightest of each of the military services are selected to serve in the experimentation headquarters. He can create positions for senior executive service members to go directly from DoD to the Command to maintain his personal influence. He can insist that the leaders of the organization be taken care of by their services, with key follow-on assignments and promotions. Through personnel and budgetary incentives, along with active personal involvement, the Secretary of Defense can create a success in one key area of transformation.

Error #7: Declaring Victory Too Soon.

Kotter researched transformation efforts over seven-year periods.[72] He noted that the amount of change peaked at around five years, or 36 months after the first set of visible wins. Thus, he encourages leaders to use short-term wins to tackle larger problems.

A cure: In DoD for example, creating the successes in the experimentation command could be used in the manner Kotter suggests. Conducted correctly, the experiments should lead to proposals for systemic and structural changes in military force structures and equipment requirements. Implementing those changes may require major changes to the services in terms of resources, organizations, personnel, equipment and doctrine. Potentially, these will require subsequent changes to the services priorities regarding budgets, force structures, training, and weapons systems acquisitions. Simply setting up the experimentation command, without preparing for the major battles ahead will be shortsighted. The DoD leadership will have to link experimentation to implementation and move the goal posts well beyond complying with the expected legislative initiatives.

Error #8: Not Anchoring Changes in the Corporation's Culture.

Kotter points to two factors that are particularly important in "institutionalizing change in corporate culture" or seeping change into the "bloodstream of the corporate body."[73] The first factor is actually showing the improved performance resulting from new approaches, behaviors, and attitudes. The second factor is making sure that the next generation of top management personifies the new approach. Again, it is important to recall the importance of the leadership of Elihu Root during the earlier reform period. While he had enemies within the War Department and Congress, he was able to work skillfully and patiently to implement the needed reforms.

A cure: Perhaps the wisest advice to the Secretary would be to study Root's example. The lessons are there for highlighting necessary executive leadership skills to reform those areas of DoD management that are suited to scientific and business-like practices. At the same time, to avoid obstacles to past transformation attempts, the politics of recruiting and sustaining a viable coalition for change must include building strong civil-military relations among political, military, and agency leaders.

Anchoring the transformation initiatives in the cultures of the Department of Defense, as well as the services, will require as much executive leadership as will finding the right organizational structures and processes. The Secretary of Defense should look closely at the National Defense Panel recommendations for broadening the scope of initiatives, to include reforming the PPBS process. The historic conditions, in part shaped by Gore's NPR, as well as changes in the international security environment, seem right for reform. If DoD truly intends to be entrepreneurial in its approach to public management, then the Secretary will have to employ a full range of individual skills to build a political coalition that will transform the Department of

Defense on a scale that rivals the lasting reforms of Elihu Root.

ENDNOTES - CHAPTER 5

1. Richard D. White, "Civilian Management of the Military: Elihu Root and the 1903 Reorganization of the Army General Staff," *Journal of Management History,* Vol. 4, No. 1, 1998, pp. 43-59. For the history of Army reforms, see Russell F. Weigley, *History of the United States Army,* New York: Macmillan, 1967; Allan R. Millett and Peter Maslowski, *For the Common Defense,* New York: Free Press, 1984; and James E. Hewes, Jr., *From Root to McNamara: Army Organization and Administration, 1900-1963,* Washington, DC: Center of Military History, United States Army, 1975.

2. White, p. 46.

3. White identifies the author of this label as Samuel Huntington. See *The Soldier and the State,* Cambridge: Belknap Press, 1957, p. 270.

4. White, p. 48.

5. *Ibid.,* p. 55.

6. *Ibid.,* pp. 51-52.

7. *Ibid.,* pp. 56-57.

8. For a critical assessment of concerns regarding the current nature of civil-military relations, see Richard H. Kohn, "Out of Control: The Crisis in Civil-Military Relations," *The National Interest,* Vol. 35, Spring 1994.

9. For a recent examination of the National Security Act of 1947, see David Jablonsky, *et al.,* "U.S. National Security: Beyond the Cold War," Carlisle, PA: Strategic Studies Institute, U.S. Army War College, and The Clarke Center, Dickinson College, July 26, 1997.

10. Enthoven and Smith, p. 2. See also Schick, p. 274.

11. *Ibid.,* pp. 33-47.

12. Enthoven and Smith devote considerable attention to the problems of interservice rivalry and military analysts. They believed greater objectivity was possible with civilian defense intellectuals. Chapter 3 focuses on "Why Independent Analysts," pp. 73-116.

13. Enthoven and Smith, p. 13.

14. Schick, 276.

15. Alain C. Enthoven and K. Wayne Smith, *How Much is Enough,* Millwood, NY: Kraus Reprint, p. 6.

16. Enthoven and Smith, p. 80.

17. For a detailed description of DoD and Army PPBS, see *How the Army Runs: A Senior Leader Reference Handbook, 1999-2000,* Carlisle, PA: U.S. Army War College, April 1999.

18. Enthoven and Smith, pp. 21-27.

19. Hal G. Rainey, *Understanding & Managing Public Organizations,* 2nd ed., San Francisco, CA: Jossey-Bass, 1997, p. 327.

20. Rainey, p. 328.

21. Allen Schick, "A Death in the Bureaucracy: The Demise of Federal PPB," *Public Administration Review,* Vol. 33, No. 2, March/April 1973, p. 146.

22. Schick, 1973, pp. 148-149.

23. Schick, 1973, p. 149.

24. See Charles E. Lindblom, "The Science of 'Muddling Through'," *Public Administration Review,* 1959, as reprinted in Shafritz and Hyde, eds., *Classics of Public Administration,* 4th ed., Fort Worth, TX: Harcourt Brace College Publishers, 1997.

25. Schick, 1973, p. 150.

26. Schick also provides a review of Nixon's 1971 plans to make major reforms in the cabinet by creating single organizations for community development, human resources, natural resources, and economic affairs. These initiatives were overcome by the Watergate scandal. While these proposals are beyond the scope of this paper, they would be interesting to review in light of ongoing reinvention efforts. See Schick, 1973, p. 151.

27. *Ibid.,* 1973, p. 154.

28. Alasdair Roberts, "Performance-Based Organizations: Assessing the Gore Plan," *Public Administration Review*, Vol. 57, No. 6, November/December 1997, p. 474.

29. James E. Hewes, Jr., *From Root to McNamara: Army Organization and Administration, 1900-1963*, Washington DC: Center of Military History, United States Army, 1975, p. ix.

30. Enthoven and Smith, p. 310.

31. Rainey, p. 339.

32. John P. Kotter, "Leading Change: Why Transformation Efforts Fail," *Harvard Business Review*, March-April 1995, p. 61.

33. Al Gore, "The Gore Report on Reinventing Government," Washington, DC: Random House, September 7, 1993, p. i.

34. *Ibid.*, p. 7.

35. *Ibid.*, p. i.

36. For a review of this criticism, see Rainey, pp. 367-8. Rainey's assessment of the NPR is positive. He writes:

Controversy over the sincerity, design, and effects of the initiative will continue for years. The NPR is nevertheless a major development in the effort to enhance excellence in public management.

37. *Ibid.*, p. ii.

38. *Ibid.*, p. 1. The data from the polls are footnoted. Of course, the nature of these kinds of survey can be subjected to various interpretations.

39. *Ibid.*, p. i.

40. *Ibid.*, p. 6.

41. *Ibid.*, p. 1.

42. *Ibid.*, p. 35.

43. *Ibid.*, p. 54.

44. *Ibid.*, p. 73.

45. *Ibid.*, p. 9.

46. *Ibid.*, p. 133.

47. *Ibid.*, pp. 136-7.

48. William S. Cohen, "Defense Reform Initiative Report," Washington, DC: U.S. Government Printing Office, November 1997, p. i.

49. *Ibid.*, p. ii.

50. *Ibid.*, p. iii.

51. *Ibid.*, p. iv.

52. *Ibid.*, p. 1.

53. *Ibid.*, p. 15.

54. *Ibid.*, p. 17.

55. *Ibid.*, p. 17.

56. *Ibid.*, p. 18.

57. *Ibid.*, p. 25. The initiative only calls for a reduction of "approximately 170 billets" for the Joint Staff and does not specify the CINC staff reductions.

58. *Ibid.*, p. 27.

59. *Ibid.*, p. 29.

60. *Ibid.*, p. 37.

61. S.1814, "Department of Defense Reform Act of 1998" (Introduced in the Senate); Sec. 704, "Closure and Realignment of Military Installations," *http://thomas.loc.gov*, May 3, 1998. The National Defense Authorization Act for Fiscal Year 1998 Report on the Base Closure and Realignment Commission (BRAC) Process, by the Senate Armed Services Committee, notes that:

It was extremely disappointing that politics prevailed and prevented the Committee from approving additional base closure rounds.

The report points out that the amendment to authorize two additional BRAC rounds was defeated on a 9-to-9 tie in committee. The Committee Report agrees with Secretary Cohen's initiative for a continuation of BRAC and concludes with a call for pursuing BRAC in the future.

62. William S. Cohen, Secretary of Defense, "Annual Report to the President and the Congress," Washington, DC: U.S. Government Printing Office, 1998, p. 14.

63. For instance, the SASC Report on the BRAC Process notes the "politicization in the last BRAC process which permitted the President to implement privatization in place at Kelly [Texas] and McClellan [California] Air Force Bases."

64. This section summarizes Kotter's discussion of transformation errors, pp. 59-67.

65. Philip A. Odeen, *et al.*, "Transforming Defense: National Security in the 21st Century," Report of the National Defense Panel, December 1997, p. 2.

66. *Ibid.*, p. vi.

67. Kotter, p. 63.

68. *Ibid.*, p. 63.

69. Rainey, p. 368.

70. Personal interview with Frederick M. Downey, Office of Senator Joseph Lieberman, Washington, DC, April 29, 1998.

71. Odeen, p. 57. Two specific proposals call for "A Broad National Security Approach," p. 67; and "Institutionalizing Change" through joint field tests, Joint Forces Command responsibility, Joint Battle Lab headquarters, Integrated service battle labs and establishing joint national training centers, p. 68.

72. Kotter, p. 67.

73. *Ibid.*, p. 67.

CHAPTER 6

TIME FOR A REVOLUTION: THE TRANSITION FROM NATIONAL DEFENSE TO INTERNATIONAL SECURITY

Grant T. Hammond

Introduction: On Evolution and Revolution.

Though there are many definitions of the terms, *The Oxford English Dictionary* in one of its entries defines evolution as "the process of evolving, developing or working out in detail what is implicitly or potentially contained in an idea or principle." It defines revolution, the way it is used here, as "an instance of great change or alteration in affairs or in some particular thing."[1] This chapter contends that mere evolution will no longer suffice in the organization and process of providing for the common defense. Revolution is required.

This is true for several reasons.

1. There was less guidance and structural imperative in the U.S. Constitution for dealing with foreign and defense policy than with most other tasks of government.

2. The transformations that have occurred domestically and internationally have presented us with a fundamentally different strategic, political, economic, and technological environment.

3. The role that the United States plays in the world today is vastly different from that presumed to be the case by the founders of the Republic or by the developers of the post World War II U.S. security apparatus.

4. That security system is so fundamentally flawed that the United States can no longer afford patchwork fixes and must radically transform it in order to meet its obligations at home and abroad.

5. What the United States does cannot be radically transformed without serious reconsideration of why it does it, and without fundamental reorganization of the structures which the government relies upon to provide for the common defense.

6. What is now required is a realization that, by default more than design, the task of providing for the common defense has been redefined. The task is no longer one of providing for national defense but rather a larger and far more complex task of providing for and sustaining international security.

Doing so requires not evolution, but revolution. The longer the United States waits, the more difficult the tasks will become and the less likely its success. Not making major transformations invites not only national defeat of U.S. policies, however well intentioned, but also a fundamental disruption of the international system.

The reason why these contentions are true are presented below. Declaring itself "the world's last remaining superpower" and repeating the phrase in hopes that it can prolong the supposed circumstance that it implies is an insufficient policy prescription for the future. The inescapable reality of these contentions is that the politics of bureaucratic process, partisan politics and intra-service rivalries must somehow be transcended if the United States is to do what needs to be done. It is not just a matter of military force structure and capabilities at the moment. It is much more a matter of strategic thinking and reorganization, in order to provide for the common defense that is, or should be, under review. It has been over a decade since the end of the Cold War and the end of the Gulf War. The United States is still unsure of its role and its strategy. This chapter argues that we need a revolution in national security affairs, describes what such a revolution would entail, and then sketches in broad strokes what the post-revolutionary regime might look like. It is purposely broad and provocative, in order to stimulate discussion on the issues involved. It calls for creative adaptation to both a world and a domestic political context that, in many ways, have already passed us by.

The Environment—International.

This is not our forefathers' world. Instead of a world dominated by several great Empires (British, French, Austro-Hungarian, Russian, Ottoman, Dutch, and Spanish), we now contend with a world that has roughly 200 states and is globally interconnected. What is more, there are approximately 800 international governmental organizations (IGOs), which were virtually nonexistent in the 18th century. In addition, there are nearly ten times that number—nearly 8,000—international non-governmental organizations (INGOs).[2] Whereas isolationism in the strict sense was at least possible in the 18th century, we now live in a world where such a strategy is virtually impossible—politically, economically, and even culturally. The center of power in the 18th century was unquestionably European. It is now located in North America and, in many ways (population size, markets, financial growth, and trade) in the Asia-Pacific region.

The international system has changed not only in size and nature. It has also changed in more fundamental ways. Increasingly, traditional conventional war is no longer a paying proposition—even for the victor.[3] As a result, while still of great importance, political and military capabilities are not as all consuming as they once were. Instead, what might be called "technomic vitality," the pace of technological advances and economic health, determines the pecking order in world affairs.[4]

The basic characteristics of the United States and its relations with the rest of the world have also changed

135

considerably. At the end of the 18th century, the United States was a nation of newly independent colonies with few major international commitments. It now finds itself in a world with defense obligations to 47 countries and personnel of the U.S. armed forces deployed to 144 countries.[5] It has millions of our citizens who regularly travel abroad and millions more who live and work abroad. The Department of State estimates that there are over 3 million Americans living abroad—working for American companies, foreign-owned subsidiaries or foreign businesses, studying abroad or retired abroad.[6] This was unimaginable in 1787 and relatively rare even in 1947.

American economic ties are considerable, and not just in terms of resources and markets for American business. Something on the order of 1 in 6 Americans depends on exports for his or her job. Foreign capital—in excess of $10 billion a month—is absolutely essential; to finance the national debt, to fuel the stock market, and to keep businesses expanding.[7] As seen recently in Russia, East Asia, and Latin America, the condition of foreign markets and financial circumstances have an impact on U.S. financial well being as well. Furthermore, as the dissolution of Yugoslavia, and events in Rwanda, Haiti, and Somalia have revealed, there is a definite correlation between economic well being, the maintenance of civil law and order, and ethnic and factional hostilities. The United States may indeed be the most powerful nation on earth. But this does not mean that it is not vulnerable, and even fragile, under certain circumstances.

There are perils in being the last remaining superpower that the United States has not fully confronted. Most important among these is the decision on just what the American purpose in the world should be. Without some sense of purpose it is difficult to know what to do or how to proceed. The Commission on Roles and Missions (CORM) of DoD was greatly hampered in many ways, not the least of which was the lack of a clear national consensus or directive on just where the United States was headed and why.

Deciding how best to go about getting there is a secondary consideration.

This is not a novel problem for the republic. The United States has never decided which dimension of its split personality is to be paramount in its relations with the world. On the one hand, for much of its history it has sought to be aloof and isolationist, preferring to be the "shining city on a hill"[8] of Reagan rhetoric, for others to emulate. Serving as a passive example while shunning the messy business of actually making the world a better place has had great appeal. On the other hand, more recently, the United States has given way to a renewed fit of Wilsonian interventionism. America now is apparently more willing, if not exactly ready or able, to go off on crusades to remake the world in its own image. "Engagement and Enlargement," was the first National Security Strategy of the Clinton administration. The expansion of choice in all aspects—democracy in politics, market economies in economics, tolerance in religion, multi-culturalism in society—is its mantra, however differentially applied.

The confusion and moral quandaries which are created by this strategy are highlighted by numerous policy dilemmas. These include: the tension between the administration's concern about human rights abuses and its desire to grant most favored nation status for China; the friction between political, military, and economic considerations relating to India and Pakistan and nuclear testing by these governments; and the contradictions between the Department of State's responsibility for certifying countries on drugs and the administration's desire for trade and good neighborly relations with Mexico and Colombia. In all of these cases, it is less the principles than the exceptions that cause difficulties. And what right do we have to hold others to "our" standards? The United States may think this a matter of claiming the moral high ground, but others may view our policies as blatant discrimination and cultural imperialism. These are not easy questions to solve when implementing policy. Consistency and constancy are both difficult.

The world in 1947, when the National Security Act was passed, was a vastly different place than it is today. The National Security establishment that it created was never fully implemented. It was born of the experiences of the coming of war in the late 1930s and the waging of World War II. The United States was not yet fully frozen into a Cold War with the Soviet Union. The world's population was a little over 2.5 billion, far less than half what it is today. Decolonization was in its early stages, and colonial empires still colored the maps of the world. There were 53 members of the United Nations, only about a fourth of what it is today. The North Atlantic Treaty Organization (NATO) did not exist, nor did supersonic aircraft, intercontinental missiles or precision guided munitions. Computers were rare, "software" was not a word, the internet was non-existent, and "hardware" meant a hammer and nails. Global interdependence existed only in a negative way—the spread of global conflict—and was neither a positive economic nor informational reality.

The biggest problem facing the world in the years following World War II was recovery from that global disaster—economically, politically, socially, and psychologically. There were still millions of refugees to be repatriated, Britain was still under food rationing, and civil war raged in China. The international drug trade was not a major problem, nor was illegal immigration. World trade and finance were relatively anemic. In the United States, segregation was still law. Such ubiquitous features of everyday life as cell phones and television, CNN and satellites were nonexistent, not to mention genetic engineering and space exploration. The United States had an atomic monopoly, nearly 50 percent of the planetary Gross National Product (GNP), and a merchant marine. The single biggest change in the last 50 years has been the relative decline of the lead of the United States in so many political, military, social, and economic indicators *vis-à-vis* the rest of the world. The international arena has changed so greatly, quantitatively and qualitatively, that it is virtually unrecognizable in many ways. Given that degree of change, why shouldn't our national security organization also undergo fundamental change as well?

The Environment—Domestic.

The Constitution of the United States of America calls upon both the executive and legislative branches of government to "provide for the common Defense," albeit in different ways.[9] The "common Defense" was defense of the nation and of the noble experiment in "American exceptionalism" that had to be preserved and nurtured. Granted, the authors of the Constitution never envisioned the sort of growth in the defense establishment that has occurred since the founding of the republic. Nor could the founding fathers have seen that two principles to which they were firmly committed—relative isolationism in world politics and the absence of a large standing military force—would be so thoroughly displaced by what they sought to avoid.

The Constitution has served us extremely well in most areas of concern for the state. Where it falls short is in the areas of foreign affairs and military preparedness.[10] This is no fault of the drafters of the document for the world in which they lived and the principles that guided their thinking have been changed virtually beyond recognition. There are no other areas where the shortfall in guidance has been so great. Thus, there is little in the way of Constitutional prescription to govern how we organize to provide for the common defense or the manner in which we pursue that goal.

Furthermore, providing for the common defense is big business and big politics. DoD is the largest single fungible element in the annual budget. It represents, through basing, procurement and hiring in both the civilian and military sectors, a roughly $300 billion enterprise which affects every state and Congressional district in the nation. It provides ample opportunity for not only checks and balances but vicious intra-governmental, inter-service and partisan rivalries of monumental proportions. The services are charged with having to train, organize, and equip. The regional commanders-in-chief (CINCs) are the ones who deploy and employ military force, but they have relatively little say in the budgetary process. The Office of the Secretary of Defense and numerous other offices in the Pentagon massage the service requests. The President must include the defense budget in his annual budget request from the executive branch. But it is the members of Congress who must decide on funding, priorities, amendments, and such. They do so based largely on their understanding of the interests of their states and districts rather than on the needs of the nation or the international community. The opportunities for conflict are legion.

The era in which the National Security Act of 1947 was passed was characterized as one of bi-partisanship in foreign and defense policy following World War II. It had nowhere near the impact on the economy that it now does. The politics of defense have also changed considerably over the last five decades. Since 1947, the pendulum of political power has swung to the "Imperial Presidency" of the Nixon era, then to what could be characterized as an "Imperial Congress" during the Clinton era. Given these shifts, it is amazing that the defense budget makes as much sense as it does.

That said, there has been no dearth of studies, recommendations, reviews, and reform initiatives addressing these concerns. The most recent efforts, beginning with the Goldwater-Nichols Act, are well known. In the post-Cold War/post-Gulf War era, defense reform efforts have become a virtual national pastime for retired officers and politicians, members of the defense intelligentsia, Congress and the Executive Branch. There have been, in rather rapid succession, the Base Force (BF), the Bottom Up Review (BUR), CORM, the Quadrennial

Defense Review (QDR), the National Defense Panel (NDP) and the Commission on National Security for the 21st Century as well as several rounds of Base Realignment and Closure (BRAC) studies. Curiously, the QDR is coterminous with presidential elections, which magnifies rather than mitigates partisan political influence. There is great argument about more rounds in the BRAC process, with the military seeking to cut needless infrastructure and Congressmen reluctant to have their districts lose federal money or jobs.

The process of assessing the shortfalls of the defense establishment, the calls for a variety of reforms, the need to reorganize the defense department or national security organization as a whole have been a long-standing feature of the American defense establishment. There have been concerns expressed about the lack of truly strategic long range planning; the failure of the budgeting, procurement and accounting systems; the need for a new command and force structures; and the necessity for reorganization of the machinery providing for national security and the defense industry which supplies it.[11] The Reports and Commissions, their titles and chairmen, and the debates they have inspired have been continuing features of both executive and congressional concern for over 50 years. Some of these have been acted upon but most have not. To them must be added the scores of journalistic reports, academic books, congressional hearings, and efforts at reform which have been a steady drum beat in our national life.[12] Indeed, there have been charges of fraud, waste and abuse, corruption, or merely poor organization and institutionalized inefficiencies since the country was founded.[13] Nearly all have concluded that there are serious flaws in the way in which we organize to provide for the common defense. Yet relatively little has been done to address the major criticisms of these myriad reports, studies, and charges. Why? More appropriately, why not?

The answers, as with most explanations, are at once simple and complex. Recently, on the simple side of the ledger, is the historical reality that the United States has lived for over half a century with a set of compromises in the organization of our national defense establishment that were built into the National Security Act of 1947. As Robert Art has explained it, the United States "created a defense organization that has a host of organizational inefficiencies built into it. Unification of the armed forces was purchased at the price of permitting duplication and overlap in function."[14]

> Four characteristics capture the manner in which the United States has organized its defense establishment since 1947. First, the defense establishment remains a system of half measures, falling somewhere between a truly integrated, highly centralized system on the one hand and a loosely coordinated, committee-run structure on the other. Second, the organizational changes that have been made since 1947 have been modest on the military side but radical on the civilian side. Third, through the three major reorganizations since 1945 (in 1947, 1949, and 1958), the services have managed to retain considerable autonomy to develop war plans and to allocate resources in a manner that each judges best suited to its own interests, without due regards for what the other services need or are doing, much less what the overall national defense requires. Fourth, since the 1958 Defense Reorganization Act, when the Secretary of Defense was given considerable powers to assert real operating control over the entire defense establishment, a fundamental imbalance has persisted between the centralizing powers of the Office of the Secretary of Defense (OSD) and the coordinating powers of the Chairman of the Joint Chiefs.[15]

Despite the passage of the Goldwater-Nichols Act in 1986 (after these remarks appeared in print) the same charges are largely true today.

The Goldwater-Nichols DoD Reorganization Act of 1986 did have a big impact on the U.S. military. Among other things, it made the Chairman of the Joint Chiefs the principal military advisor to the President, thus creating a competition with the Secretary of Defense. It increased the strength of the regional CINCs, but did not give them real power in the budgeting process. It also further emasculated the civilian service secretaries. While the military continues to repeat the mantra of jointness, and J-7 writes joint doctrine for nearly every task one might be asked to perform, the realities are far less than the appearance would suggest. A cynic would say Goldwater-Nichols is the way to guarantee that all the services participate in every major use of military force. A booster would say that wars of the future are likely to be both joint and combined and jointness is only rational and prudent. Both would be correct. Indeed, many of the problems with today's American defense establishment are similar to those that were identified by James Fallows in his 1980 book *National Defense*—a book that was written prior to the passage of the Goldwater-Nichols Act.

The Perils of Being the Last Remaining Superpower.

However much we may like the sound of it and however soothing it may be to bask, albeit temporarily, in the glow of being the self-proclaimed last remaining superpower, this reality is fraught with difficulties and burdened with some rather substantial obligations and responsibilities. Is the United States up to the task? Just how should it go about doing it? Some would like it to retain this mantel permanently and to actively promote a "Pax Americana" for the next century, while others think the moment has passed. Some would like to make William Wohlforth's "Unipolar World" a manifest reality of some duration while others seek a more limited role for the United States, such as that favored by Robert Art and others who see "Selective Engagement" as the answer.[16] In between are other prescriptions for and images of America which range from being lonely to being a bully.[17] Some see the United States as ready but reluctant. Others see it as not unwilling but unable to exert leadership in the world. There is some truth in most of these views.

Regardless of one's views on America's proper role in the world, there is another issue. The test of national security used to be the ability and willingness of the nation to act unilaterally, to include the use of force if deemed necessary, in defense of the nation's interests. However, both the National Security Strategy of the United States and the National Military Strategy assume that when force is used by the United States in the future, it will be as part of a coalition, either permanent or ad hoc. Americans want others to assist them in their international actions. The United States needs others to permit (via U.N. Resolutions), pay for (through NATO burden sharing; Saudi or Japanese cash payments), and participate (regional states in the area of intervention, if not the U.N.) in the application of American military power abroad. But international action by committee is often slow, cumbersome, belated, and ineffectual.

The other options are "selective engagement" based on principles and precepts which can be stated in advance and generally adhered to in policy execution. However, all this takes place in a circumstance where the American public may not perceive or care about international security. Since others will be paying for the investments that the United States makes in the world—in physical, financial, and human terms—some Americans believe that they need not be overly concerned. But, it would be helpful if there were a consensus on why a specific action is important, and some general agreement on how best to go about it. Such a consensus would be easier to develop if it could be guided by another "Long Telegram," the equivalent of the "Mr. X" article for the current era. The problem is that without an all-consuming peer competitor on which to focus, it is highly unlikely that such a document will be created and accepted.

There are risks and opportunity costs associated with the adoption of any of the proffered strategies for the long haul. They need to be debated thoroughly and weighed carefully. The opportunity costs revolve around the misuse of our current strategic situation. It is a relatively benign period, in terms of threats to the United States, which gives us the time to catch our breath and decide how best to contend with the future without having to worry about a serious, immediate threat to the nation. America has the luxury of not having to fight a war of necessity and being able to decide upon wars of choice. As George Bush observed after the Gulf War, America finds itself for the third time in a century in a position of being able to help shape the security regime for the future. It is an opportunity that should not be squandered and one that may not occur again, at least for some time.

On the other hand, it is a situation that is also full of danger. In promoting engagement and a philosophy of choice, the United States stands, if not guilty by intent, closely associated with the charge of cultural imperialism. Worse, in the eyes of many, America is the bully on the playground of international relations. It can afford neither the labels nor the reality if it hopes to have a benign and peaceful impact on the world. Yet both its short-term rhetoric and its actions seem to get in the way of America's long-term goals and preferences. The United States stands accused in some quarters of seeking world domination, by default if not by design. It is seen as the engine responsible for the homogenization and Americanization of the globe in nearly every aspect; from finance to movies, food to religion, clothing to music.

Americans also suffer from a feeling of perpetual guilt regardless of our actions. We feel damned if we do and damned if we don't intervene. The nonlogical but compelling emotional rationalizations of "if not here, where?" and "if not now, when?" are difficult to refute and tug at the heartstrings of American sensibilities that abhor famine, the slaughter of innocent civilians, genocide, etc. What we think of as assistance is usually intended to be short term, for humanitarian reasons and well-intentioned on our part. The fact that others may see such efforts as part of a "Pox Americana" rather than a "Pax Americana," is difficult for many Americans to understand. To many in the rest of the

145

world, particularly the Islamic world, it is increasingly a matter of "The West Against the Rest."[18] The fact that this is not our intention is essentially irrelevant.

Americans must confront the fact that despite good intentions, there are many problems in the world that the United States just cannot solve. The current experience in Kosovo is a case in point. An air campaign to punish Serbian President Slobidan Milosevic for ethnic cleansing in Kosovo is not likely to solve the problem for Albanian refugees fleeing the area. In the name of democracy and self-determination, principles Americans hold dear, the United States and its NATO allies may well be writing the requiem for a "new world order" in the wars of succession and secession in Yugoslavia. The fact that this is an unintended consequence may be of little solace to all concerned.

The System is Broken.

As defined in *Joint Publication 1-02*, "national security" is

> a collective term encompassing both national defense and foreign relations of the United States. Specifically, the condition provided by: a) a military or defense advantage over a foreign nation or group of nations, or b) a favorable foreign relations position, or c) a defense posture capable of successfully resisting hostile or destructive action from within or without, overt or covert.[19]

This is a matter for national decision. But increasingly, during and particularly after the Cold War, the United States is more concerned about creating a global environment in which it can survive and prosper and in which the ideals of the American political system can flourish. Doing so constitutes an effort to shape not merely national security but an international security environment. That is both a larger, and more problematic, agenda.

The scope, scale, and magnitude of the problems confronting the United States are much larger than they used to be. So, too, is the supposed "system" of government that has grown out of all proportion to what was initially envisioned in 1947. DoD has 36 separate organizations in the Office of the Secretary of Defense. In addition, it has 17 Defense agencies, 10 field activities, 10 laboratories, and 9 unified and combatant commands. DoD is divided into three service secretaries and departments, each with their own sizeable staffs; four services, each with a Reserve component and two with Guard components; as well the Inspector General, the Joint Chiefs of Staff (JCS) and an eight-division Joint Staff. The Army has 113 separate installations, the Air Force has 93, the Navy has 74, and the Marines has 19, both at home and abroad. Instead of an Office of the Secretary of Defense with a staff of 100, as established by the 1947 National Security Act, there are now hundreds of staff officers working for the secretary, and thousands in the service and joint staffs in the Pentagon.[20]

Add to this the executive and congressional players in the national security process, and the picture becomes even more complicated. There are over 50 congressional committees and subcommittees that have something to do with national security. The White House has the National Security Council, the National Economic Council, the President's Foreign Intelligence Advisory Board, and the U.S. Special Trade Representative. Then there are the specialized agencies in the executive branch, such as the Central Intelligence Agency, the National Security Agency, the Defense Intelligence Agency, and the National Reconnaissance Organization, as well as a whole series of shops in cabinet departments as diverse as Commerce, Justice, Agriculture, and Treasury. To this list, one can add numerous shops in the Department of State—35 separate ones—as well as a number of related agencies such as the U.S. Information Agency and the Agency for International Development.

Two things emerge from this cursory overview of the players in the national security bureaucracy. First, because of the large number of separate components involved in information gathering, analysis, decisionmaking, and dissemination, getting a timely response from this array of governmental organizations is difficult if not impossible. Second, the notion that quick, effective, and efficient coordination can occur routinely may be fiction. Merely checking with principals—let alone deputies, related agencies, and intelligence sources— becomes a time consuming process.

Coordination supposedly occurs through the interagency process, which is surveyed by Gabriel Marcella in this volume. The interagency process coordinates among U.S. Government agencies, and occasionally International Governmental Organizations or Non-Governmental Organizations, to craft policy initiatives and responses to events as they unfold. It usually involves the delegation of a lead agency responsible for determining the agenda, extracting agreement, and implementing decisions. The phrase imparts a notion of a well-oiled policy machine. It is largely a myth. Neither adaptation nor control is possible given the crazy quilt of organizations and players in the national security arena. The sheer difficulty of holding a meeting, even a conference call, is daunting. The "system" that we now have is too large, unwieldy, and complex to respond effectively or initiate the changes that are required. Both the purpose and the process are in need of attention. We need to start over.

America's Role in the World.

Virtually every aspect of our role in the world has changed. The chart below summarizes the transition—in both definition and focus—in the role of the United States in the world and the changing requirements for the common defense.

Former Focus	Current/Future Focus
National Defense	International Security
Unilateral Action	Coalition Diplomacy
Threat Based Policy	Objective Based Policy
Control	Adaptation
Capabilities	Intentions
Domestic Politics the Key	International Politics the Key
Force Application	Statecraft and Negotiation
War Preparation	Peace Preservation
Win by Out-producing Foe	Win by Outwitting Foe

I will survey each of these changes before proceeding to the next set of issues. What is the cumulative impact of these trends?

The fundamental transformation relates to the need to move from a system which provides for national defense to one which provides for international security. This latter task is larger in context, continuous in attention, and more complex in execution, particularly for a multi-cultural democratic republic such as the United States. Providing for the common defense used to be defined as protecting the nation from attack by other states. War would be declared when the nation was threatened, the citizenry and the economy would be mobilized, and Americans would sally forth beyond their ocean moats to give battle. Now the problem is more complex. The United States must shape an international environment conducive to the survival and prosperity of American values, institutions, citizens, and assets. The assumption of the National Security Strategy and the National Military Strategy of the United States is that the

The United States will employ force only as a part of a coalition. Since the Gulf War, the United States has needed others to permit, pay for, and participate in the application of American military force. That is a fundamental transformation. Similarly, throughout the Cold War, the United States focused on the identification of threats from the Communist world and the formulation of contingency plans to counteract these threats.

At present, by contrast, it is increasingly obvious that we cannot control all of the possible threats to the United States. The array of hypothetical threats is limited only by the imaginations of contractors and members of the armed services, and, in any event, America does not possess the will or the resources to counteract them all. What the United States can, and should, control, however, are the objectives we wish to accomplish in the world. Knowing what we wish to accomplish must necessarily precede the effort to do so.

The United States has always been more focused on capabilities than intentions. For much of the Cold War, the United States measured threats by the capabilities others possessed because it could. This gave logic to budgetary requests—the USSR has this, so the United States needs that. It was a costly and inefficient way to attempt to insure readiness for war. At present, it is increasingly important to pay attention to the intentions of others—of both allies and adversaries—as well as to their capabilities. Assessing intentions as well as capabilities may produce interesting opportunities as well as threats, and requires an investment in human intelligence (HUMINT) as well as overhead imagery. The United States has tended to place far more assets in the latter than in the former. It tried for much of the Cold War to control the pace, nature, intensity, scope, and outcome of the competition with others. But in a chaotic, nonlinear, unknown and largely unknowable global environment, seeking to control events may be a fool's errand and may be part of the problem, not part of the solution. Most organisms and organizations that have survived and prospered have been those that were able to adapt well and quickly to changing circumstances.

Improvisation and "work-arounds" are a hallmark of the American military. Why not train and educate an adaptable force rather than seeking to control what cannot be controlled?

For most of its history, the United States has been able to afford the luxury of doing much as it pleased and following its domestic agenda which has been the driver in American decisionmaking. It has not had to worry greatly about others and the general international climate. Increasingly, however, we are linked and interdependent with international forces, actors, and events. Pretending we can ignore or override them is both wrong and dangerous. Furthermore, contending in the international arena during our mostly isolationist past was seen as the application of the ultimate sanction of superior force. After the aberration of war was finished, we would return home to peace. But increasingly, the application of force doesn't pay, even for the victor. Statecraft, diplomacy, and negotiation are far better means of conflict resolution, and less costly. But others are far better at this and its tangential skills—language fluency, long-term views, pragmatic dealings—than Americans, who have disinvested in the capacity to conduct routine skillful diplomacy on many fronts.

The ultimate threat and final arbiter in international relations has been the act of war. As Charles Tilly has commented, "States make war, and wars make states."[21] But the stakes and costs have escalated beyond the capacity of most states to absorb them. Increasingly, it is peace preservation, not war waging, that is the problem for the international system. How can the United States allow transformation of the international system by force of arms, and thereby legitimize the use of force, while at the same time trying to preserve the *status quo* and promote only peaceful change? It is not strong states with aggressive designs on neighbors, totalitarianisms from both the left and the right, that threaten the international system today. Rather, it is the weakness of states and their disintegration that rocks the international system. But war, when it has come for the United States, has generally been good business. America won by outproducing the adversary. The German Panzer tanks were unquestionably better than the American Sherman tanks in World War II. The Germans produced a total of roughly 21,500 of the former in 7 years while the United States built over 40,000 of the latter in 4 years. Moreover, the United States built nearly as many tanks in a month—over 2,000—as the Germans did in some years.[22] Given the high cost of war material, the United States may not be able to afford the luxury of an economically profligate solution to its problems. Increasingly, America needs to be able to outwit our enemies, not merely out-produce them. This is particularly true in an era in which social security has defeated national security as the primary concern of the body politic.

These general trends are supplemented by yet another set of trends which also have significant implications for America's ability to provide for the common defense. These are as follows.

Former Focus	Current/Future Focus
Politico-Military Emphasis	Economic-Social-Psychological Emphasis
Regional	Global
Military Jointness	Civilian & Civil-Military Jointness
Technology	Strategy
Competition	Cooperation
Military Intelligence	Cultural Anthropology/Ethnology
The Services	The CINCs
Department of Defense	The U.S. Government
Right Place	Right Time

The collective imperative of these transformations is revolutionary change in the way the United States organizes to provide for international security as well as national defense.

It is no longer mainly about political and military problems and solutions. These are increasingly irrelevant to many global problems. It is often the other elements of national power—ones in which the United States has disinvested, relatively speaking—that are more pertinent. A better understanding of the realities that underlie both international problems (Somalia, the Balkans) and their ultimate solutions would go a long way towards making U.S. actions more appropriate and effective. For example, while containment led the United States to pursue a virtual "pactomania" approach to global problems—through regional military arrangements in the 1950s—these are not necessarily the most appropriately sized entities to deal with current and future problems. Most transnational problems involve regions that are smaller than states but involve many of them, or larger than states and thus not susceptible to national solutions. Increasingly, other issues—the availability of fresh water, global warming, pollution—are global in their consequence and hence, their solution. The political-military alignments of the Cold War are insufficient to the tasks at hand. A global data gathering, assessment, and dissemination process is required, along with a global vision to address these issues.

Since the passage of the Goldwater-Nichols Act, the U.S. military has been driven toward the realization of "jointness." As discussed by Douglas Lovelace in this volume, jointness is the increasing integration of the Armed Services, and the quest for common solutions to military problems that confront all of the services. It is meant as a direct challenge to the traditional parochial approach that the Services have brought to debates about national security. While much progress has been made with the development of joint doctrine, there is still more lip service than reality associated with this concept. Furthermore, there is little jointness among the active duty forces and the reserve and national guard components, and even less among the military and their civilian counterpart agencies and institutions. There is also no equivalent effort at jointness among the civilian government agencies, to align functions, integrate effort, and eliminate duplication. Most regrettable of all, there is a growing gap between the military and civilian society where neither understands the other as they should.

Traditionally, and increasingly, given the commitment to *Joint Vision 2010* and its follow-on documents,[23] the United States has placed its faith in science, engineering, and technology to achieve and sustain a qualitative edge over current or future adversaries. While this is a reasonable choice, it masks the reality that not all problems are technological nor have technological solutions. Understanding the strategic environment, and knowing if, when, how, why, and where to employ technological means, is a far more difficult challenge than the mere acquisition of the technology, however sophisticated it might be. Developing the strategy that underlies the selection and employment of technology is the more important part of the problem. Americans tend to be captivated by things, and not by their purpose. We tend to focus on the hardware at hand rather than the second and third order consequences that may flow from its application. Furthermore, an American strategy may require more than intermittent competition with adversaries. It may demand sustained competition and cooperation with allies and adversaries alike, something that Americans are not comfortable doing and with which we have little experience. Because of our capitalist system, and the American emphasis on individual effort, competition seems the norm to Americans. There is less of an understanding of the necessity to cooperate as well as compete with both adversaries and allies. The yin and yang of the international system over the long haul require both capacities.

The United States has invested massive amounts of time, money, and effort in military intelligence using national technical means to identify threats to the nation. It has invested less in thinking about just who our potential adversaries might be and what makes them tick. Overhead imagery, multi-spectral imaging, and electronic data capture and assessment may not reveal what needs to be known about what another society, polity, or economy really values or how and why it functions as it does. Unfortunately, the United States has spent far less time, money, and effort trying to understand the perceptions, languages, and values of those who share the planet with us than many of them have invested in trying to understand us. Knowing these things—about friend, foe, and bystander alike—will be increasingly important in our interdependent world. Cultural anthropology and ethnology are as important, if not more important, than military intelligence in understanding others and our relations with them.

America's military requirements have traditionally been interpreted through the eyes of the major service components who train, organize, and equip the U.S. military in DoD. There are three departments, four services, four Reserve, and two Guard systems, which we attempt to integrate with the armed forces of other nations in joint and combined operations as necessary. But it is the regional and unified CINCs that deploy and employ forces, not the services. The services have the primary control of the budget, despite some CINC inputs to the Joint Resource Operations Command (JROC). The CINCs have forces "chopped" to them when action is required, but this is a complicated and cumbersome system. More power should devolve to the CINCs, as a logical extension of Goldwater-Nichols. But beyond that, both national defense and international security demand the effective use of more than the assets of DoD. For more than half a century, DoD has functioned as the major guarantor of national security. But it is too big in size and too narrow in focus to compete effectively in today's world. The policymaking process requires data fusion and information integration from not only DoD, Central Intelligence Agency (CIA), National Security Agency (NSA), National Reconnaissance Office (NRO), Defense Intelligence Agency (DIA) and other security agencies in the U.S. Government but also the agencies and functions of other departments. These include not only State, Justice, Commerce, and Treasury, but also Agriculture, Transportation, and Education as well as agencies such as the Federal Trade Commission, Federal Emergency Management Agency (FEMA), and others, to be integrated into a U.S. Government—wide focus on international security. The international aspects of many of these agencies are under-funded and understaffed at precisely the time of greatest need for specialized information and competencies.

Lastly, and most generally but importantly, the United States may be focused on the wrong part of many of the problems it faces. In the past, winning wars and preventing a *fait accompli* against our allies and policies required that the United States be in the right place to thwart an adversary's plans. But the United States has withdrawn from much of the world. It does not have nearly as many bases abroad nor as many people stationed permanently overseas as it used to have. The real BRAC process actually occurred overseas—with 65 percent of U.S. bases in Europe and 24 percent of those in the Far East being closed. Increasingly the speed, range, and accuracy of weapons, and improvements in communications, surveillance, and transportation mean that time and timing are critical. Doing things at the right time is as important, or more important, than doing them in the right place. Establishing or preventing a *fait accompli* is time dependent as well as place dependent. Global reach is necessary, but if it cannot be achieved at the right time, it may be worthless. This places a premium on rapid, adaptive Observation-Orientation-Decision-Action (OODA) loops and decision processes, something that is increasingly difficult for the U.S. Government to accomplish.

The cumulative impact of the issues raised above has been largely ignored. It is time to address the collective implications and act accordingly. Failure to do so will contribute to the ebb of American power and prestige and the erosion of America's capability to act. It is not American capabilities that may be called into question as much as American intent. Thinking through what we wish to accomplish and why, and how this may or may not unfold, are critical tasks. The United States may be as much in need of an entrance strategy as an exit strategy when it prepares for the next Gulf War or Kosovo operation. If the United States does not know what it seeks to accomplish, as well as why and how, then perhaps its intervention will be stillborn from the outset.

War may be too important to be left to the generals, but peace is too important to be left only to the politicians. This is true because, increasingly, peacetime preparedness is the key to victory in war. There are also an increasing number of "less than war" applications of military force occurring during ostensible periods of peace. The real struggle may be the peacetime competitions that war only validates. If the United States hopes to compete and cooperate successfully in this century to help manage a relatively peaceful international security system, it needs to pay more than lip service to the imperatives of the National Military Strategy of shape, respond, and prepare now. It needs to devise a strategy that is principled, affordable, and adaptive for the long haul. Such an effort is not, and should not be, dependent on having a peer competitor to plan against. Rather it requires vision, commitment, and leadership that is positive, sustainable, and inclusive.

It also requires an organization designed to accomplish the task. The national security machinery of over 50 years ago is part of the problem, not part of the solution. It is time not just for a conceptual revolution to understand better what it is we are about, but also for an organizational revolution to accomplish what we seek to do. This is a problem of political leadership for the president, political

157

courage for Congress, and political change for the country. A failure to address these problems—and soon—will lead to both our demise as a nation and the failure of the effort to establish a modicum of international security in the world in the 21st century.

ENDNOTES – CHAPTER 6

1. The Compact Edition of the Oxford English Dictionary, 22nd ed., Oxford: Oxford University Press, 1982. Vol. I, "Evolution," entry I, 5, p. 354; Vol. II, "Revolution," entry III, 6, b, p. 617.

2. The number of "non-state actors" is over 40 times larger than the number of states, and they play an increasingly important role in international affairs whether as U.N. agencies, terrorist groups, economic unions, producer cartels, or private voluntary organizations such as *Medecins Sans Frontieres*, Oxfam, and the like.

3. See Grant T. Hammond, "The Paradoxes of War," *Joint Forces Quarterly*, Vol. 2, No. 2, June 1994, pp. 7-16.

4. "Technomic vitality" was a term coined in the research done on two Chief of Staff Air Force (CSAF) directed studies entitled "Spacecast 2020" and "Air Force 2025." It refers to the synergy, growth, and degree of change in technology and economic growth and was seen as a major factor in determining national capabilities in the future.

5. The number of countries with some U.S. military deployed covers a wide range of circumstances ranging from NATO allies in whose countries we have bases, detachments involved in fighting the "drug war," National Guard partnership programs with countries in Eastern Europe and former Soviet Socialist Republics, listening posts and satellite ground stations around the world, peace keeping and humanitarian relief operations, forward support locations, prepositioned equipment stocks and personnel to monitor them, naval bases and gunnery ranges, aerial ranges, space monitoring facilities, etc.

6. U.S. Department of State, "Overseas Digest for Americans Abroad," located at *http://overseasdigest.com/amercian*.

7. See Table No. 838, "Foreign Purchases of Sales of U.S. Securities, by Type of Security, 1980-1998, and by Selected Country, 1998," in *U.S. Bureau of the Census, Statistical Abstract of the United States*, 1999, p. 533. The total foreign investment in the U.S. in 1998 was $278.2 billion.

This does not include an additional $201 billion of foreign purchases of U.S. businesses through mergers and acquisitions. See Bureau of Economic Analysis News Release, Wednesday, June 9, 1999. "Foreign Investors' Spending to Acquire or Establish U.S. Businesses Tops $200 Billion for the First Time in 1998," available at *http://www.bea.doc.gov*.

8. This is a quotation from John Winthrop, "A Model of Christian Charity," 1630, which is itself a Biblical reference to Matthew, 5:14.

9. The legislative powers are spelled out in Article I, Section 8. The executive powers are detailed in Article II, Section 2.

10. The current national security structure and organization of the United States is not authorized in the Constitution nor are many of the constituent portions of the U.S. Armed forces—the U.S. Air Force, the National Guard structure, or the Reserve components of the U.S. military. For that matter, neither are DoD, the NSC, the NRO, the CIA, the NSA, DIA, or a host of other entities. None of the Amendments to the Constitution deal with issues of national security.

11. See, for example, some of the more recent books and articles such as David E. Snodgrass, "The QDR: Improve the Process to Improve the Product," *Parameters*, Vol. XXX, No. 1, Spring, 2000, pp. 57-68; James R. Schlesinger, "Raise the Anchor or Lower the Ship: Defense Budgeting and Planning," *The National Interest*, Fall 1998, pp. 2-12; Paul Davis, David Gompert, Richard Hillestad and Stuart Johnson, *Transforming the Force: Suggestions for DoD Strategy*, Santa Monica, CA: RAND Issue Paper, 1998; Peter Trubowitz, *Defining the National Interest: Conflict and Change in American Foreign Policy*, Chicago, IL: University of Chicago Press, 1999; Eugene Gholz and Harvey Sapolsky, "Restructuring the U.S. Defense Industry," *International Security*, Vol. 24, No. 3, Winter 1999/2000, pp. 5-51; and John Hillen, "Defense's Death Spiral, *Foreign Affairs*, Vol. 78, No. 4, July/August 1999, pp. 2-7.

12. Among these, Ashton B. Carter and William James Perry, *Preventive Defense: A New Security Strategy for America*, Washington, DC: Brookings Institution Press, 1999; Richard N. Haas, "What To Do With American Primacy," *Foreign Affairs*, September/October 1999, pp. 37-49; *Transforming Defense: National Security in the 21st Century*, Report of the National Defense Panel, December 1997; Barry R. Posen and Andrew Ross, "Competing Visions for U.S. Grand Strategy," *International Security*, Vol. 21, No. 3, Winter 1996/1997, pp. 5-53; Franklin C. Spinney, "Defense Spending Time Bomb?," *Challenge*, July-August 1996, pp. 23-33.; and The United States Commission on

National Security/21st Century, *New World Coming: American Security in the 21st Century*, September 15, 1999.

13. The problem is an old one, indeed, almost as old as the Republic itself. In 1782 the Congress instructed Superintendent of Finance Robert Morris to investigate "fraud, negligence, or waste of public property" in Revolutionary War procurement. It sought competitive bidding, but got cronyism among Morris's friends instead. Nearly a decade later, it had instructed Alexander Hamilton in 1791 to report on

> the encouragement and promotion of such manufactures as will tend to render the United States independent of other nations for essential, particularly for military supplies.

These instructions are cited in Richard F. Kaufman, *The War Profiteers*, New York: Bobbs Merrill, 1979, p. 7; and Drew McCoy, *The Elusive Republic*, New York: W. W. Norton, 1980, p. 148, respectively. Thus, the military–industrial complex and both its evils and its necessity were a matter of concern well over 200 years ago. During the Cold War, uttering the phrase "national security" could invoke money, secrecy, and massive resources—public and private—often with little public scrutiny or debate. See the overview by Kate Doyle, "The End of Secrecy: National Security and the Imperative for Openness," *World Policy Journal*, Vol. XVI, No. 1, Spring 1999, pp. 34-51.

14. Robert J. Art, "Introduction: Pentagon Reform in Comparative and Historical Perspective," in Robert J. Art, Vincent Davis, and Samuel P. Huntington, eds., *Reorganizing America's Defense: Leadership in War and Peace*, Washington, DC: Pergammon Brassey, 1985. p. xii.

15. *Ibid.*, p. xiii.

16. See William C. Wohlforth, "The Stability of a Unipolar World," *International Security*, Vol. 23, No. 1, Summer 1999, pp. 3-41; Samuel P. Huntington, "Why International Primacy Matters," *International Security*, Vol. 17, No. 4, Spring 1993, pp. 71-81; Joshua Muravchik, *The Imperative of American Leadership: A Challenge to Neo-Isolationism*, Washington, DC: AEI Press, 1996; Condoleezza Rice, "Promoting the National Interest," *Foreign Affairs*, Vol. 79, No. 1, January/February 2000, pp. 45-62; Robert J. Art, "Geopolitics Updated: The Strategy of Selective Engagement," *International Security*, Vol. 23, No. 3, Winter 1998/99, pp. 79-113; and Joseph Nye, "The New National Interest," *Foreign Affairs*, Vol. 78, No. 4, July/August 1999, pp. 22-35.

17. Samuel P. Huntington, "The Lonely Superpower," *Foreign Affairs*, Vol. 78, No, 2, March/April 1999, pp. 35-49; Garry Wills, "Bully of the Free World," *Foreign Affairs, Ibid.*, pp. 50-59. See also Richard Haas's notion in his *The Reluctant Sheriff: The U.S. After the Cold War*, New York: Council on Foreign Relations, 1998.

18. See Matthew Connelly and Paul Kennedy, "Must It Be the Rest Against the West?," *The Atlantic Monthly*, Vol. 274, No. 6, December 1994, pp. 61-84.

19. *Joint Publication 1-02, Department of Defense Dictionary of Military and Associated Terms*, March 23,1994, as amended through January 24, 2000, Washington, DC: Joint Staff (Documents Division), 2000, p. 305.

20. These, and information about them, can be found at *http://www.defenselink.mil.*

21. Charles Tilly, "Reflections on the History of European State Making," in Charles Tilly, ed., *The Formation of National States in Western Europe*, Princeton: Princeton University Press, 1975, p. 42. See also Bruce D. Porter, *War and the Ruse of the State: The Military Foundations of Modern Politics*, New York: Free Press, 1996.

22. For information see *www.shadowsfolly.com/wwII/Germany* and *www.valourandhorror.com/DB/SPEC/tanks_2.html.*

23. See *Concept for Future Joint Operations: Expanding Joint Vision 2010*, Ft. Monroe, VA: Joint Warfighting Center, May 1997; and *Joint Vision 2020*, June 2000.

CHAPTER 7

NATIONAL SECURITY
AND THE INTERAGENCY PROCESS:
FORWARD INTO THE 21st CENTURY

Gabriel Marcella

Power is the capacity to direct the decisions and actions of others. Power derives from strength and will. Strength comes from the transformation of resources into capabilities. Will infuses objectives with resolve. Strategy marshals capabilities and brings them to bear with precision. Statecraft seeks through strategy to magnify the mass, relevance, impact, and irresistibility of power. It guides the ways the state deploys and applies its power abroad. These ways embrace the arts of war, espionage, and diplomacy. The practitioners of these three arts are the paladins of statecraft.[1]

Chas W. Freeman, Jr.

The Interagency Process and Purposeful Adaptation.

The comments of Ambassador Chas W. Freeman, Jr. speak to the skillful use of influence and power to promote the national interests in a competitive world. It is a tall order even for the United States, the only fully equipped, globally deployed, interagency superpower. America is the indispensable anchor of international order and the increasingly globalized economic system. Nothing quite like it has ever existed. Indeed such great powers as Rome, Byzantium, China, Spain, England, and France achieved extraordinary sophistication, enormous institutional and cultural influence, and longevity, but they never achieved the full articulation of America's global reach.

Today the United States forward deploys some 250 diplomatic missions in the form of embassies, consulates, and specialized organizations. It possesses a unified military command system that covers all regions of the world and even outer space. It is the leader of an interlocking set of alliances and agreements that promotes peace, open trade, the principles of democracy, human rights, and protection of the environment. American capital, technology, and culture influence the globe. American power and influence is pervasive and multidimensional. All the instruments of national power are deployed. Yet the challenge of strategic integration, of bringing the instruments into coherent effectiveness, remains. Presidents and their national security staffs strive to achieve coherence, with varying levels of success, through the use of the "interagency process."

The interagency decisionmaking process is uniquely American in character, size, and complexity. Given ever expanding responsibilities and declining resources in dollars and manpower, it is imperative that national security professionals master it in order to work effectively within it. The complex challenges to national security in the 21st century will require intelligent integration of resources and unity of effort within the government.

The United States first faced the challenge of strategic integration within an embryonic interagency process during World War II. Mobilizing the nation and the government for war and winning the peace highlighted the importance of resources and budgets, of integrating diplomacy with military power, gathering and analyzing enormous quantities of intelligence, conducting joint and combined military operations, managing coalition strategies and balancing competing regional priorities. From the war and the onset of the Cold War emerged a number of institutional innovations, including: The structure of the modern Department of State, the Department of Defense, the Air Force, a centralized intelligence system and unified military command system, the predecessor of the U.S. Agency for International Development (Point Four), North Atlantic Treaty Organization (NATO) and other alliances, and the United States Information Agency.

There is probably no period in American history like the late 1940s and early 1950s that is so formative of the kind of national and institutional learning that John P. Lovell calls "purposeful adaptation." He defines it as "the need to develop and pursue foreign policy goals that are sensitive to national needs and aspirations and to the realities of a changing world environment."[2] The evolution of the interagency process parallels America's purposeful adaptation to the changing global realities of the last five decades. But it has not been an orderly evolution, in part because of serious structural and cultural impediments, such as poor institutional memory.[3] Prominent historical markers along this path include such documents as NSC 68, the intellectual framework for the containment strategy against the Soviet Union, and the Weinberger Doctrine, which articulated criteria for the use of military power that dramatically influenced the shape of American strategy in the 1980s and 1990s.

In 1945, American statesmen faced three challenges: forging a system of collective security, promoting decolonization, and building a stable international financial order. These, and 4 decades of intense threat from the other superpower, had a decisive impact on the interagency process. With the end of bipolar ideological and geopolitical conflict, the foreign policy and defense agenda is captured by free trade, democratization, subnational ethnic and religious conflicts, failing states, humanitarian contingencies, ecological deterioration, terrorism, international organized crime, drug trafficking, and the proliferation of the technology of weapons of mass destruction. At the dawn of a new era, is the policymaking system which was developed and refined for the strategic imperatives of the Cold War adequate to meet a very different set of challenges?

The National Security Council: Coordination vs. Policymaking.

To bring strategic coherence, consensus, and decisiveness to the burgeoning global responsibilities of the emerging superpower, the National Security Act (NSA) of 1947 created the National Security Council (NSC). Its mandate was:

> . . . to advise the President with respect to the integration of domestic, foreign, and military policies relating to the national security so as to enable the military services and the other departments and agencies of the Government to cooperate more effectively in matters involving the national security.

> . . . other functions the President may direct for the purpose of more effectively coordinating the policies and functions of the departments and agencies of the Government relating to the nations security. . .

> . . . assess and appraise the objectives, commitments, and risks of the United States. . .

> . . . consider policies on matters of common interest to the departments and agencies of the Government concerned with the national security . . .

The statutory members are the president, the vice president, secretaries of State and Defense. All others present are advisors: Chairman of the Joint Chiefs of Staff, Director Central Intelligence, and cabinet members. The Council need not convene formally to function. Indeed, by late 1999 the Clinton NSC had met formally only once: March 2, 1993. There are alternatives to formal meetings, such as the "ABC" luncheons of Secretary of State Madeleine Albright, Assistant to the President for National Security Affairs Sandy Berger, and Secretary of Defense William Cohen, and the deputies breakfasts and lunches. The "NSC system" of policy coordination and integration operates 24 hours a day. The Assistant to the President for National Security Affairs directs the staff. The emergence of

166

the modern "operational presidency,"[4] brought to the NSC greater authority over the development and implementation of policy, thus creating a new power center that competes for jurisdiction with the Departments of State and Defense.

The NSC staff, known as the Executive Secretariat, has varied in size and function. In 1999 the staff comprised about 208 (of which 101 were policy personnel and 107 administrative and support personnel) professionals covering regional and functional responsibilities. Staffers are detailed from the diplomatic corps, the intelligence community, the civil service, the military services (12 in policy positions in September 1999), academia, and the private sector. The staffing procedures are personalized by the president's style and comfort level. The structure of the staff, its internal and external functioning, and the degree of centralized control of policy varies. Presidents Jimmy Carter and William Clinton have favored a very centralized system, Presidents Ronald Reagan and George Bush less so. The first two Presidential Decision Directives of the Clinton administration, dated January 20, 1993, set forth the structure and function of the NSC staff and groups that report to it, as depicted below:

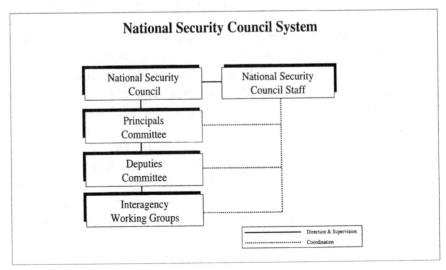

The day-to-day policy coordination and integration is done by the NSC Staff, divided into functional and geographic directorates:

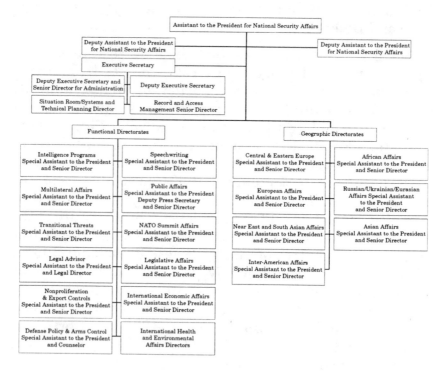

National Security Council Staff.

The Principals Committee members are the cabinet level representatives who comprise the senior forum for national security issues. The Deputies Committee includes assistant secretary level officials who monitor the work of the interagency policy formulation and articulation process, do crisis management, and, when necessary, push unresolved issues to the Principals for resolution. Interagency Working Groups (IWGs) are the heart and soul of the process. They may be *ad hoc*, standing, regional, or functional. They function at a number of levels, meet regularly to assess routine and crisis issues, frame policy responses, and build consensus across the government for unified action. The fluid nature of the process means that IWGs do not always have to come to decisions. The system prefers that issues be decided at the lowest level possible. If issues are not resolved there, they are elevated to the next level and, when appropriate, to the Deputies Committee. Who chairs the different IWGs and committees can vary between the NSC director and a senior State Department official.

Policy is often made in different and subtle ways. Anthony Lake, writing in *Somoza Falling: The Nicaraguan Dilemma, A Portrait of Washington At Work*, discusses how the answer to an important letter can help set policy. Hence the importance of interagency coordination and the importance of being the one (bureau, office, agency) that drafts it.

> ... policy flows as much from work on specific items—like the letter from Perez [to Carter]—as it does from the large, formal interagency "policy reviews" that result in presidential pronouncements.[5]

Each action is precedent for future actions. Speeches, press conferences, VIP visits, and presidential travels are also important. Lake elaborates:

> Policy is made on the fly; it emerges from the pattern of specific decisions. Its wisdom is decided by whether you have some vision of what you want, a conceptual thread as you go along.[6]

The NSC staff does the daily and long-term coordination and integration of foreign policy and national security matters across the vast government. Specifically, it:

1. provides information and policy advice to the president;

2. manages the policy coordination process;

3. monitors implementation of presidential policy decisions;

4. manages the interdepartmental dimensions of crises;

5. articulates the president's policies;

6. undertakes long term strategic planning;

7. conducts liaison with congress and foreign governments; and,

8. coordinates summit meetings and national security related trips.

There is a natural tension between the policy coordination function of the NSC and policymaking. Jimmy Carter's Director of Latin American Affairs at the NSC, Robert Pastor, argues that:

> . . . tension between NSC and State derives in part from the former's control of the agenda and the latter's control of implementation. State Department officials tend to be anxious about the NSC usurping policy, and the NSC tends to be concerned that State either might not implement the president's decisions or might do so in a way that would make decisions State disapproved of appear ineffective and wrong.[7]

The NSC staff is ideally a coordinating body but, in fact, it oscillates between the poles—taking policy control over some issues while allowing the State or Defense to be the lead agency on most national security and foreign policy issues. On some key issues, such as the Kosovo crisis of 1998-99, the NSC staff may take over policy control from State. Similarly, policies toward Cuba and Haiti in 1993-95 were handled directly out of the White House because of the deeply rooted domestic dimension of these issues. The Oliver North Iran-Contra caper created an autonomous operational entity within the NSC staff. But this was an aberration that does not invalidate the general rule. The salient point is that proximity to the president gives the NSC staff significant policy clout in the interagency process. Such clout must be used sparingly lest it cause resentment and resistance or overlook the policy wisdom and skills available elsewhere in the executive departments.

By late 1999, the Clinton administration had established other formal bodies under the umbrella of the NSC:

1. Executive Committees, established by PDD 56 for complex humanitarian contingencies;

2. Peacekeeping Core Group, established by PDD 25;

3. Counter-terrorism Security Group, established by PDD 42, amended by PDD 62;

4. Special Coordination Group, established by PDD 42 for international crime;

5. Weapons of Mass Destruction Preparedness Group, established by PDD 62; and,

6. Critical Infrastructure Coordinating Group, established by PDD 62.

These groups have reached across the network of executive departments.

Towards a Theory of the Interagency Process: How Does the President Mobilize the Government?

The interagency is not a place. It is a process involving human beings and complex organizations with different cultures, different outlooks on what's good for the national interest and the best policy to pursue—all driven by the compulsion to defend and expand turf. The process is political (therefore conflictual) because at stake is power—personal, institutional, or party. The "power game" involves the push and pull of negotiation, the guarding of policy prerogatives, the hammering out of compromises, and the normal human and institutional propensity to resist change.[8] Regardless of the style of the president and the structures developed for the management of national security policy, the NSC-dominated interagency process performs the same basic functions: identifies policy issues and questions, formulates options, raises issues to the appropriate level for decisions, makes decisions where appropriate, and oversees the implementation of decisions throughout the executive departments.

It is helpful to view policy at five interrelated levels: conceptualization, articulation, budgeting, implementation, and post-implementation analysis and feedback. Conceptualization involves the complex intellectual task of policy development, such as a Presidential Decision Directive (PDD). Articulation is the public declaration of policy by the president or his subordinates. This is critical in a democracy in order to engage public support. Budgeting involves testimony before Congress to justify policy goals and to request funding. Implementation is the programmed application of resources in the field in order to achieve the policy objectives. Post-implementation analysis and feedback is the continuous effort to assess the effectiveness of policy and to make appropriate adjustments.

The ideal system would have perfect goal setting, complete and accurate intelligence, comprehensive analysis and selection of the best options, clear articulation of policy and its rationale, effective execution, thorough and continuous assessment of the effects, perfect learning from experience and the ability to recall relevant experience and information.

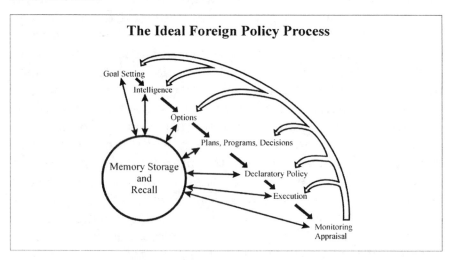

The Ideal Foreign Policy Process

Source: John P. Lovell, *The Challenge of American Foreign Policy: Purpose and Adaptation,* p. 26.

Such perfection is impossible. The reality is:

POLICY IN PRACTICE

TASK	CAPABILITY
Goal Setting	National interests are object of competing claims; goals established through political struggle
Intelligence	Always incomplete, susceptible to overload, delays and distortions caused by biases and abiguity in interpretation
Option Formulation	Limited search for options, comparisons made in general terms according to predispositions rather than cost-benefit analysis
Plans, Programs, Decisions	Choices made in accordance with prevailing mind sets, often influenced by groupthink and political considerations
Declaratory Policy	Multiple voices, contradictions and confusion, self-serving concern for personal image and feeding the appetite of the media
Execution	Breakdowns in communication, fuzzy lines of authority, organizational parochialism, bureaucratic politics, delays
Monitoring and Appraisal	Information gaps, vague standards, regidities in adaption, feedback failures
Memory Storage and Recall	Spotty and unreliable, selective learning and application of lessons

Effective policy requires vision, control, resources, and a system of accountability. The most compelling challenge for the executive is to retain policy control. Since presidents don't have the time and expertise to oversee policymaking in detail (though Jimmy Carter tried), they delegate responsibility. But "nobody is in charge" is an often-heard criticism of the interagency process. By delegating responsibility, control becomes more diffused, and the policy effort is diluted. Moreover, the quest for resources brings in another stakeholder, Congress, which has the constitutional responsibility to scrutinize policy initiatives and vote monies for foreign affairs and national defense. At this point, a literal Pandora's box of players and expectations are opened. The numerous congressional committees and their staffs have enormous impact on national security and foreign policy.

The president begins to mobilize his government immediately upon election. A transition team works closely with the outgoing administration for the purpose of continuity. The incoming president begins nominating his cabinet, which must then be confirmed by the Senate. Some 6,000 presidential level appointees will fill the subcabinet positions, staff the White House and the NSC, take up ambassadorships (serving ambassadors traditionally submit their resignation when the occupant of the White House changes), and move into second, third, and fourth level positions in the executive departments. The purpose of these nominations is to gain control and establish accountability to the president and his agenda. In his first administration, Clinton faced problems associated with never finishing the staffing of his government.

Thus there is a high turnover and the injection of new talent, at times inexperienced and equipped with new predispositions about national security, at the top echelons of American government every time the part that controls the White House changes. Continuity of government resides in the non-partisan professionals of the federal civil service, the diplomatic service, the military, and the intelligence

174

community. The transition to a new administration is a period of great anticipation about the direction of policy. Consequently, the entire interagency produces transition papers to assist and inform the newcomers, and to also protect the institutional interests of the various departments from unfriendly encroachment.

The first months of a new administration are a period of learning. Newly appointed people must familiarize themselves with the structure and process of policymaking. This necessity invariably leads to a trial-and-error atmosphere. In anticipation of the passing of the mantle, think tanks and the foreign policy and defense communities write papers recommending specific policies. These help to inform the new administration about the central commitments of U.S. policy and provide opportunities for departments and agencies to define institutional turf and stake a claim to resources. The administration itself will also mandate policy reviews (Presidential Review Directives) that eventually produce new guidance for policy.

Making speeches and declaring policy and doctrines are other ways in which the incoming administration establishes its identity. The State of the Union message is one of the preeminent sources of presidential activism that engages the interagency. The congressionally-mandated National Security Strategy (NSS) document, which bears the president's signature and is supposed to be produced annually, is also eagerly awaited (though not with equal intensity across departments) as an indicator of an administration's direction in national security and foreign policy. The NSS is eagerly awaited for another reason as well. It is the best example of "purposeful adaptation" by the American government to changing global realities and responsibilities. It expresses strategic vision—what the United States will stand for in the world, what the administration's priorities are, and how the diplomatic, economic, and military instruments of national power will be arrayed.

Since it is truly an interagency product, the NSS also serves to provide direction to the interagency system to understand the president's agenda and priorities and develops a common language that gives coherence to policy. It is also more than a strategic document. It is political, because it is designed to enhance presidential authority in order to mobilize the nation. Finally, the NSS tends to document as well as drive policy initiatives, especially in election years.

The first NSS in 1987 focused on the Soviet threat. The Bush administration expanded it by including more regional strategies, economic policy, arms control, and transnational issues and the environment. The Clinton document of 1994 proposed "engagement and enlargement," promoting democracy, economic prosperity, and security through strength. The 1995 version added criteria for judging when and how military forces would be used. By 1997, the integrating concepts of "shape," "prepare," and "respond" came into prominence. To the core objectives of enhancing security and promoting prosperity and democracy were added fighting terrorism, international crime and drug trafficking, and managing the international financial crisis. Homeland defense against the threat of mass casualty attacks and regional strategies completed the agenda in 1997.

Another instrument used by the Clinton team is the aforementioned Presidential Decision Directive process. Previous administrations have titled these documents differently, such as Bush's National Security Decision Directive. The two Clinton administrations produced 71 PDDs by February 2000 (Bush, 79 National Security Directives; Reagan, 325 National Security Decision Memoranda; Carter, 63 presidential Directives; Nixon-Ford, 348 National Security Decision Memoranda; and Kennedy-Johnson, 372 National Security Action Memoranda). Each administration attempts to use these documents to put its own stamp on national security and foreign policy, though there is great continuity with previous administrations. Thus, whereas Reagan emphasized restoring the preeminence of American military power and rolling back the "evil empire," Clinton focused on open trade, democratization, conflict resolution, humanitarian assistance, fighting drug trafficking and consumption, counter-terrorism and non-proliferation.

PDDs are macro-level documents, normally classified, that take much deliberate planning to develop. They result from intensive interaction among the agencies. The process begins with a Presidential Review Directive, which tasks the relevant agencies to develop a new policy based on broad guidance. For example, Clinton's PDD 14 for counternarcotics, the "Andean Strategy" of November 1993, emphasized greater balance between supply and demand strategies. PDD 25, "U.S. Policy on Reforming Multilateral Peace Operations" (May 1994), set down an elaborate set of guidelines for U.S. involvement in peace operations. It became so effective that the United Nations adopted it for planning its own peace operations, an excellent example of the international transfer of American purposeful adaptation.

An instructive example of the Clinton administration's application of one of its Directives is PDD 21 which took effect on December 27, 1993. This document emphasized democracy promotion and free trade in Latin America. It was addressed to more than twenty departments and agencies: Vice President, Secretary of State, Secretary of the Treasury, Secretary of Defense, Attorney General, Secretary of Commerce, Secretary of Labor, Director of the Office of Management and Budget, United States Trade Representative, Representative of the United States to the United Nations, Chief of Staff to the president, Assistant to the president for National Security Affairs, Director of Central Intelligence, Chair of the Council of Economic Advisors, Assistant to the president for National Economic Policy, Chairman of the Joint Chiefs of Staff, Administrator of the Agency for International Development, Director of the Arms Control and Disarmament Agency, Administrator of

177

the Environmental Protection Agency, and Director of the United States Information Agency.

The point of listing departments and agencies is to identify the interagency stakeholders relating to one regional policy. Inevitably, the size of the stake will vary greatly among regions and issues. The stakeholders are related **by functional interdependence**; they have different resources, personnel, and expertise that must be integrated in order for policy to be effective. It is an iron rule of the interagency that **no national security or international affairs issue can be resolved by one agency alone**. For example, the Department of Defense needs the diplomatic process that the Department of State masters in order to deploy forces abroad, build coalitions, negotiate solutions to conflicts, conduct noncombatant evacuations (NEO) of American citizens caught in difficult circumstances abroad, and administer security assistance. The Department of State in turn depends on the logistical capabilities of Defense to deploy personnel and materials abroad during crises, conduct coercive diplomacy, support military-to-military contacts, and give substance to alliances and defense relationships. The Office of National Drug Control Policy, a new cabinet position, must rely on a range of agencies to reduce the supply abroad and consumption of drugs at home. Finally, all require intelligence input to make sound decisions.

Ideally in response to the promulgation of a PDD, all agencies will energize their staffs and develop the elements that shape the policy programs. But this takes time and seldom creates optimum results, in part because of competing priorities of policymakers, limited time, constrained resources, and congressional input. For example, with respect to U.S. Latin American policy, the Haiti crisis of 1992-1994 and congressional passage of the North America Free Trade Act consumed most of the kinetic energy of the Clinton Administration's NSC staff and the Bureau of Inter-American Affairs of the Department of State during 1993-94.

In theory, once the policy elements are put together and costs are calculated, they are submitted to Congress for approval and funding, without which policy is merely a collection of words of expressions of hope. The reality, however, is that a PDD is not a permanent guide to the actions of agencies. Rarely is it fully implemented. It can be overtaken by new priorities, new administrations, and by the departure of senior officials who had the stakes, the personal relationships, the know how, and the institutional memory to make it work. A senior NSC staffer, Navy Captain Joseph Bouchard, Director of Defense Policy and Arms Control, remarked in 1999 that one cannot be sure about whether a PDD from a previous administration is still in force because for security reasons no consolidated list of these documents is maintained. Moreover, PDDs and other presidential documents are removed to presidential libraries and archives when a new president takes over. A senior Defense Department official states that PDDs are rarely referred to after they are final, are usually overtaken by events soon after publication, and are rarely updated. In this respect the interagency evaluation of PDD 56's effectiveness, published in May 1997, is instructive: "PDD 56 no longer has senior level ownership. The Assistant Secretaries, Deputy Assistant Secretaries, and the NSC officials who initiated the document have moved on to new positions."[10]

PDD 56: Ephemeral or Purposeful Adaptation?

PDD 56, *The Clinton Administration's Policy on Managing Complex Contingency Operations*, is perhaps the mother of all modern PDDs. It is useful to examine PDD 56 as an example of an interagency product and as a tool intended to influence the very process itself. PDDs normally deal with the external world of foreign policy and national security. PDD 56 is radically different, for it goes beyond that and attempts to generate a cultural revolution in the way the U.S. Government prepares and organizes to deal with these issues. It is a superb example of codifying lessons

179

of "purposeful adaptation" after fitful efforts by American civilian and military officials in the aftermath of problematic interventions in Panama (1989-90), Somalia (1992-1994), and Haiti (1994-1995).[11] The intent was to institutionalize interagency coordination mechanisms and planning tools to achieve U.S. Government unity of effort in complex contingency operations. It tried to institutionalize five mechanisms and planning tools:

1. An Executive Committee chaired by the Deputies Committee (Assistant Secretaries),

2. An integrated, interagency Political-Military Implementation Plan,

3. Interagency Rehearsal,

4. Interagency After-Action Review,

5. Training.

The philosophy behind the document is that interagency planning can make or break an operation. Moreover, early involvement in planning can accelerate contributions from civilian agencies that are normally culturally impeded from strategic and operational planning.[12] PDD 56 was applied extensively and adapted to new contingencies, such as Eastern Slavonia (1995-1998), Bosnia from 1995, Hurricane Mitch in Central America, the Ethiopia-Eritrea conflict since 1998, and the Kosovo contingency of 1998-99. The March 1999 review commented:

> PDD 56 is intended to be applied as an integrated package of complementary mechanisms and tools . . . since its issuance in 1997, PDD 56 has not been applied as intended. Three major issues must be addressed to improve the utility of PDD 56.

It recommended:

1. greater authority and leadership to promote PDD 56,

2. more flexible and less detailed political-military planning, and

3. dedicated training resources and greater outreach.

Imbedded in the three recommendations are the recurring problems of the interagency: the need for decisive authority ("nobody's in charge"), contrasting approaches and institutional cultures (particularly diplomatic versus military) with respect to planning, and the lack of incentives across the government to create professionals expert in interagency work. PDD 56 is a noble effort to promote greater effectiveness. It may yet bear fruit, if its philosophy of integrated planning and outreach to the interagency takes root. It is encouraging that, in late 1999, the PDD 56 planning requirement became an annex to contingency plans.

The Operational Level of the Interagency Process: Ambassador, Country Team and Regional Military Commanders.

Up to this point this chapter has discussed the national strategic level of the interagency process, that is, what occurs in Washington. Actually, the interagency process spans three levels: the national strategic, the operational, and the tactical. In the field, policy is implemented by ambassadors and their country teams, often working with the regional unified commanders. The embassy country team is a miniature replica of the Washington interagency system, with which it is in constant communication. At the country team, the rubber literally meets the road of interagency implementation. Ambassadors and commanders-in-chief (CINCs) rely on each other to promote policies that will enhance American interests in a country and region. CINCs have large staffs and awesome resources compared to the small staffs and resources of ambassadors. Moreover, their functions are different. The ambassador cultivates ties and is a conduit for bilateral communications through the art of diplomatic discourse. He or she promotes understanding of U.S. foreign policy, promotes American culture and business, and is responsible for American citizens in that country. The ambassador is the personal emissary of the president, who writes the ambassador's formal letter of instruction.

The letter charges the ambassador,

> to exercise full responsibility for the direction, coordination, and supervision of all executive branch officers in (name of country), except for personnel under the command of a U.S. area military commander . . . .

There is enough ambiguity in the mandate to require both ambassador and CINC to use common sense and, in a non-bureaucratic way, work out issues of command and control over U.S. military personnel in the country. In effect control is shared, with the ambassador having policy control and the CINC having control over day-to-day operations. It is essential that both work closely together to ensure that military operations meet the objectives of U.S. policy.

This is particularly the case in military operations other than war. Before and during noncombatant evacuations, peace operations, exercises, disaster relief and humanitarian assistance, such cooperation will be imperative because of the different mixes of diplomacy, force, and preparation required. A successful U.S. policy effort requires a carefully calibrated combination of diplomatic and military pressure, with economic inducements added. The security assistance officer at the embassy (usually the commander of the Military Advisory Group) can facilitate communication and help to bridge the policy and operational distance between the ambassador and the CINC. So can State's Political Advisor to the CINC, a senior ranking foreign service officer whose function is to provide the diplomatic and foreign policy perspective on military operations.[13] The personal and professional relationship between the Political Advisor and the CINC is the key to success.

The CINC represents the coercive capacity of American power through a chain of command that goes to the president. He and his sizable staff command the operational tempo, deployments, readiness, exercises, and training of divisions, brigades, fleets, and air wings—resources, language, and culture that are the opposite of the art of diplomacy. CINCs also have a regional perspective, strategies, and programs while ambassadors are focused on advancing the interests of the United States in one country. Since all military activities have diplomatic impact, it is necessary that the CINC work harmoniously with the ambassador in order to achieve common purpose. Ambassador and CINC interests intersect at the Military Advisory Group (MAAG, also called Military Liaison Office, Office of Defense Coordination) level. The commander of the MAAG works for both the ambassador and the CINC.

In the spectrum from peace to crisis to war, the ambassador will tend to dominate decisions at the lower end of the spectrum. As the situation moves toward war, the CINC assumes greater authority and influence. Haiti 1994 is an excellent example of how the handoff from ambassador to CINC takes place. The American ambassador in Port-au-Prince, William Swing, was in charge of U.S. policy until General Hugh Shelton and the U.S. military forces arrived in September of that year. Once the military phase was completed, policy control reverted to Swing, thus restoring the normal pattern of military subordination to civilian authority. In the gray area of military operations other than war, or in what is called an "immature" military theater such as Latin America, disputes can arise between ambassadors and CINCs about jurisdiction over U.S. military personnel in the country. The most illustrative was in 1994 between CINC of the U.S. Southern Command General Barry McCaffrey, and U.S. Ambassadors to Bolivia Charles R. Bowers and Colombia Morris D. Busby. The dispute had to be adjudicated in Washington by the Secretaries of State and Defense.[14] This situation demonstrates very clearly that ambassadors and CINCs must work closely together to coordinate U.S. military activities.

The Continuing Problems of the Interagency Process.

The tensions generated by cultural differences and jealousy over turf will always be part of the interagency process. The diplomatic and the military cultures dominate the national security system, though there are other cultures and even subcultures. The former uses words to solve problems while the latter uses force. Cultural differences are large but communicating across them is possible.[15] Table 1 compares the cultures of military officers and diplomats.

The principal problem of interagency decisionmaking is **lack of decisive authority; there is no one in charge**. As long as personalities are involved who work well together and have leadership support in the NSC, interagency efforts will prosper, but such congruence is not predictable. The world situation does not wait for the proper alignment of the planets in Washington. There is too much diffusion of policy control. This is why it is time to implement an NSC-centric national security system, with appropriate adjustments that align budget authority with policy responsibility. This system would consolidate in the NSC the functions now performed by the Policy Planning Staff at State and the strategic planning functions done at Defense. Such reorganization recognizes the reality that the White House is where an integrated approach to national security planning must take place.

Asymmetries in resources are another impediment. The Department of State, which has the responsibility to conduct foreign affairs, is a veritable pauper. Indeed, the military has more money to conduct diplomacy. The State Department's diplomats may have the best words in town, in terms of speaking and writing skills, and superb knowledge of foreign countries and foreign affairs, but it is a very small organization that has been getting smaller budget allocations from Congress in recent years. The corps of foreign service officers equates in number to about an

Military Officers	Foreign Service Officers
Mission: prepare for and fight war	Mission: conduct diplomacy
Training is a major activity, important for units and individuals	Training is not a significant activity, not important either for units or individuals
Extensive training for episodic, undesired events	Little formal training, learning by experience in doing desired activities (negotiating, reporting)
Uncomfortable with ambiguity	Comfortable with ambiguity
Plans and planning--both general and detailed--are important core activities	Plan in general terms to achieve objectives but value flexibility and innovation
Doctrine: important	Doctrine: not important
Focused on military element of foreign policy	Focused on all aspects of foreign policy
Focused on discrete events and activities with plans, objectives, courses of action, endstates	Focused on on-going processes without expectation of an "endstate"
Infrequent real-world contact with opponents or partners in active war fighting	Day-to-day real-world contact with partners and opponents in active diplomacy
Officer corps commands significant numbers of NCOs and enlisted personnel	Officers supervise only other officers in core (political and economic) activities
NCOs and enlisted personnel perform many core functions (war fighting)	Only officers engage in core activity (diplomacy)
Leadership: career professional military officers (with the military services and in operations)	Leadership: a mix of politicians, academics, policy wonks, and career Foreign Service professionals at headquarters and in field
All aspects of peace operations, including civilian/diplomatic, becoming more important	All aspects of peace operations, including military, becoming more important
Writing and written word less important, physical actions more important	Writing and written word very important. Used extensively in conduct of diplomacy
Teamwork and management skills are rewarded, interpersonal skills important internally	Individual achievement and innovative ideas rewarded, interpersonal skills important externally
Accustomed to applying large resources, manpower, equipment, and money to achieve goals	Accustomed to applying meager resources to achieve goals

Adapted from Robert Johnson, Foreign Service Officer, "Teaching Notes," Department of National Security and Strategy, U.S. Army War College.

Comparing Military Officers and Foreign Service Officers.

Army brigade (a typical brigade is about 3,600). The Department of State's technology is primitive and professional development of the kind that the military does is not promoted. Moreover, unlike the military, State lacks a strong domestic constituency of support.

The **resource barons**, those with people, money, technical expertise, and equipment reside in the Department of Defense (DoD) and the military services. Consequently, the military, especially the Army, is constantly being asked to provide resources for nation-building purposes in such places as Haiti and Panama. It is tempting to reach out to DoD because it is the only institution with an **expeditionary** capability and fungible resources and expertise. It can get there quickly, show the flag, bring significant resources to bear, stabilize a situation, and create an environment secure enough for other agencies to operate. Other baronies exist, of course, including the Agency for International Development, the intelligence community, the Departments of Justice and Commerce, and the Office of National Drug Control Policy.

Finally, the personnel systems of the various agencies of the U.S. Government **do not promote professionalization and reward service in interagency jobs**. What is needed is a systematic effort to develop civilian and military cadres that are experts in interagency policy coordination, integration, and operations. Some of this already takes place. Military officers are assigned to various departments (for example, 35 officers from all services work in the regional and functional bureaus of the Department of State). Likewise, diplomats are allocated to military and civilian agencies, such as Political Advisors at the regional unified commands, the Special Operations Command, to peacekeeping and humanitarian missions, various key positions in the Pentagon, and the war colleges. These programs must be expanded. There ought to be incentives for national security professionalism, as there are for service and joint activities. For civilians, including employees of the Department of State, something akin to

186

the 1986 Goldwater-Nichols Act for jointness in the military is needed. Promotions should be based not only on performance at Foggy Bottom and in embassies abroad, but on mandatory interagency tours as well. Similarly, professional development incentives should apply to civil servants who work in the national security arena.

Admittedly, mandatory interagency tours would require significant changes in personnel systems and career tracking. The Report of the National Defense Panel of 1997, *Transforming Defense: National Security in the 21st Century*, recommended creating "an interagency cadre of professionals, including civilian and military officers, whose purpose would be to staff key positions in the national security structures."[16] The Report also recommended a national security curriculum for a mix of civilian, military, and foreign students. The Defense Leadership and Management Program of the Department of Defense, a Master's level initiative in national security studies for civilian personnel, is an important step in this direction.

Implications for the Military Professional.

The changing strategic environment has critical implications for career military professionals. The nature of future warfare is likely to be more military operations other than war, requiring more mobile, flexible, and light forces. Future war will also require a more intellectual military officer, one who understands the imperative of having to work with the panoply of civilian agencies, non-government organizations, the national and international media, and with foreign armed forces. It is a commonplace of strategy that American forces will rarely fight alone again; they will do so in coalition. Thus, the strategic Clausewitzian trinity of the people, the armed forces, and the government now encompasses the global community. The implications are clear; the military officer will have to develop greater diplomatic and negotiating skills, greater understanding of

187

international affairs, greater facility in foreign languages, and more than a passing acquaintance with economics.

Tomorrow's warrior will likely work with civilian counterparts across a spectrum of activities short of war. These include: strategic planning and budgeting, humanitarian assistance, peace operations, counter narcotics, counter terrorism, security assistance, environmental security, human rights, democratization, civil-military relations, arms control, intelligence, war planning and termination strategy, command and control of forces, continuity of government, post-conflict reconstruction, technology transfer, crisis management, overseas basing, alliances, non-combatant evacuations, and homeland defense.

The future officer will also need greater appreciation of the institutional diversity and complexity of government, because of the need to advise a diversity of civilians on the utility of military power in complex contingencies that are neither peace nor war, as Americans are accustomed to think of them. He or she will have to work in tandem with civilian agencies and non-government organizations unaccustomed to command systems and deliberate planning, and who often do not understand the limits of military power.[17] Lastly, instruction on the interagency system and process should be mandatory for civilians and military alike. It must have a sound theoretical foundation in national security decisionmaking, strategic planning, and organizational behavior, expanded by sophisticated case studies of relevant historical experiences.

What attributes should the military officer bring? Above all, the ability to think in terms of all the instruments of national power and respect for the functions and cultures of diverse departments and agencies. Communication skills are paramount. The effective interagency player will have to write and speak well. He or she will be bilingual, able to function in military as well as civilian English. Bureaucratic jargon is the enemy of interagency communication. The military briefing, though an excellent vehicle for quickly transmitting a lot of information in formatted style, is not acceptable. One must be less conscious of rank because ranks will vary among the representative around a table. A person of lower rank may be in charge of a meeting. A sense of humor, patience, endurance, and tolerance for ambiguity will help. The ability to "stay in your box" and articulate the perspective of your department will be respected. The capacity to anticipate issues, to consider the second and third order effects from the national level down to the country team and theater levels, will be invaluable. Finally, the interagency requires diplomatic and negotiating skills, the ability to network, and mastery of the nuances of bureaucratic politics and language.[18]

The most evolved democracy in the world has the most cumbersome national security decisionmaking process in the world. Inefficiency is the price the founding fathers imposed for democratic accountability. But some of the inefficiency is the result of American strategic culture, with its multiplicity of players, plentiful but diffused resources, and the propensity to segment peace and diplomacy from war and military power. Major structural changes must be made in the interagency system in order to harness intelligently human talent and resources. It is time to move away from a system designed for the problems of 1947 toward one that is appropriate to the challenges of the next century.

U.S. Departments and Agencies
Involved in Foreign Affairs

White House
      National Security Council
      Office of the Special Trade Representative
      Office of National Drug Control Policy
      National Economic Council

Department of Defense
      Office of Secretary of Defense
      Joint Chiefs of Staff
      Army, Navy, Air Force, Marines
      On-Site Inspective Agency

Department of Treasury
      Internal Revenue Service
      United States Customs Service
      Secret Service
      Bureau of Alcohol, Tobacco, and Firearms

Department of Agriculture
      Foreign Agricultural Service

Department of Commerce
      Foreign Commercial Service
      Travel and Tourism Administration
      National Oceanic & Atmospheric Agency
      National Marine Fisheries Service
      International Trade Admininistration
      Trade Commision

Department of Justice
      Federal Bureau of Investigation
      Immigration and Naturalization Service
      Border Patrol
      Drug Enforcement Administration
      U.S. Marshals Service
      Foreign Claims Settlement Commission
      National Central Bureau--International
      Criminal Police Organization

Department of Transportation
      Coast Guard
      Federal Aviation Administration

Department of Energy
Assistant Secretary for Defense Programs

Department of Labor
Deputy Undersecretary for International Affairs

Department of State
U.S. Foreign Service
United States Information Agency
Agency for International Development
Overseas Private Investment Corporation

Department of Health & Human Services
Social Security Administration
Public Health Service
Centers for Disease Control and Prevention

Department of the Interior
Assistant Secretary for Territorial & Intl Affairs

Office of National Drug Control Policy

Independent Agencies
Central Intelligence Agency
Environmental Protection Agency
Export Import Bank
Federal Communications Commission
Federal Maritime Commission
Federal Trade Commission
National Aeronautics & Space Administration
National Science Foundation
National Transportation Safety Board
Nuclear Regulatory Commission
Panama Canal Commission
Peace Corps
U.S. Postal Service

Congress
General Accounting Office

(Those with personnel stationed overseas are indicated in bold. These personnel are stationed at U.S. embassies, consulates, missions, U.S. military headquarters, U.S. military bases, multilateral organizations and deployed in peacekeeping and other roles.)

ENDNOTES - CHAPTER 7

1. Chas W. Freeman, Jr., *Arts of Power: Statecraft and Diplomacy*, Washington, DC: United States Institute of Peace Press, 1997, p. 3.

2. John P. Lovell, *The Challenge of American Foreign Policy: Purpose and Adaptation*, New York: Collier MacMillan, 1985, p. 7.

3. A 1987 report of the National Academy of Public Administration noted:

> . . . the institutional memory of the United States Government for important national security affairs was worse than that of any other major world power and had resulted in mistakes and embarrassments in the past which would be bound to recur.

Strengthening U.S. Government Communications: Report of the National Academy of Public Administration, Washington, DC, 1987, p. 227, cited in Margaret Jane Wyszomirski, "Institutional Memory: Improving the National Security Advisory Process," in James Gaston, ed., *Grand Strategy and the Decisionmaking Process*, Washington, DC: National Defense University, 1991, p. 194.

4. Anthony Lake, I.M. Destler, and Leslie Gelb, *Our Own Worst Enemy: The Unmaking of American Foreign Policy*, New York: Simon and Schuster, 1985.

5. Anthony Lake, *Somoza Falling: The Nicaraguan Dilemma, A Portrait of Washington At Work*, Boston: Houghton Mifflin, 1989, p. 32.

6. Lake, p. 114.

7. Robert Pastor, *Condemned to Repetition: The United States and Nicaragua*, Princeton, NJ: Princeton University Press, 1987, p. 81.

8. Hedrick Smith, *The Power Game: How Washington Works*, New York: Random House, 1988.

9. Adapted from John P. Lovell, *The Challenge of American Foreign Policy*, p. 32.

10. Institute of National Strategic Studies, National Defense University, "Improving the Utility of Presidential Decision Directive 56: A Plan of Action for the Joint Chiefs of Staff," Washington, DC: National Defense University, March 1999, p. 16.

11. For an excellent analysis of lessons learned and prudent policy recommendations from recent U.S. military interventions, see: John T. Fishel, *Civil-Military Operations in the New World*, New York: Praeger, 1997; John T. Fishel, *The Fog of Peace: Planning and Executing the Restoration of Panama*, Carlisle Barracks: Strategic Studies Institute, April 15, 1992. A penetrating analysis of the operational and tactical dimensions of the interagency process, particularly as they apply to the U.S. Army at the operational and tactical levels, is Jennifer Taw Morrison, *Interagency Coordination in Military Operations Other than War: Implications for the U.S. Army*, Santa Monica: RAND Arroyo Center, 1997.

12. An excellent *Handbook for Interagency Management of Complex Contingency Operations* issued in August 1998, contains in easy and digestible form much wisdom about how to do it right.

13. Excellent advice on how the ambassador and the regional unified commander should work together is found in Ted Russell, "The Role of the Ambassador, the Country Team, and Their Relations with Regional Commanders," in U.S. Army War College, *Course Directive: Regional Appraisals*, AY 97, Carlisle Barracks, PA, 1997, pp. C1-C9. A Memorandum of Understanding (MOU) between the Department of State and the Department of Defense covers the function of the Political Advisor. The MOU,

> recognizes the valuable role POLADs render to the Department of Defense and the Department of State in assessing the political implications of military planning and strategy and in serving as the principal source of counsel on international issues to their respective Commanders-in-Chief . . . the deep level of commitment and cooperation acknowledged by the Secretary of State and the Secretary of Defense in executing foreign and security policy established by the President.

14. For specifics, see the telegrams dated June 6, 1994, from USCINCSOUTH, June 8, 1994, from Embassy La Paz, and June 9,1994, from Embassy Bogota.

15. The classic study of the role of culture and turf in government is James Q. Wilson, *Bureaucracy: What Government Agencies Do and Why They Do It*, New York: Harper Collins, 1989. Pertinent are the excellent studies: George T. Raach and Ilana Kass, "National Power and the Interagency Process, *"Joint Forces Quarterly*, Summer 1995, pp. 8-13; Douglas A. Hartwick, "The Culture at State, the Services, and Military Operations: Bridging the Communication Gap," Washington, DC:

National War College, April 12, 1984; Rosemary Hansen and Rick Rife, "Defense is from Mars and State is from Venus: Improving Communications and Promoting National Security," Palo Alto: Stanford University, May 1998. Other impediments to sound decisionmaking are: groupthink, information overload, insufficient information, lack of time, faulty analogy, insufficient analysis of options, and the personal predispositions of the decisionmaker. The interaction of these factors are explored in the writings of Irving L. Janis, Alexander George, and Graham Allison.

16. National Defense Panel, *Transforming Defense: National Security in the 21st Century*, Arlington, VA, 1997, p. 66.

17. There are indications that even the Department of State, the first among equals of the executive departments, is beginning to understand the value of strategic planning. See: Secretary's Office of Resources, Plans, and Policy, U.S. Department of State, *U.S. Department of State Strategic Plan*, Washington, DC, September 1997. Excellent advice on how military culture should interact with the culture of nongovernment organizations during humanitarian relief operations, peacekeeping, and stability operations is Judith Stiehm, "The Challenge of Civil-Military Cooperation in Peacekeeping," *Airman-Scholar*, Vol. IV, No.1, Winter 1998, pp. 26-35.

18. Military officers contemplating assignment to the Pentagon or civilians wishing to understand how to work with counterparts there should read the advice in Perry Smith, *Assignment Pentagon: The Insider's Guide to the Potomac Puzzle Palace*, 2nd ed., rev., Washington, DC: Brassey's, 1992.

CHAPTER 8

IMPROVING NATIONAL SECURITY DECISIONMAKING

Constantine Menges

As we look at the issue of improving national security decisionmaking, it is important to take a moment to recognize that overall, since the end of World War II, the United States has been extremely successful in its national security policy. The most important example of that success is the fact that the Soviet Union, despite its enormous military strength, its range of instruments and its cunning, was in fact contained and deterred from launching either a nuclear or a conventional war and that, in time, the Soviet Union unraveled peacefully. Another example of America's enormous success has been the democratic reconstruction after World War II of Germany, Italy, Austria, and Japan. This was an exceptional act of statesmanship on the part of the United States which made it possible for the men and women in those countries to establish stable democratic political systems. In fact, the history of the last 50 years illustrates clearly a fundamental axiom of international politics, which is that the political character of governments is most important in determining the foreign policy of states.

Turning to the topic—improving national security decisionmaking—I shall provide a few perspectives, offer a few examples of problems that have arisen over the last decades, briefly analyze the reasons for these problems, and conclude with some suggestions for improving the decisionmaking process.

Perspectives.

My former colleague, Dr. Carnes Lord, has written an excellent book on this issue, and I agree with him that the president is at the center of decisionmaking. The president has not only the right but also the duty to lead in national security decisionmaking since the Constitution specifies that it is his fundamental task to assure the "common defense". All of the executive branch directly work for the president whom we elect. We understand that the president has essentially four full time jobs: he is the symbolic leader of our country, the leader for domestic policy, the leader for national security policy, and the leader of his political party. So presidents are always very, very busy and very challenged to use their time and authority to greatest effect.

Furthermore, each member of the president's cabinet is also charged with a range of responsibilities that are exceptionally demanding. First, he or she has to implement the policies that have already been decided upon. Second, each cabinet member has to manage his or her organization while at the same time managing relations with Congress. Third, those managing institutions involved in foreign policy making have to develop relations with their counterparts among our allies and in other key countries. This does not leave a lot of time for the fourth task that is, in a sense, written in invisible ink: to look to the future in prudent anticipation of new problems, issues, and opportunities.

It is also worth emphasizing that there is something about all issues of national security decisionmaking that is somewhat different from other domains of policy. The difference is that conflicting views and judgments among the president's advisers are an intrinsic aspect of national security decisionmaking. Different individuals, different organizations are going to approach the same problem from different perspectives. Often they will have different understandings about the current facts and trends. But the most important reason for conflict is that views about actions taken or not taken today, and about their effects in the future, are always matters of judgment—there is usually no way of proving the validity of one or another policy choice in advance.

This does not mean that foreign policy judgments are derived from guess work, or that the opinion of an individual who has not thought deeply about a particular situation is equal to the opinion of one who has spent his or her professional career dealing with similar issues. But it does mean that, in the end, conflict—both within and among the participants—is intrinsic to national security decisionmaking. Under these circumstances, the issue always is: will the conflict be fair and open and honorable, or will it be characterized by manipulation and deception, perhaps including the manipulation of the president?

My 1988 book, *Inside the National Security Council*, was written because, in my experience as a national security advisor to the president, I witnessed important members of the Executive branch who sought to substitute their foreign policy views for the decisions made by the president and who also sought to manipulate the decisions made by the president. Perhaps this was also part of the reason why Dr. Lord wrote his book. We both saw a great deal of deception and manipulation, which only compounded the intrinsic challenges to good decisionmaking.

National security issues can be divided into four types. The first are issues relating to ongoing policy matters—the annual budgets for defense, relations with the North Atlantic Treaty Organization (NATO) governments, etc. These are important issues, but they are regularized and in a sense predictable. The second type are issues relating to the use of force. Some well-known examples are: Berlin, 1948; Korea, 1950; Cuba, 1962; Iran, 1979; Panama, 1989; Iraq, 1990; and Kosovo, 1999. I would suggest that, on issues relating to the use of force, there is a regularized process that more or less works when the issue gets to the top and is acted upon. The third kind of issue relates to major policy shifts, where there is a reconsideration of policies which have been established toward major countries (Russia, China) or on major issues (national missile defense). These are issues involving large consequences, where there tends to be a policy that has been settled and perpetuated year after year. Nonetheless, there are times when there is a need to consider changing these policies. The fourth type of issue involves emerging threats or opportunities that may require a fundamental reassessment of U.S. interests and goals.

Among the four types of issues listed above, issues involving major policy shifts as well as issues involving emerging threats or opportunities are the two areas where change in the decisionmaking process is most needed. Some examples will help to illustrate this view.

Examples.

The first example is from 1968 when I was at the RAND Corporation. At that time, one could look at the long established right wing dictatorships in Spain and Portugal and say that the authoritarian rulers were likely to leave in the next few years because of their advanced age. It was also clear that when these leaders passed away there would be an opportunity for democratically inclined individuals in these countries to press for political democracy. At the same time, however, there would also be an opportunity for the clandestine but well-organized Communist parties in these countries to move those countries into the Communist sphere. It was also reasonable to expect that the Soviet Union would try to make this happen.

My suggestion in 1968 was that in the few remaining years before the crisis hit, the West should begin to identify, analyze, and assess which groups and individuals favored democracy, and then use appropriate means to encourage and help them. There were institutions in Europe, especially in Germany, that could have been helpful in doing this. Unfortunately, in Washington, DC, there was no interest and no proactive strategy.

What happened? What happened is illustrated by the revelation of former Central Intelligence Agency (CIA) Director William Colby, whom I respect very much. In his memoirs, Colby notes that in 1974 the CIA closed its station in Lisbon, Portugal to save two job slots because there was a temporary government freeze or job reduction at the time. Concurrently, the Soviet Union worked to radicalize a small element of the Portuguese military which staged a coup in 1974. The Soviet Union conducted with skill a major covert operation in support of the Portuguese Communist Party, flying the Portuguese Communist Party leader back home from Moscow. The result was that in a matter of months, Portugal began to move rapidly into the Communist orbit. If Portugal had become communist in 1974-1975, it is my judgment that Spain, following Franco's death in 1975, could well have followed and NATO could have been faced with two new Warsaw Pact members, with populations totaling 35 million people, on its western border. Given Soviet assertiveness in the 1970s, its military buildup, its success in helping 11 new pro-Soviet regimes take power (including Vietnam, Afghanistan, and Nicaragua) such a defeat in Western Europe could have had very negative consequences. Fortunately, the situation was turned around in time, but it took quite a bit of last-minute effort. If it had not been turned around, it could have been an extremely dangerous situation.

In the late 1970s, a destabilization process began in Iran. In this case, there were essentially three competing groups. A group of moderates who wanted constitutional government, radical Islamic elements, and the Iranian Communist Party and allied groups supported, as it had been in 1944 and again in 1953, by the Soviet Union. For many months in 1977 and 1978, I urged the Carter administration to give serious attention to the events in Iran and I proposed a strategy of political preventive action designed to help the Iranian moderates in coalition with the military to move toward a constitutional transition, perhaps under a constitutional monarchy as in Spain. Unfortunately, the U.S. Government's response to this was—no time, no interest, and no action—until the final weeks when it was too late. And here we are, more than 20 years later, with a regime in Iran that hopefully might become more moderate, but one that remains a serious threat to the United States and its allies and is seeking weapons of mass destruction. I believe that this situation could have been prevented if there had been timely action, but none was taken.

Another example of missed opportunities has been Russia since 1992. With the dissolution of the Soviet Union and Russian president Boris Yeltsin's ascent to power, the United States was presented with an enormous opportunity to help encourage the building of genuinely democratic parties, democratic labor unions, and democratic institutional infrastructure that could have supported both the democratic transition process and the efforts led by Senators Samuel Nunn and Richard Lugar to radically reduce the Russian nuclear threat. The remarkable thing about the Russian case is that, in spite of the fact that presidents George Bush and Bill Clinton publicly espoused these goals, and in spite of the fact that the United States invested more than 25 billion dollars in direct assistance to the former Soviet Union, and more than 140 billion dollars in overall assistance to the democracies, very little was done to help build democratic political parties and trade unions. In October 1992, the U.S. Congress enacted the Freedom Support Act, proposed by President Bush, which provided billions in assistance for post-Communist Russia. Taking office in January 1993, these funds were available to President Clinton, but he did not take hold of this issue and really lead national policy, as President Harry S. Truman had done with the Marshall Plan. There was a large but ineffectual effort to help the Russian people succeed in their aspirations for an effective democratic transition. This was probably the highest national security priority of the United

States during the 1990s in light of the fact that Russia, with its remaining 6,000 operational strategic nuclear missiles continues to pose such a potential military threat and because the political character of the regime in Moscow makes such an enormous difference for the world.

Another example that the national security decisionmaking system is regrettably flawed in the domain of anticipating events is the tragedy of former Yugoslavia during the early 1990s. In the spring of 1991, right after the end of the Gulf War, there was an attempt to inform the Executive branch leadership that there was a high probability of war in Yugoslavia, and that this might be the time for preventive diplomacy. As we now know, preventive diplomacy did not occur. In fact, the U.S. Secretary of State flew to Yugoslavia the day before the war began—a little late.

Likewise, in 1993 after 2 years of war and enormous suffering, a plan was presented to two members of the Clinton foreign policy cabinet, to help those in Serbia and other parts of the former Yugoslavia who wanted democracy: to help them to organize; to help them to set up broadcasting facilities; to help them end the dictatorship of Serbian President Slobodan Milosevic through political means by providing political assistance, as the United States knows how to do and has done in the past. This was not done in 1993 or for years thereafter. We know the consequences have included much more suffering, bloodshed, displacement of populations in this region and, in 1999, the very real risk of a major confrontation with Russia (and perhaps its "strategic partner" China) following the NATO attacks against Serbian forces.

Last, a current example: starting in the fall of 1998, it was suggested to senior officials in the Clinton administration that Colonel Hugo Chavez of Venezuela, a candidate for the presidency of that country, would in all likelihood establish a radical military based dictatorship that would be allied with the Castro regime, the communist guerillas in Colombia, and other anti-democratic groups in Latin America. The strategic consequence for the United States could be highly negative because Colonel Chavez would control approximately two to three billion dollars annually in oil revenues which would give him the ability to finance his radical activities including destabilizing appeals to elements of the military in other Latin American countries and possible geopolitical cooperation with anti-U.S. oil producers such as Iraq, Iran, and Libya.

This assessment was based upon the fact that Colonel Chavez had been a leftist radical ever since his days as a military academy student, had for years attempted to organize a radical movement within the Venezuelan military, had in 1992 allied with the small Castro-supported Venezuelan armed Communist movements and elements of the Venezuelan military to attempt a coup against a democratically elected president, and had worked closely with the Colombian Communist guerillas after he received amnesty in 1995. The judgment, which was repeated to senior U.S. government officials in February and March 1999 (a month before this analysis was presented) was that as President of Venezuela, Chavez would use pseudo-constitutional means and disguised coercion to establish his *de facto* dictatorship but would seek to remain on rhetorically good terms with the United States, continue as a major foreign oil supplier to the United States, and would not interfere with U.S. and other foreign business operations in Venezuela. Essentially, Chavez would use the Chinese approach of deriving economic benefits from the United States and other democracies while pursuing those internal and international policies he decided upon.

Given Venezuela's 40 years as a political democracy and the existence of two strong democratic political parties, independent labor unions, media, and the institutions of civil society, the proposal made to the U.S. Government was that encouragement should be given to the democratic parties of Venezuela—discredited by poor performance and some corruption—to choose new leadership and unite to compete in the presidential election and thereafter use the political and other institutions of Venezuela to restrain and counter the authoritarian tendencies and actions of Colonel Chavez. It was also proposed that under the terms of a unanimous 1991 Organization of American States decision, all member governments would work together to preserve democracy if threatened from within by any member country, and that the United States would work discreetly to support a coalition of Latin American democracies to help the democratic movement in Venezuela and closely monitor the negative actions of Colonel Chavez. The U.S. Government decided to take no action, and the coming months and years will reveal how seriously this may threaten U.S. national security interests.

Analysis.

What explains a frequent pattern where the national security decisionmaking institutions, staffed by individuals who are well meaning, experienced, and intelligent, do not take the time to examine seriously emerging potential future threats?

The following are four possible explanations. First is what I call the paradox of foresight. This involves the irony that, when a problem is still small enough to be dealt with preventively it is usually too small to generate interest, let alone consensus, at any level in the national decisionmaking process. Second, there is the intrinsic unprovability of judgments about future opportunities or threats. The present is the present, but the future is conjectural. Most people tend to view the future as a continuation of the present, and discontinuities are always seen as somewhat anomalous and unlikely. This is a natural reflex, and usually correct.

Third, most emerging national security problems are complex, multifaceted, and very political in nature. This means that they do not fall easily within any one agency's jurisdiction. The Department of State always seeks to

203

control all aspects of foreign policy, but in fact it prefers to conduct diplomacy—that is, negotiate with governments. The Department of Defense is very focused on its primary functions of deterring serious threats, preparing to prevail in nuclear and conventional wars, and managing current deployments and ongoing operations. Defense tends not to be looking for new problems and issues. The CIA, which has the primary responsibility for looking ahead, is at times limited by the "mindset" problem of prevailing consensus thinking within the organization, as well as by its reluctance to bring unproven and therefore low probability contingencies to the attention of policymakers. As an organization, it is also often reluctant to move toward new tasks and responsibilities in direct political action, given the problems that it confronts with congressional oversight and public criticism when there are visible setbacks.

A fourth reality that undermines the ability of decisionmakers to respond to new threats and opportunities has to do with the indispensability of presidential leadership in a situation when every president is faced with immense demands on his attention and time. Understandably, presidents are not looking for new problems and issues. On the other hand, they do not want to be surprised by events. President Jimmy Carter illustrated this fact in a letter which he wrote to then CIA Director Stansfield Turner (which, remarkably enough, was quoted in the national media about an hour or two after it was sent). To paraphrase, the handwritten note said: Dear Stan, I am so disappointed that the CIA failed to alert me to the problems in Iran and that now we face this enormous crisis.

When it comes to issues involving major policy shifts, all of the problems that I have just mentioned apply, but they are compounded by two other difficulties. The first is that current policy obviously has its strong supporters both within the government and outside the government. Second, the risks of continuing a policy always seem to be much less than the risks of changing it.

Suggestions.

We now come to the question, how do we improve the decisionmaking process? How do we move toward doing better in the future? Let us start with the fact that, in the post World War II era, the national security decisionmaking process virtually always involves four organizations and three different decisionmaking levels within the main institutions. The National Security Council, Department of State, Department of Defense, and the CIA are the four principal organizations. The three decisionmaking levels above the operational level are:

1. the interagency group at the assistant secretary level;

2. the undersecretary/deputy secretary level (often called the senior interagency group); and

3. the National Security Council as the convening group in which members of the cabinet and their key staff discuss issues with the president.

If one studies all of the presidential administrations since the enactment of the National Security Act of 1947, whatever the particular nomenclature, this is essentially how things have worked. This system, in my view, is likely to stay with us. The question then becomes—how does one improve the system so that it performs more effectively?

My recommendation is that, to cope with emerging potential threats and opportunities, the government should establish a system of monthly interagency meetings at which time would be set aside for discussion and analysis relating to emerging threats and opportunities. This would occur in two phases. First there would be an unclassified discussion which would draw upon the skills and judgments of experts who are not currently in the Executive branch but who have concerns about specific major issues. This could include individuals at universities, at the military analysis and educational institutions, at the RAND Corporation, Center for Naval Analysis, and so forth. There would need to be staff that winnows out suggestions, papers, published articles and op-eds in order to have a reasonable range and number of presentations, but the meeting should certainly involve people who feel that current policy should be changed.

Government participants would be the interagency principals at both the assistant secretary and the under/deputy secretary levels. They would listen to the presentations, discuss them with the experts who have presented, but not necessarily offer their views. Immediately following (or perhaps a week or so later), there should be a classified meeting of the principals at the assistant and under/deputy secretary level to discuss the issues raised by the outside experts and to decide whether any of these issues should lead to new analytic work within the government or whether any should be brought to the president at a National Security Council meeting. This approach allows the government to reconsider the existing consensus views by drawing upon the enormous wealth of talent that exists in the country—informed experts who are not busy with the day-to-day activities of government.

When it comes to major policy shift issues, such as U.S. policy toward Russia, China, or national missile defense, I would recommend that these issues be reviewed in the same way, no less than once every 6 months. Once again, the review process should start at the interagency level and then move up to the National Security Council level. And once again, the system should be designed so that experts are brought in from the outside to provide different perspectives in the unclassified meeting. This is one way in which the policy leaders within the U.S. Government could obtain a wide range of opinions and advice in order to test and stretch their own thinking. At the same time, the system needs to be flexible enough to allow individuals in the government to consult candidly with each other about whether they want to move a particular issue up to the presidential level.

A last point is that, when we think about the decisionmaking process, the key organization serving the president needs to be the National Security Council staff, which acts as the president's eyes and ears in the Executive branch. It is the group of individuals who do not have day-to-day program management responsibilities; instead they work directly for the president who is accountable to the American people for the results of national security policy.

The National Security Council staff has four intrinsic responsibilities. First, to assure that the president has full information to make the key decisions that need to be made, and that the policy debate is fair, with all relevant agencies having a fair hearing before the president. Second, to monitor the implementation of decisions made by the president (which are usually written in the form of national security decision directives). Third, to coordinate the political, economic, military, and intelligence aspects of the U.S. policy. And fourth to provide information that helps the president of the United States deal effectively with emerging threats and opportunities and make major policy changes when they are needed. Therefore the National Security Council staff should serve as the custodian of the two-stage process that I have outlined.

In order for the NSC staff to perform these functions effectively for the president, the senior staff members for each part of the world and for each major functional area should be individuals who are independent of the existing executive agencies. A Foreign Service Officer or a military or CIA officer on a 1-year or 2-year assignment can make an important contribution to the National Security Council (NSC) staff. But he or she is going to be tied, to some extent, to the perspectives of his or her agency which also will decide on their promotions and future assignments. I believe that the pattern that has grown out of having mostly Foreign Service Officers staff the key positions in the NSC essentially gives the president two Departments of State. One Department of State may have much to contribute, but two is one too many for any president. The issue of the independence of the senior NSC officials is very important because every president depends on these individuals to keep him in charge of foreign policy.

These suggested changes would not place an unreasonable burden on the national security institutions. The open meetings I am suggesting would be of no more than two hours duration, perhaps ten times each year. If they helped to prevent one major crisis over a three-year period, this would have been time well spent. Obviously, doing this would require a National Security Council staff that is fair-minded, brings issues forward, and reaches out to people with different points of view. This innovation might well significantly improve the national security decisionmaking process in the domains of policy change and prudent foresight.

CHAPTER 9

SERVANTS, SUPPLICANTS, OR SABOTEURS: THE ROLE OF THE UNIFORMED OFFICER AND THE CHANGING NATURE OF AMERICA'S CIVIL-MILITARY RELATIONS

John Hillen

> Nations which develop a properly balanced pattern of civil-military relations have a great advantage in the search for security. They increase their likelihood of reaching the right answers to the operating issues of military policy. Nations which fail to develop a balanced pattern of civil-military relations squander their resources and run uncalculated risks.
>
> Samuel Huntington
> *The Soldier and the State*

The North Atlantic Treaty Organization's (NATO's) 1999 war against Serbia over Kosovo has been analyzed in many different contexts. Much has been made over the conflict's implications for NATO's future, transatlantic relations in general, humanitarian intervention policy, Balkan stability, and many other areas. But the way in which Kosovo illuminated the contemporary angst over America's civil-military relations is worth highlighting. In the end, more questions were raised than answered about the role of the uniformed officer in the nation's strategic affairs. Kosovo showed that America has not yet found the post-Cold War civil-military boundaries between dissent vs. disloyalty, political identity vs. politicization, and advice vs. interference.

When viewing Kosovo through a civil-military prism, an inescapable irony becomes clear. Although Kosovo was a war waged by a governing elite whose formative political experience was protesting American involvement in Vietnam, the strategy was eerily similar. Like Vietnam, the United States decided to use coercive force in Kosovo to induce a change in the behavior of one party to an internal conflict. Like Vietnam, U.S. military power was applied incrementally—gradually escalating as it became obvious that preceding actions were failing. Like Vietnam, there was considerable ambiguity over how the military pressure—even if "effectively" applied—could lead to a sustainable political solution. Like Vietnam, few were sure what "effective" meant, or how it could be measured.[1] Like Vietnam, the Joint Chiefs of Staff were fairly united in their early opposition to the president's strategy. It appears that, at least in the early stages of both conflicts, the main difference between these episodes was that only in Kosovo did the Joint Chiefs immediately disassemble in public by leaking their displeasure to the press.[2]

The lessons of Vietnam were very much in the minds of America's military leaders at the start of the Kosovo Operation. Indeed, the single most influential book among senior military leaders in this country over the past several years has been H.R. McMaster's *Dereliction of Duty: Lyndon Johnson, Robert McNamara, the Joint Chiefs of Staff, and the Lies That Led to Vietnam*. In the book, McMaster brings to light the way in which the Joint Chiefs accepted the strategy of graduated pressure in Vietnam even though they felt, from the very beginning, that the effort was fatally flawed. McMaster concludes that President Johnson got exactly the advice he wanted because he made clear to the chiefs that he would accept only military advice that conformed with his political agenda. The chiefs complied.

Only months before the start of the Kosovo operation McMaster briefed the Joint Chiefs and the Commander's in Chief of the military's regional commands. These men had all been junior officers during Vietnam. He told them,

> In telling the story of how and why decisions were made in the
> period 1963 to 1965 that slowly transformed our commitment

210

[in Vietnam] from an advisory and support effort into an American War, I found that the nature of the civil-military relationship prevented the Joint Chiefs of Staff from providing their best military advice to the National Command Authority. Indeed, an insidious relationship between the nation's top civilian and military officials rendered President Lyndon Johnson's Administration incapable of dealing effectively with the complexity of the situation in Vietnam.[3]

It was with this denouement in mind that the Joint Chiefs of Staff confronted Kosovo. For military planners, Kosovo meant ambiguous, contradictory, and unattainable goals, self-imposed constraints designed to fit political agendas, and the incremental and indecisive application of force. The conflict was waged in a way that was so fundamentally at odds with contemporary military thinking that the Pentagon was quite happy to have the press attach responsibility directly to the Secretary of State—labeling it "Madeleine's War." One can only speculate whether the Joint Chiefs were keeping in mind the regrets of the Vietnam era's "five silent men" when they sent a clear public message to the President in the first weeks of the campaign: "If this fails, we are not going down with you."

Was this the real civil-military lesson of Vietnam? That the role of senior uniformed military officers is to give the President their honest military advice, and upon it not being taken, cover their reputations through the good offices of the *Washington Post*? One would hope not. And yet there is tremendous confusion among both communities—political and military—about the relationship between their respective leaders over matters strategic. Much of the confusion stems from some recent episodes that have pushed civil-military relations toward a post-Cold War nadir. Observers are familiar with the (sometimes thinly) veiled strain between an administration whose political elite struggled to avoid service in Vietnam and a military elite who fought there as junior officers. Besides that, the relationship between Congress and the senior military is particularly strained. The extraordinary timing of military actions against Iraq and Sudan/Afghanistan in 1998 led many on the Hill to think that the Joint Chiefs were complicit in "Wag the Dog" strategies. Recent hearings have been marked by acrimonious challenges to senior military leaders' integrity.[4] Many congressional leaders seem to privately view the Joint Chiefs as obsequious executive branch "yes-men" rather than objective leaders with the best interests of the country and the **entire** government in mind.

To repair these views and bridge these gaps, the role of the uniformed officer must be recast in the context of America's new civil-military environment. While Samuel Huntington, S. E. Finer, Morris Janowitz, and others provided early markers, today's environment requires that new thought be given to the same questions they sought to answer in their time.[5] The extraordinary changes in the strategic environment and the domestic political scene have rendered their classic works models rather than guides. There is not the space here for a complete exposition of the new civil-military environment and what is likely to shape it over the next decades. It is helpful, however, to survey the state of the debate about this environment and lay the foundation for some recommendations about the role of the uniformed officer in the future.

America's Civil-Military Future: Crisis or Transition?

Two schools of thought dominate the contemporary debate over the civil-military present and future. One school maintains that there is a crisis in civil-military relations. There are four basic elements to this crisis.

The first sign of crisis is that the military is becoming more outspoken on matters of strategy and policy—areas in which the military is merely to advise civilian leaders before executing their decisions.[6] This school holds former Chairman of the Joint Chiefs Colin Powell in particular disdain for his very public resistance to newly elected

President Bill Clinton's decisions regarding homosexuals serving in the military and the possibility of an armed intervention in Bosnia in 1993. Powell has since been succeeded by a more pliant set of Chairmen appointed by the Clinton administration, but adherents to this school of thought still maintain that the problem has been institutionalized. With the passage of the Goldwater-Nichols Act in 1986, the Chairman has received a disproportionate amount of influence that could well lead to challenges to civil authority.

The second element of crisis is the growing gap between the military and civilian cultures in America.[7] Those who warn of this trend speak not only of a physical disconnect between the military and society (due to a smaller professional force serving an ever growing country) but of a "nearly unbridgeable cultural divide."[8] The military and society will not only have less contact with each other in the future, they will develop diametrically opposing cultural values. Adherents to these ideas maintain that this will lead to an insular and resentful military that will hold a deteriorating American society in contempt. Moreover, this military will hold itself in too high a regard to be the humble servant and protector of American society. These ideas have captivated many public leaders. The Secretary of Defense, among other top officials, has stated that "reconnecting the military to society" is a top priority.

The third element is related to the first two in that a separate crisis could develop from the growing divide between military and civilian leadership. Increasingly, the two communities are "raised" apart and do not share formative experiences that might give them compatible world views and values when they come to leadership positions in their respective communities. Many observers maintain that this is a long-term trend and not a phenomenon particular to the Clinton Administration.

Finally, the fourth element of a continuing civil-military crisis is the overt politicization of the uniformed military.

Warnings here are painted against a somewhat idealized backdrop of a professional military that was scrupulously apolitical until the past 25 years. Adherents maintain that since the 1970s, the uniformed military—especially the officer corps—has become overwhelmingly and actively Republican, conservative, and evangelically Christian.[9] A separate observation has been made about the politicization of recently retired military officers whose endorsements are sought by political leaders and who are then rewarded with political spoils for their services.

As one might expect, there is a separate set of observers (of whom I am one) who maintain that there is no civil-military crisis. According to this group, what the United States is experiencing is merely the pains of transition due to changes in the political and strategic landscape.

In response to the first "charge" of unreasonable military dissent from civilian dictates, I would answer that professional dissent is required at times, while disloyalty in the execution of civilian orders can never be tolerated. Despite the warnings of the crisis school of thought, there has been no evidence of the latter—even in its smallest form. In fact, the greater danger to the civil-military balance comes from the opposite, when senior military leaders feel obliged to be policy lap-dogs for civilian officials, or when they work their dissent through disingenuous channels of bureaucratic obfuscation and under-cutting. As McMaster warned about Vietnam, the suppression of honest dissent can accumulate with nefarious effect. In the best recent defense of an active "voice" for senior military leaders, Sam Sarkesian wrote,

> Disagreements that arise among the military, the president, and members of Congress should not be stifled, as was the case during the Vietnam War, but should be aired honestly without prejudice to the military's obedience to, and implementation of, civilian directives. Nor should the armed forces wait until a debate occurs before presenting its perspective and objections to a given policy line. Military professionals ought to be as free to

214

make known their technical judgments as engineers, scientists, or doctors without conjuring fears that they are trying to escape civilian control. The alternative, after all, is to perpetuate the timidity, extreme defensiveness, and fear of criticism from the public and Congress that seems to pervade the military today.[10]

Promoting such a role for the uniformed military will undoubtedly cause friction—something that the senior political and military officials seem determined to avoid in the politically correct and thoroughly "spun" world in which they operate. This sort of friction, however, is natural and healthy in a democracy. Moreover, it is part and parcel of America's civil-military history—a successful tale in general but one not without the friction that accompanies constructive political engagement on the part of the military. As General Matthew Ridgway warned in his memoirs,

> Civilian authorities must scrupulously respect the integrity, the intellectual honesty, of its officer corps. Any effort to force unanimity of view, to compel adherence to some politico-military "party line" against the honestly expressed views of responsible officers . . . is a pernicious practice which jeopardizes rather than protects the integrity of the military profession.[11]

I will not dwell on the second "charge" of the crisis school, as I have written on it elsewhere.[12] It is worth noting here however that the three principal tenets of this charge are all eminently disputable. First, while there is a growing gap between the military and society, it is characterized by a divergence in shared experience and understanding—not an antagonistic cultural divide. Despite declining participation from the populace, the military remains one of the most admired institutions in America and there is little evidence that any segment of the population other than a small portion of the elite begrudges the armed services their martial culture and particular ethos. Second, it is not fundamentally unhealthy, nor remotely dangerous *ipso facto*, for a democracy to have a military and a greater society that differ from each other in their values, culture, and ethos. What serious observer would maintain that they must have exactly congruent cultures in order to co-exist in a free society? Last, momentum gained from the first two tenets, which results in calls to "close the gap" by making the military accommodate contemporary societal mores, will in the end hurt society more than help it. Not only will such calls force a lowest cultural common denominator approach on the military, they will remove from the military the very ethos that it needs for the missions that alone justify its existence.

On the matter of the third charge, I agree that military and civilian leadership today has less in common than at any other time in recent American history. Similarly, on the fourth charge, I agree that the officer corps is more overtly Republican and conservative than in the past. **But both of these facts are phenomena, not necessarily civil-military emergencies.** The distinction is profound. Both facts are rooted in the Vietnam conflict and can be explained by the socio-political evolution of this country over the past 30 years. In that short span, one political party (which has held the White House for the last 7 years) accommodated the anti-war movement, neo-Marxism, radical environmentalism, feminism, multiculturalism, gay rights, and other socio-political movements that were anathema to a conservative, traditional institution such as the military. To many in uniform during this period, it seemed that the Democrats left the military and then blamed it for looking Republican. I suspect that the friction between civilian and military leaders and the political imbalance in the services will re-adjust themselves over time. The effects of the "cultural wars" that started in 1968 will take at least another generation to wash out. More important, despite these alleged "problems," there have been no civil-military incidents of any note that have resulted. Some bruised egos and political sensibilities aside, these issues appear to be sociological phenomena that have had no discernible negative impact on civil-military relations.

Nonetheless, the fact that there has been no "Seven Days in May" occurrence does not mean all is well. Indeed, it is incumbent on both the civilian and military communities—as well as adherents to both schools of thought about the current state of affairs—to join in producing a set of rules for civil-military relations in the future. In order to do this, one must place the immutable aspects of American civil-military relations in the context of the changing civil-military environment. This exercise makes clearer the questions that need to be asked about the shape of America's civil-military future. I offer here some thoughts on how to understand and evaluate the shifting dynamics that will shape this future. By better understanding the context in which they will emerge, American leaders can begin to discern the parameters of successful civil-military relations much as Huntington and others did two generations ago.

The New Landscape and What it Portends.

Ultimately, the new boundaries of civil-military relations —while rooted firmly in the Constitution and the rule of law—will be subjective in nature. The lines between political engagement and political interference, between political identity and politicization, and between constructive dissent and destructive disloyalty will be hotly debated and not clearly seen. There are six variables shaping the development of those lines today and in the near future.

- The lack of consensus over strategy and the use of military force. Ultimately, civil-military relations are determined by three sets of pressures: legal, societal, and functional. Disagreement over the functional role of the military in America's affairs will keep civil-military relations in a constant state of agonizing flux. The famous exchange between Colin

217

Powell and Secretary of State Madeleine Albright over the use of the military is perhaps the best known example of this. Fundamental differences over the use of the military in so-called Operations Other Than War are likely to continue and perhaps even get worse. This is curious for historians, who know for instance that in over 275 shooting military deployments since 1789, the U.S. military has been in only five declared wars. Despite that history, "warfighting" remains the dominant physical and psychological template on which the nation builds and drills its forces. This split between what the military is doing day-to-day and who it thinks it is at its core will continue to tear at the fabric of civil-military relations for the foreseeable future. A clear and cohesive national security strategy (rather than the public relations pabulum the White House issues today) would go a long way toward reconciling these strains.

- The relative sophistication of the political and military communities have gone in opposite directions.[13] Since the end of the Vietnam conflict, which the military views as being lost by a combination of McNamara's whiz kids and feckless political leaders, the uniformed services have struggled mightily to increase their own political acumen and sophistication. It is not unusual today to see dozens of junior officers destined for headquarters staff jobs gaining advanced degrees in public policy and political science at the best universities in America. On the other hand, civilian leaders are increasingly unaware of military science, or of the history, culture, and traditions of the armed forces. Programs to encourage participation and education in military affairs should be a top priority for the upper ranks of the civil service dealing with strategic matters. Without them, the uniformed military will fill the knowledge vacuum with savvy officers who will take the political initiative and thereby incur the distrust and resentment of civilian leaders.

- Goldwater-Nichols merely fired the first salvo in an organizational war between the services over the issue of jointness. The continuing evolution of this set of policies and processes will shape civil-military relations for some time to come. Since Goldwater-Nichols, the powers and prestige of the Joint Staff, the Chairman, and the Secretary of Defense have risen. Ironically, the powers of the civilians in the office of the Secretary of Defense have diminished. This is principally because while the civilians are busy setting policy, the individual services—armed with over 85 percent of the Pentagon budget and under almost no constraints on how they spend it—are building the forces they wish to see in order to execute their particular vision. In a large bureaucracy, those with the budget authority make the policy. So long as the policy makers (civilians) are separated from those who plan and build the forces (military), a fundamental disconnect will remain that will skew not only America's strategy—but its civil-military relations.[14]

- The growing gap between the military and society is real and must be addressed by policy. As noted above, the gap between the military and society on issues of culture and values is one that has always existed and should remain. It should, of course, be managed by good civil-military policies but there is certainly no need to "close the gap" by making the military look more like society at large. There is, however, a need to address the gap in shared experience, understanding, and appreciation that comes from fewer and fewer Americans having contact with their military. Along with others, I have written about potential solutions to this problem.[15] In general, the military must adopt much bolder personnel and public relations policies in order to cycle more of America—both physically and psychologically—through its ranks. With a series of eminently achievable policies directed at a related problem—the lack of interest in public service among American elites—the military could make great strides to fix this area of friction as well.

- Finally, the uniformed military can help reduce its civil-military angst by reconnecting not only with America at large, but also with the rest of its government. As General Fred Weyand has noted, "The American Army is not so much an arm of the Executive Branch as it is an arm of the American people."[16] Improving the relationship with Congress—to include consultation over policy and not merely budgetary issues—would restore the proper structure of the Clausewitzian trinity between the military, the people, and the government. Congress, after all, represents two sides of the trinity—the people **and** the government. In recent times, our civil-military relationship has treated the President as the government and polls or editorial pages as the will of the people. This is a profoundly anti-constitutional set of devices and has thrown our entire civil-military system out of balance. As one constitutional scholar noted, the American system is "an invitation to struggle" between the branches of government over issues relating to foreign and defense policy. Thus Madison and others accepted some inefficiencies for the sake of democratic governance and civilian control. McMaster noted that the Joint Chiefs of the Vietnam era were complicit in helping the President to "circumvent the constitution." If the nation does not restore the proper role of Congress and the relationship between Congress and the military, we could face this problem again.

By recognizing the shifting variables that shape America's civil-military relations, both the political and military communities can work to restore a proper role for the uniformed officer and a healthy relationship between these two parties. It should be emphasized that the military must be involved in this process and not merely accept new rules of civil-military relations. Civilian control of the military is a hallmark of modern democracies but it does not mean that the military cannot participate in deciding on the nature of a healthy civil-military balance. In the past few years, most senior uniformed leaders have shrunk from entering the contemporary debates outlined here. It is, for instance, amazing to me that the only public officials who have taken the opportunity to address the "gap" issue from the perspective of the military are those civilians whose seminal experience was in avoiding military service. Uniformed leaders must participate in the discussions and decisions that will shape America's civil-military future. To not do so is to doom civil-military relations to a rocky road for some time to come.

ENDNOTES - CHAPTER 9

1. To this day, the American public is not even quite sure what caused our ultimate victory. Most of the players involved in the campaign have offered theories trumpeting almost exclusively the significance of their role and actions.

2. See Bradley Graham, "Joint Chiefs Doubted Air Strategy," *The Washington Post*, April 5, 1999, p. A1. Showing their political acumen, the intelligence community was actually the first rat off the ship, beating the JCS by a few days in the "I told you so" game.

3. McMaster presentation to the CINC's conference, 1998.

4. Among many others, I am reminded in particular of the exchange in September of 1996 between General John Shalikashvili and Senator John McCain. McCain, who knew full well that Bosnia planning was continuing apace (several Hill staffers had already been mobilized for 1997 reserve tours in theater), was aghast when the Chairman of the Joint Chiefs assured him that there were no plans to continue the

Bosnia mission past the promised 1-year duration. McCain stormed out of the hearing room.

5. I am, of course, referring to the classics *Soldier and the State* (1957), *The Man on Horseback* (1962), and *The Professional Soldier* (1960).

6. See especially Richard Kohn, "Out of Control: The Crisis in Civil-Military Relations," *The National Interest*, Vol. 35, Spring 1994, pp. 3-17.

7. See Thomas Ricks, "The Widening Gap Between Military and Society," *The Atlantic Monthly*, July 1997, pp. 66-78.

8. James Kitfield, "Standing Apart," *National Journal*, June 13, 1998, p. 1352.

9. See Andrew J. Bacevich and Richard H. Kohn, "Grand Army of the Republicans," *The New Republic*, December 8, 1997; and Ole Hosti, *International Security*, 1999.

10. Sam C. Sarkesian, "The U.S. Military Must Find Its Voice," *Orbis*, Vol. 42, No. 3, Summer 1998, p. 428.

11. General Matthew Ridgway, *Soldier: The Memoirs of Matthew B. Ridgway*, New York: Harper and Brothers, 1956, p. 270.

12. See "Must U.S. Military Culture Reform?," *Orbis*, Vol. 43, No. 1, Winter 1999. Reprinted in *Parameters*, Autumn 1999.

13. See Don Snider's presentation at this conference for some data and analysis on this phenomenon.

14. I detail this issue in "Defense's Death Spiral," *Foreign Affairs*, July/August 1999.

15. See Charles Moskos, "Overcoming Military Recruitment Woes Without the Draft," *The Washington Post*, March 3, 1999; and my paper, "The Gap Between American Society and the Military: Keep It, Defend It, Manage It," presented to the American Bar Association on November 13, 1998.

16. Quoted in Harry Summers, *On Strategy: The Vietnam War in Context*, Carlisle Barracks, PA: Strategic Studies Institute, U.S. Army War College, 1981, p. 7.

CHAPTER 10

DoD IN THE 21st CENTURY

Lawrence J. Korb

Introduction.

The organization and operation of the Department of Defense (DoD) in the 21st century, like the last half of the 20th century, will be a product of the conflicting and often contradictory objectives that it must achieve. For purposes of analysis, these cross pressures may be placed into four categories.

First, DoD must be organized and operated to ensure civilian control while not undermining or diluting military professionalism. Therefore, civilian control must not be exercised in such a manner that military opinions and expertise are excluded from or downgraded within the decisionmaking process. On the other hand, military considerations cannot be allowed to dominate the process. Maintaining a proper balance or equilibrium in this area has been and will be both a delicate and challenging task.

Second, DoD must serve the needs of both the executive and legislative branches simultaneously. While the president is the chief executive and commander-in-chief of the armed forces, the Congress has the constitutional mandate to raise armies and maintain navies, establish personnel policies for the armed services, and declare war. Since the branches are often controlled by different parties and most often have different perspectives and constituencies, high-level DoD officials find it difficult to serve both branches equally well. If they defer to the needs of the president, the Congress often criticizes them for slighting the legislature's constitutional responsibilities.

But if DoD's executives, particularly uniformed leaders, air their complaints about the executive branch's policies in legislative hearings, the president, in the words of President Dwight D. Eisenhower, will accuse them of "legalized insubordination."

Third, the political system wants DoD to be unified and efficient without undermining the independence, uniqueness, and statutory responsibilities of the three separate and very different military departments and four armed services. Whether it be in procurement, logistics, training, or strategy, the politicians and the public expect to receive the advantages of centralization and decentralization at the same time.

Fourth, the department must be organized to function efficiently and effectively during both war and peace. An organizational structure designed to optimize the Planning, Programming, and Budgetary System (PPBS) most probably will be able to handle equally well a peacekeeping mission or the enforcement of a no-fly zone.

To make a prediction or projection about how DoD will cope with these conflicting pressures in the next century, it is useful to take a look back at the last half-century of DoD's operations. While history will not repeat itself exactly, it is reasonable to assume that DoD will respond to these conflicts in a similar manner.

The Civil-Military Balance.

For the most part, the balance between civilian and military concerns has been well maintained. However, on occasion strong individuals have upset the balance. For example, Robert McNamara, Secretary of Defense from 1961-68, made use of the powers granted to the secretary and his office by the 1949, 1953, and 1958 reorganizations to dilute the impact of the military professionals within the policy process. McNamara employed a decisionmaking process, PPBS, and an analytical technique, systems analysis, that diminished the influence of military expertise in deciding how and where to spend defense resources. However, the military professionals eventually learned how to employ PPBS and systems analysis to enhance their military perspectives, and none of McNamara's successors has been able or willing to use the powers of the office to exclude military input to the extent that McNamara did. Ironically, while most of McNamara's successors eschewed his methods, they continued to employ his decisionmaking tools, i.e., PPBS' and systems analysis.

General Colin Powell, Chairman of the Joint Chiefs of Staff (JCS) from 1989 through 1993, became the military equivalent of McNamara. Relying on the powers granted to the Chairman of the JCS by the Goldwater-Nichols Act of 1986 and the political and bureaucratic skills he developed at the Office of Management and Budget (OMB), Office of the Secretary of Defense (OSD), and the White House, Powell dominated the policy process in the immediate post Cold War period. U.S. military strategy and force employment doctrine were developed by him. So great was his impact that we now speak of the "Powell Doctrine." Moreover, he openly and successfully challenged, even writing op-ed pieces and giving public speeches, President Bill Clinton on his campaign promises to allow gays to serve openly in the military, reduce military spending, and stop the Serb onslaught in Bosnia. However, Powell's two successors, Generals John Shalikashvili and Henry Shelton, have assumed a much more low key role. They have deferred to President Clinton on such controversial issues as deploying forces to Bosnia and conducting an air war against Kosovo.

While neither McNamara nor Powell did permanent damage to the civilian-military balance, they have demonstrated that the potential now exists for upsetting the balance. This potential exists because the reorganizations of 1949, 1953, 1958, and 1986 have enhanced significantly the powers of both the secretary and chairman. Therefore, since there is little prospect of undoing these reorganizations, the president and the Congress must guard against strong individuals using those powers to overwhelm either military or civilian considerations. Moreover, as fewer and fewer civilians have military experience, the President must ensure that the secretary and his key advisors are not afraid to challenge the uniformed military.

The Executive-Legislative Balance.

Because of the separation of powers and the system of checks and balances which is built into our political system, senior military and civilian officials in DoD are in a no-win position when it comes to satisfying the needs of both the President and the Congress. The problems usually arise from DoD officials supporting the executive line on policy while being less than candid with the Congress. Over the past 50 years, senior Pentagon officials have been less than forthcoming with Congress on such controversial subjects as the progress of the war in Vietnam, the killing of the marines in Lebanon, opinions regarding the war in the Gulf, the length of the deployment in Bosnia and the readiness of the armed forces in the late 1990s. With the end of the Cold War, however, Congress has become increasingly assertive in national security policy and will continue to insist on more candor from DoD officials, particularly the uniformed military.

Moreover, the resurgent Congress will continue to establish its own bodies, like the National Defense Panel and the Commission on National Security/21st Century, to provide it with an alternate source of advice, particularly from retired military. The executive may find this development troubling, but, just as in other areas like balancing the budget and welfare reform, it will be reduced to reacting rather than initiating. For example, in late 1998, President Clinton and Secretary William Cohen reacted to the anticipated testimony of the Chiefs before the Congress by agreeing to a large increase in their own defense program.

Centralization vs. Decentralization.

Because it has within it three departments and four armed services whose existence predated it, DoD will never be totally unified or completely efficient. The Pentagon will always have a myriad of accounting and procurement systems, training practices, personnel policies, and duplicative weapon systems, (including four air forces), laboratories, and missions. Nonetheless over the past 50 years, the power of the Central government (OSD and JCS) has grown at the expense of the services. DoD now allocates resources on the basis of programs or missions rather than by individual service. OSD can, if it wishes, control the personnel, logistic, and even acquisition policies of the individual departments. For all practical purposes, the main function of the service secretaries and the service chiefs is to implement the policies of OSD and the JCS. For example, after the Lieutenant Kelly Flinn episode, OSD made all the services adopt a common fraternization policy; the Air Force, Navy, and Marines are developing a common fighter, the Joint Strike Fighter; and, finally, it is the Secretary and the Chairman who represent and speak for the Department at interagency meetings.

Military operations are now conducted jointly and military officers aspiring to higher command must complete a specified number of joint assignments. The military chiefs of service have become advisers to the Chairman, who alone ensures that a military point of view, his, is inserted into the policy process. Indeed, the service chiefs were not even consulted by General Henry Shelton prior to the cruise missile attack on Osama Bin Laden in August 1998.

If anything, these trends will accelerate in the next century because the scarcity of resources will compel even more consolidation, most probably in such areas as logistics and intelligence. However, there will never be a completely unified department or a single armed services along the Canadian model. The individual services have too much tradition and too much clout—both in Congress and with the American public—to be completely ignored. This is probably the reason why Secretary of Defense Cohen refused to challenge the Marines on the issue of gender integrated basic training, and why Secretary of Defense Dick Cheney was not able to prevent the Marines from obtaining the V-22. These service "victories" will nonetheless be few and far between in the future, and it would not be surprising if the next DoD reorganization did not completely eliminate the service secretaries.

Peace and War.

The system for providing the Secretary of Defense with advice on policy, strategy, and budgets works reasonably well. He has enough civilian advisers with the necessary expertise to balance the individual and joint military perspectives. But when it comes to such technical areas as military operations and the readiness of the armed forces, he must rely primarily on the JCS for advice. Theoretically, his civilian advisers could challenge estimates of what it would take to conduct an operation or make a unit ready for battle, but OSD is not organized or equipped to do so. Moreover, as fewer and fewer civilians in OSD have military experience, they will be less inclined to do so. Therefore, OSD needs to establish an organization of analysts with operational expertise and experience to challenge the military professionals on why it takes 400,000 military people to bring peace to Bosnia or why an army tank unit must drive 800 miles a year to be "ready."

Conclusion.

In the next century DoD will continue to deal with these cross pressures and continue to be criticized for leaning too much or too little in one direction or another. At times, the Pentagon will also probably go too far in one direction or another. However, if history is any guide, this tilting will generate an equal or opposite reaction that will restore the proper balance between military and civilian, executive and legislative, centralization and decentralization, and war and peace.

CHAPTER 11

THE NATIONAL SECURITY ACT OF 2002

William A. Navas, Jr.

> It must be realized that there is nothing more difficult to plan,
> more uncertain of success, or more dangerous to manage than
> the establishment of a new order of government; for he who
> introduces it makes enemies of all those who derived
> advantage from the old order and finds but lukewarm
> defenders among those who stand to gain from the new one.
>
> Machiavelli, *The Prince*

Introduction.

In the life of a nation, the end of war marks a new
beginning. There is a marked parallel, almost surreal,
between the events after the end of World War II which led
to the National Security Act of 1947 and the situation today,
as we struggle to reform our national security policymaking
process and organization to deal with the challenges of the
new century. Actually there are those who posit, and I tend
to agree with them, that the end of the Cold War is actually
the end of a 75-year-long conflict, which started in 1914 and
ended in 1989 with the collapse of the Soviet Union and the
symbolic crumbling of the Berlin Wall. The failure of
Versailles and the emergence of Weimar Germany set the
stage for the unfinished business of the "war to end all
wars."

As with the end of every major war (the Cold War not
being an exception), changes are deemed necessary to
support a new security strategy. These changes reflect the
perceptions of what the new realities are and the "lessons
learned" from the last war. President William J. Clinton has
made this argument in his December 1999 National

231

Security Strategy.[1] Today we are at a juncture, whether we realize it or not, where forces are being set in motion for a major revision of our national security structure. This paper offers a case for those changes.

Background.

In 1945, the soldiers, sailors, marines, and airmen of the Army and the Navy returned triumphant from their battles in Europe and the Pacific. But success was no insurance against change. There would be painful years ahead as the U.S. military modernized both its organization and its philosophy. The idea of change was anathema to most in uniform (except for the Army Air Forces, who wanted their own military branch and got it). The Army and the Navy had never been part of the same military command structure. In fact, their internal command and management systems and cultures were as different as the uniforms they wore. Making them so was to be a painful process of compromise. Periodically over the years, various leaders had proposed reform, but only a national disaster of the magnitude of Pearl Harbor was impetus enough to force change. This was the "burning platform" of 1945—the horrific event was blamed on incredibly poor coordination and communication between the Army and the Navy, which together had shared defense responsibility for the Hawaiian Islands. The result was a bias for change among the American public.

The National Security Act of 1947 and its amendment in 1949 implemented that change. The act and the debate preceding it also gave new meaning to the term national security. In the 1940s, national security was seen primarily as protection from external invasion. Clearly the military dimension of national security was first among equals.

The new concept saw national security as a decisional discipline that is neither primarily foreign nor defense policy. Rather, national security is treated as an overarching, interdisciplinary paradigm embracing elements and responsibilities of a number of departments in a dynamic relationship. This new concept was institutionalized in the national security bureaucracy that was established in 1947, and, in particular, in the new National Security Council (NSC).

Breaking Old Paradigms.

Today America faces significant technological, economic, political, and social challenges in the national security environment. Adapting our strategy to this new environment will place great demands upon all of our national security institutions, including Congress, the Defense Department, the Department of State, the intelligence community, the National Security Council, but in particular the military services. Any major change will require commitment from all involved. To succeed in such an endeavor we must understand the motives that lie behind the puzzling and often contradictory behavior of America's military forces. Carl Builder[2] has observed that this has little to do with what party controls the White House or who writes the budget.

An understanding of the motives of the three services must begin with an appreciation of their entrenched institutions and distinct "personalities" or cultures.

- The Navy sees itself mainly as heir to a glorious tradition dating back to the British navy. Equipped with its own land and air force, it jealously guards its independence and is happiest when left alone.

- The Air Force is the embodiment of a single idea—one that also happens to be a strategy of war. Not love of "the Air Force" but love of flight and flying machines binds it's members together.

- Traditionally the Army has considered itself the nation's servant, charged with teaching citizen-soldiers the art of war in times of crisis. But a heady memory of triumph in the closing months of

World War II and the need for a large forward deployed Army during the Cold War contradict this modest role and have exacerbated the historical tension between the Army and its principal reserve component, the National Guard.

- If the operational concept before World War II was that:

- the Navy was the instrument for wielding sea power as the most important and flexible kind of military power for the United States as a maritime nation;

- and the Army, as the nation's obedient and loyal military servant, was the neutral instrument of state policy, keeping itself prepared to meet the varied demands that the American people have historically imposed upon it, but especially prepared to forge America's citizenry into an expeditionary force to defeat America's enemies overseas;

- then the establishment of the Department of Defense (DoD) might have had the effect that some feared in the tumultuous days before the reorganization of 1947.

One exasperated spokesman for the Army expressed this fear very well,

> . . . the only way to overcome the Navy's resistance [to reorganization] would be to do away with the War Department, transfer all its elements to the Navy, and redesignate that organization as the Department of Defense.[3]

Those words, uttered in frustration, have proven to be somewhat prophetic.

The demands of the Cold War, with the need to project power overseas, maintain forward deployed forces (of all services), contain the spread of communism, and engage in what we call today Major Regional Conflicts (Korea,

Vietnam) made DoD the *defacto* U.S. Navy—the instrument for wielding U.S. military power across the globe. Meanwhile, the role of the Army changed from that of a "soldier in support of the nation" to that of an "instantly ready armored defender of Western Europe." And the Air Force, the new service, found its own niche, in particular, as the instrument for the delivery of our nuclear power in an era of strategic war and deterrence and, later on, as the advocate of the supremacy of air power. On the other hand, the Navy and Marine Corps remained comfortable with their traditional roles. The last Secretary of the Navy before the reorganization, James Forrestal, would become the first Secretary of the newly established DoD.

The Goldwater-Nichols DoD Reorganization Act of 1986 (some say it accomplished what Truman wanted to do in 1947 and fell short) reinforced this situation by taking more power from the Service Secretaries and concentrating it in the Office of the Secretary of Defense, who was advised by a very strong Chairman and a Joint Staff with a direct command line to the Unified and Specified Commanders-in-Chief (CINCs). The strong personalities of individuals like Admiral William Crowe and General Colin Powell established the primacy of the Chairman within this system. That is where we were when the Cold War ended in 1989, more than a decade ago.

A Decade of "False Starts."

The last 10-plus years have been no less traumatic for the American Military than the years after World War II. In October of 1989, the Soviet Union collapsed and the Berlin Wall came down. We were getting ready to deal with the "New World Order" and to distribute the "Peace Dividends." We had started our "downsizing" (another of our fashionable euphemisms), had gone through the "Commission on Roles and Missions," and were considering the permutations and combinations of the "Base Force." Then in August 1990, the same day that President Bush

235

was delivering a major national security speech at the Aspen Institute in Colorado, Iraqi President Saddam Hussein invaded Kuwait. In 100 days, the United States led a coalition that stopped the aggression, expelled the aggressors from Kuwait, and caused major damage to the war fighting capabilities of Iraq. For the first time in more than 40 years, American military forces returned victorious from war. The overwhelming support of the American people and the quick victory over Iraq had a euphoric effect on the U. S. Military services, in many ways similar to the atmosphere in 1945. Once again there were parades and national heroes. There was even talk of re-establishing the five-star rank. But once again, as at the end of World War II, success was not an insurance against change.

This time change came in the political landscape as well. In 1992, a very popular president during the Gulf War lost his bid for re-election to a candidate with no military service. "It's the *economy*, stupid" was one of the most popular slogans during that political campaign. The American people had once again put the war behind them and were looking at domestic issues and challenges. There were no major threats looming out there. Threats to the survival of the United States, such as those posed by the Soviet Union during the Cold War, would be at the top of a hierarchy and would be an "A list." But that list is empty today. According to Dr. Bill Perry in his recent book, co-authored with Mr. Ash Carter,

> the emptiness of the A list is disorienting for Americans who made the huge transition from defeating aggression, to deterring aggression after World War II, but who now, in consequence, tend to conceive national security exclusively in terms of threats to be deterred or defeated.[4]

They go on to say that what is left are the two Major Regional Contingencies in the Persian Gulf and the Korean Peninsula that undergird Pentagon planning and budgeting that form the "B list" of imminent threats to U.S. interests, but do not threaten the survival or the way of life of Americans. A third place is occupied by the Kosovos, Bosnias, Somalias, Rwandas, and Haitis. They compose a "C list" of important contingencies that indirectly affect U.S. security but do not directly threaten U.S. interests. I call these contingencies "wars of conscience" or "wars of interest" depending on how they are portrayed by either *The Wall Street Journal* or *CNN*.[5]

It appears that Americans, in times of international tensions and instability (when we have an "A list"), prefer a Republican administration, strong in national security, with a Democratic congressional majority to provide the balance of power and advocate for domestic issues. The perception of the United States being the only remaining superpower shifted that equation to where we have had two consecutive Democratic administrations and a Republican controlled Congress.

This interesting phenomenon (the reversal of the traditional political roles between parties and who controls which branch of government) will be very important in the years ahead as we attempt to establish a new framework to allow us to pursue a national strategy for the next century. For after all, it is the Congress that raises armies, maintains a navy, disciplines the militia and declares war, in addition to the more mundane tasks of appropriating and authorizing, on a yearly basis, the "ways and means" for the execution of what by definition should be a long term strategy to provide for the "common defense." Up to this point DoD has developed the strategies, prepared the programs, and submitted the budgets to Congress. The services, executing their Title 10 functions, have manned, equipped, trained, and sustained the forces. Will Congress have the political will to "break some crockery" in order to provide the necessary legislation (and internal restructuring of their own committee and sub-committee structures) to effect the required changes, as it did in 1947?

In 1993 the incoming administrations' efforts to re-structure defense culminated with Secretary Les Aspin's

Bottom-Up Review, which downsized the armed forces and provided a strategy to fight two nearly simultaneous major regional contingencies, while generating funds for investments in modernization and recapitalization. It is interesting that this was accomplished early in his tenure, prior to the appointment and confirmation of the service secretaries. This further weakened the position of the service secretaries, who did not participate in the policy debate but still had to execute the decisions.

During the second term of the Clinton administration, initially under Secretary William Perry, and reported out by Secretary William Cohen, DoD published the results of the *Quadrennial Defense Review (QDR)* in the summer of 1997[6]. This report, mandated by the Goldwater-Nichols Act, was, as many have stated, "dead on arrival" when it was delivered to Congress. Most of the policy issues were vetted at DoD and Joint Staff levels with modest participation from the service secretaries (the Army's in particular).

The National Defense Panel, also mandated by Congress, submitted its report on December 1997, making a series of recommendations for the United States to launch a transformation strategy to meet the range of security challenges in 2010 to 2020. The report stated that:

> Transforming the armed forces into a very different kind of military from that which exists today, while supporting U.S. near-term efforts, presents a significant challenge. **Beyond Defense** (emphasis added), we must also transform the manner in which we conduct foreign affairs, foster regional stability, and enable projection of military power.

It concluded that:

> In the increasingly complex world that we foresee, DoD and its armed services cannot preserve U.S. interests alone. Defense is but one element of a broader national security structure. If we are to be successful in meeting the challenges of the future, the entire U.S. national security apparatus must adapt and become more **integrated** (emphasis added), coherent and proactive."[7]

They were right on the mark on these issues.

If "form follows function" and we have a stated strategy to enhance our security, to bolster America's economic prosperity and to promote democracy abroad—as stated in the White House's National Security Strategy, then the question that Congress needs to ask is . . . Do we have the adequate systems, processes, and organization to accomplish the tasks required by the strategy?[8] It is a sobering task indeed. For at stake is the survival of the nation itself. There are great risks but also great opportunities because experts tell us that we have a period of about 20 years (a strategic pause) before the next peer competitor appears. If the United States is going to make fundamental changes, intuition tells us that the time is now. There is an old adage that says, "the best time to plant a tree was 20 years ago, the next best time is now."

We have spent more than 10 years dealing with this issue at the margins, the good news is that there have been some encouraging initiatives within the Services and within DoD during this period. The bad news is that the U.S. policy making community has not yet confronted the necessity for fundamental change in the way that national security policy is formulated and managed.

The Way Ahead.

Just as the advent of nuclear power mandated a major restructuring of the National Defense Establishment at the end of World War II, so today's Revolution in Military Affairs, the threats of nuclear proliferation, domestic and transnational terrorism, weapons of mass destruction, homeland security, and the potential emergence in the future of a power that may challenge our vital national interests (a new "A list") require a comprehensive "out of the box" thinking in order to create a new National Security Establishment which is capable of meeting the challenges of the next era. Today those challenges demand close cooperation across all levels of government—federal, state,

239

and local—and across a wide range of agencies, including the Departments of Defense and State, the Intelligence Community, law enforcement, emergency services, medical providers, and nongovernmental organizations (NGOs).

The United States cannot afford to wait for a new "burning platform" like Pearl Harbor to create a bias for action. This would be criminal. What is needed is a pragmatic, bipartisan approach which deals honestly with the issue of national security as we see it evolving in the 21st century. The administration and the Congress need to make this a top priority.

The Secretary of Defense has established the U.S. Commission on National Security/21st Century, with a mandate to conduct a 2 1/2-year effort to assist the president and Congress in confronting this challenge. The work of the Commission is guided by three goals: to determine the global security environment of the first quarter of the next century; to analyze the character of the nation during that time frame and develop an appropriate national security strategy; and to recommend alternatives to the current national security apparatus and processes to implement the new strategy. The work of that group and the results thus far are encouraging. The most important question is what actions will "the powers that be" take once the final work is completed and the report is published? Congress and the National Security Council should work with the Commission to put in motion the actions that are required to effect the necessary changes. A restructuring of the scope and magnitude of 1947 might be required. We must be ready to break old paradigms and challenge entrenched interests in order to succeed. After all, the security of its citizens is the primary function of government. We need the same fervor and enthusiasm to fix our national security as we express for our Social Security.

The United States is at a historic juncture where it must lead in the world arena to protect our people and our way of life. This is accomplished by a sustained commitment to diplomacy and a strong national security posture. As stated in the preface to the National Security Strategy Report:

> At this moment in history, the United States is called upon to lead—to marshal the forces of freedom and progress; to channel the energies of the global economy into lasting prosperity; to reinforce our democratic ideals and values; to enhance American security and global peace."[9]

A new National Security Act that establishes a Department of National Security, bringing together DoD, State, Central Intelligence Agency (CIA), Justice, Energy, and the Federal Emergency Management Agency (FEMA) to be able to meet the national security challenges of the future may be the solution.

Following are some recommendations that might be worth considering as the U.S. begins to confront the need for reform the national security policy making system.

- Restructure the service staffs along functional rather than operational lines. This is consistent with the goals of the Goldwater Nichols Act and will help the services to perform their Title 10 duties of manning, equipping, training and sustaining.

- After 50 years, the NSC has taken many forms and roles under different presidents. However, the inexorable forces of the international system are driving modern presidents into more intimate involvement in national security affairs.[10] If that trend continues, then serious consideration should be given to the development of a new set of principles for the organization and functions of the NSC and NSC Staff. These principles should be adaptable enough to accommodate the desires and styles of each occupant of the White House, while at the same time assuring that the President receives well thought out, unbiased and unvarnished alternatives and courses of action for his consideration. One helpful reform of the NSC

241

would be the introduction of a Goldwater-Nichols type personnel policy in order to avoid the inevitable parochialism and careerism associated with the current system of staffing of NSC positions.

- The National Security Panel noted in their 1997 *Report* that all elements of national power, including military, diplomatic, and economic elements, needed to be integrated in order to meet the security challenges of the 21st century.[11] They also recommended, and I strongly support this proposal, that some agencies which have traditionally had a domestic focus should now play a larger international role. One example is the U.S. Coast Guard, which is part of the Department of Transportation. This service can play an important role as a model for some of the navies of the world.

- Make foreign and national security policy an issue during the current and future presidential and congressional campaigns, in order to know the candidates' views, educate the public, and express a mandate to elected officials from the American people.

- Reinstate a form of draft to provide for universal military training or some other form of national service as a means of reinforcing the sense of citizenship obligation among young Americans. This could help tremendously with the current manpower shortfalls in the Services and reduce defense costs.

- Institutionalize the Weinberger Doctrine—

1. Do not commit combat forces overseas unless the engagement is deemed vital to our national interest.

2. If combat troops are committed, do so wholeheartedly, with the clear intention of winning, and with clearly defined political and military objectives.

3. The commitment of combat forces abroad should be a last resort.

- Establish Commanders-in-Chief (CINCs) responsibilities based on the nature of the threats, operational or functional responsibilities, not geography.

- Re-engage the American people in national security matters to avoid the "law enforcement syndrome" when Americans no longer feel the obligation to help a fellow citizen in distress but lock themselves up and dial 911 for the law enforcement "professionals" to deal with the situation. Increased emphasis on the Reserve Components and reinstating some form of draft would facilitate this process.

- Sponsor a Revolution in Business Affairs to free DOD of the tyranny of the Planning, Programming, Budgeting, and Execution System (PPBES) with its 5-year "directed economy" approach to the Service Project Objective Memorandum (POMs). We need to reduce the DOD decision cycles in order to take advantage of the explosion of technology.

- Create a Homeland Security "czar" to coordinate the efforts of consequence management for chemical, biological, radiological, nuclear, and high yield explosive acts of terrorism among federal, state, local, and non-government players.

Proposals such as these need to be discussed and vetted as alternatives to the *status quo* if we are to successfully develop a unified and shared vision in support of a new National Security Act. After a 75-year period of conflict, America is the only remaining superpower. History will be harsh in her judgment if we fail to capitalize upon this opportunity.

ENDNOTES – CHAPTER 11

1. The White House, *A National Security Strategy for a New Century*. See *www.whitehouse.gov/WH/EOP/NSC/Strategy/*.

2. Carl H. Builder, *The Masks of War*, Baltimore, MD: Johns Hopkins University Press, 1989.

3. David C. Jones, "What's Wrong With Our Defense Establishment" *New York Times Magazine*, November 7, 1982, p. 70; quoted by James L. Lacy, *Within Bounds: The Navy in Postwar American Security Policy*, Center for Naval Analyses, CNA 05 83 1178, July 28, 1983, p. 596.

4. Ashton B. Carter and William J. Perry, *Preventive Defense, A New Security Strategy for America*, Washington, DC: The Brookings Institution Press, 1999.

5. Morley Saffer, on *Larry King Live*, April 6, 1999.

6. Department of Defense, *Quadrennial Defense Review*, Washington, DC: U.S. Government Printing Office, 1997; see also *http://www.defenselink.mil/topstory/quad.html*.

7. *Transforming Defense*, National Security in the 21st Century, Report of the National Defense Panel, December 1997. See *http://www.dtic.mil/ndp/*.

8. See *www.whitehouse.gov/WH/EOP/NSC/Strategy*.

9. *Ibid.*

10. Lieutenant Colonel Christopher C. Shoemaker, *Structure, Function and the NSC Staff: An Officers' Guide to the NSC*, Carlisle, PA: Strategic Studies Institute, U.S. Army War College, 1989.

11. *Transforming Defense, National Security in the 21st Century*, Report of the National Security Panel, December 1997.

CHAPTER 12

PRESIDENTIAL LEADERSHIP AND NATIONAL SECURITY POLICYMAKING[1]

Robert D. Steele

Background

The Ninth Annual Strategy Conference, held at the U.S. Army War College in 1998, addressed the theme of "Challenging the United States Symmetrically and Asymmetrically: Can America be Defeated?" In the course of that event, a number of speakers and participants, including the author, reflected on our existing policymaking process and our existing force structure, but without making recommendations for specific changes.

In the largest sense, the Ninth Annual Strategy Conference called into question every aspect of *Joint Vision 2010* and clearly identified a need to come to grips with several asymmetric threats for which our existing force structure is not well suited as a primary defense. A summary of the conference was subsequently published and is readily available online.[2]

In the aftermath of last year's conference, and again at the invitation of the Army War College, the author undertook the task of considering and integrating three aspects of presidential leadership and national security policymaking:

1. Implications of the symmetric threat;

2. Organizational pathologies in policymaking;

3. Potential Information Solutions.

Out of that reflection and in keeping with guidance to the effect that one should seek to provoke with "big ideas" that might or might not be immediately or practically amenable to adoption, the author selected the following three ideas for presentation to the Tenth Annual Strategy Conference:

1. Four threat types need four forces after next;

2. Must modify White House staff and leadership method for three departments;

3. Need a national information strategy and a virtual intelligence community approach.

When considered together, these three ideas suggest that we must simultaneously reinvent how we think of the threat, how we organize to deal with the threat, and how we communicate both internally and externally as we make plans and execute operations to confront the threat. At root, our challenge is neither technical nor financial but rather intellectual—how do we modify our perceptions, our information collection, our information processing, and our information sharing so as to permit the president to be much more effective in understanding the threat, confronting the threat, and neutralizing the threat?

Setting the Stage.

As we consider how best to restructure the manner in which the president provides leadership with respect to national security matters as well as how that leadership is implemented, we must face three realities.

First, the Department of Defense (DoD), whatever course it is directed to follow in the early decades of the 21st century, is severely underfunded. As one distinguished former Secretary of Defense stated in congressional testimony early in 1999:

> . . . the course on which we are now embarked involves increasing strains and growing costs in the short term, and is unsustainable in the long run.

... we shall need gradually to increase procurement outlays to $100 Billion per year (from $40 Billion).

(this does not address) homeland defense . . . which) would include protection against chemical and biological weapons, protection of the critical infrastructure against cyber attacks, space control . . . and certain other areas.[3]

Of special interest to us all is the noted reference to the fact that "traditional" DoD funding shortfalls are being put forward that do not provide for homeland defense. The concepts and doctrine as well as the legislation needed to determine who is responsible for homeland defense, and how that is handled in relation to DoD as well as other departments of government, do not exist.

Second, even if the president were to choose a rational course and seek to make substantive changes in how we make policy and execute national security initiatives, it will take many years—from 5 to 25—before such change is agreed to by Congress, accepted by the public, and fully institutionalized.[4]

Third and finally, we come to the complex nature of bureaucracy. No matter what the president may decide and what Congress may legislate, ultimately it will take years to effect substantive change within the U.S. Government bureaucracy if we adhere to traditional forms of change—this paper proposes a nontraditional solution that can be implemented immediately.

Four Threat Types.

As the United States prepares to enter the 21st century there is much discussion about *Joint Vision 2010* and the "force after next." Unfortunately, the net assessment process, so well-regarded during the Cold War, has failed us. Furthermore, the Revolution in Military Affairs (RMA) is nothing more than a perpetuation of our fascination with technical solutions, and fails completely with regard to the much more complex issues of human conflict, culture,

247

history, diminishing resources, and **sustainability**. We ran out of precision munitions in 8 days during the Gulf War. The North Atlantic Treaty Organization (NATO) ran out of precision munitions for Serbian attacks in just three days. There are those who feel that our stocks of conventional ammunition for plain infantry are also severely inadequate.

The net assessments process of the 21st century will have to deal with four threat types, not one; it must be able to deal easily with both domestic or home front issues that are not obviously military in nature; and it must also deal with the **human factors** associated with avoiding as well as deterring threat conditions from arising both at home and abroad. By human factors I mean historical, cultural, social, and psychological intelligence, four forms of intelligence at which we are especially poor.

Figure 1 shows that each threat type relies on different forms of power, different forms of concealment, and different objectives. At the same time, we see that between the four **types** of threat there are also four different **kinds** of nontraditional conflict.

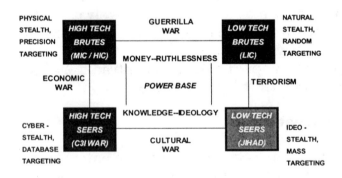

Figure 1. Four Threat Types.

248

High-Tech Brutes—The Violent State Threat.

DoD and the U.S. intelligence community dedicate the majority—well over 80 percent, if not 90 percent—of their resources to training, equipping, and organizing forces focused on dealing with the "high-tech brute," the violent state.

This warrior class relies on strategic nuclear and conventional capabilities including uniformed troops and marked equipment. It applies high-technology to achieve some physical stealth, and relies heavily on precision targeting.

This is the **only** threat that we focused on during the Cold War, and this is the threat that we understand best. Russia, China, North Korea, Iraq, India, Pakistan, and, to a much lesser extent, Cuba represent this kind of threat. The major countries in Europe, were they to become our enemies, also represent this kind of threat.

This is the **easiest** threat to monitor and the easiest threat to plan against because it is so obvious, so large, and so complex that it cannot, by and large, surprise us.

Low-Tech Brutes—The Violent Non-State Threat.

The "low-tech brute" is violent but generally does not represent a state. Transnational criminal gangs present both defense and intelligence agencies with a threat which is extremely difficult to detect in the absence of a pervasive human intelligence network. This type of threat also very "random" in nature in that it does not have obvious military goals and can rely on an unlimited fifth column of either well-paid volunteers, or volunteers recruited for one-time *in extremis* support tasks.

The low-tech brute is the most common threat to the good order and prosperity of organized states and their peoples. Unlike "low-intensity conflict" (LIC) threats for which Congress wisely created the Special Operations

Command and the new Special Operations and Low Intensity Conflict (SOLIC) Program, the low-tech brute is not state-sponsored but rather an aggregation of violent individuals who come together in random or covert ways that are extraordinarily difficult for our intelligence and law enforcement communities to detect and counter.

Perhaps more to the point, our national security structure—in policymaking terms, in acquisition terms, and in day-to-day operational capability terms—is not geared to effectively challenge this threat class.

Low-Tech Seers—The Non-Violent Non-State Threat.

This "threat" class is not inherently violent although some of its extremist elements may be. It should be viewed primarily as a challenge characterized by the unresolved and largely legitimate needs of large groups of people whose circumstances, culture, and history force them into confrontations with either established states or other non-state groups. At root, this threat class is about water, food, and freedom from fear.

Our intelligence community, with the tacit if not the active consent of our national security policymakers, has neglected this threat because it has been perceived as one that does not require the collection of secrets and one that can be adequately understood through common academic, think tank, business, and other non-governmental study.

More recently we have begun to realize the error of our ways. The Associate Director of Central Intelligence for Analysis and Production, Dr. John Gannon, has spoken publicly several times about the challenges facing us in the 2015 timeframe, and he clearly appreciates the national security implications of population growth, migration and immigration, the environment including energy and water supplies, and disease. In May 2000, the administration declared that Auto-Immune Deficiency Syndrome (AIDS) is now a national security threat. This is all to the good, but just as it took us 50 years to evolve a national security structure—including the all-important intelligence support structure—so also will it take us at least a decade, if not more, to redirect our sources and methods so as to adequately address this threat.

High-Tech Seers—The Volatile Mixed Threat.

In just the past few years, a new threat has catapulted itself to the top position in our consciousness. Although terms such as cyberwar and information warfare are in vogue, this threat is much more complex. On the one hand, we see in this threat class deliberate state-sponsored capabilities to wreak havoc with our domestic infrastructure (power, communications, transportation, and finance) as well as individual or gang capabilities to be very destructive while remaining anonymous. On the other hand, we see more subtle uses of electronic access to conduct economic espionage at the state level, "political theft" at the terrorist gang level, and plain theft at the individual level. This threat class also includes information vandalism by our own disgruntled citizens as well as outsiders, and corporate irresponsibility in failing to provide properly developed communications and computing products that are "safe" on the information superhighway.

Let us take each in turn. Winn Schwartau was the first to warn America publicly and effectively about the vulnerability of our critical infrastructures, with his books *Terminal Compromise* (1990) and *Information Warfare: Chaos on the Electronic Superhighway* (1994). I myself issued a press release in August 1994 documenting the urgent need for a $1 billion a year investment in critical infrastructure protection. We have a very long way to go before our financial, transportation, power, and communications systems are safe from attack because we have spent decades building computer-driven systems that "assumed" there was no threat other than normal

251

operational inefficiencies. The entire insurance program for such systems is geared toward "acts of God" and not acts of man. The moment one contemplates vulnerabilities to deliberate human attacks on our most fundamental electronic systems, the risk of catastrophe increases by several orders of magnitude.

We also have a grave problem in dealing with individual insider attacks against all manner of electronic systems because no one ever contemplated the possibility that a trusted employee would deliberately tamper with basic computer software and hardware. Fully 20 percent of our losses in the electronic world are attributable to insider attacks that are motivated by either dishonesty or a desire for revenge. This is four times the losses from outside attacks.[5]

Finally, we come to the whole issue of what comprises appropriate "due diligence" on the part of both the manufacturers of computer hardware and software, and on the part of organizations that install and administer electronic systems on behalf of their stockholders, employees, or members. The reality is that there are no standards today. There is nothing comparable to the accounting and other fiduciary standards for electronic systems. We are still operating our critical infrastructures on the basis of "buyer beware," or "as is" without warranty. This is completely unacceptable since the center of gravity for national security is now in the private sector—in our intellectual property and in our critical infrastructures.

Existing Organizational Pathologies.

As we contemplate presidential leadership options in the national security policymaking process, we quickly identify three major problem areas:

First, the National Security Council staff structure is too limited. It is formed along regional and issue area lines that are undeniably important, but not staffed in consonance with the emerging fault lines—the environmental element, for example, has the fewest people assigned to it, and the senior position is too easily left vacant.

Second, we have schisms among the three major Departments dealing with national security: Defense, State, and Justice. As now managed and organized, they no longer provide the United States with the most effective arrangements for: defending our population, resources and interests; for exerting necessary influence abroad; and for dealing with individual and gang threats to our prosperity and personal security. The schisms between Defense, State, and Justice are of three kinds: conceptual, financial, and informational.

1. Conceptually we have not yet devised common approaches for dealing with emerging crises such as Burundi, Somalia, Kosovo, Sierra Leone, and Sri Lanka—we are especially poor at early warning, at early resolution or deterrence, and at transitioning from diplomatic to enforcement to military means;

2. Financially we still have the bulk of the money invested in standing armies that are increasingly hollow in both personnel and technical terms; and

3. Informationally we do not have an integrated operational, resource management, or intelligence system adequate to the task of harmonizing cross-departmental inputs, decision processes, and outputs.

Third, and finally, we have a strategic vacuum overall, with no element on the National Security Council having a clear mandate and the necessary resources to marshal for the president and the Cabinet the necessary mix of private sector and other capabilities through which to achieve deep historical and cultural understandings while also assuring access to the widest possible range of multi-lingual content.[6]

Where we see major gaps in the existing White House staff structure are: with respect to policy development at the interface of external requirements and internal

253

capabilities; with respect to the deliberate introduction of "grand strategy" as well as deliberate net assessments and operational control over integrated defense, diplomatic, and transnational justice initiatives; with respect to much improved national intelligence capabilities that fully exploit open sources of information; and with respect to improved control and coordination of national investments in research.

General Organizational Changes.

Three kinds of organizational change are recommended to improve presidential leadership with respect to national security policymaking.

First, the National Security Council staffing plan needs to be modified to achieve the following objectives:

1. Provide for equal focus on each of the four threat types;

2. Provide for cross-cutting staffing between security and competitiveness issues;

3. Significantly upgrade the role of intelligence in the White House staffing process;

4. Introduce a dedicated strategy element co-equal to the policy and intelligence elements;

5. Introduce a national research element co-equal to the other elements.

Second, and this would naturally require congressional support in the form of legislation, establish the position of Secretary General for National Security. This position would have executive authority over the Secretaries of Defense and State as well as the Attorney General, and would thus be able to better realign resources and integrate programs of common interest. One of the three individuals, ideally the Secretary of State, could, if desired, be "double-hatted" as Secretary-General, if the first incumbent is to be considered a pathfinder in testing this idea.

Third and finally, we must develop an integrated Net Assessments and Operations Staff under the cognizance of the Secretary General for National Security.

These suggested changes avoid major organizational restructuring, avoid any dislocation between the existing executive structure and existing legislative authorization committees, and avoid any major new programmatic initiatives.

At root, these suggested changes are built on three simple principles:

1. Put one person in charge of the three Departments at the policy and resource level;

2. Provide for the needed day-to-day decisiveness regarding cross-departmental activities, personnel assignments, and incremental resource realignments; and

3. Provide for the needed information system integration, especially with regard to shared operational and intelligence information.

Recommended National Security Council Staff Changes.

The existing staff arrangements in the NSC handicap the president in the following ways:

1. national security and competitiveness policy are not always reconciled—some would even say never;

2. national intelligence is severely limited in its ability to exploit open sources of information and harness distributed private sector and international expertise on behalf of the president and **public** policymaking;

3. we have no global strategy office nor any means of providing continuing education to presidential appointees and their private sector counterparts—we have no effective means of "thinking in time" or across cultural and religious and ethnic boundaries;[7]

4. national research is fragmented among departments and special programs.

Block and wire diagrams are an unfortunate but necessary evil. Figure 2 is intended to illustrate some basic alterations in our concepts for approaching presidential leadership with respect to national security policymaking.

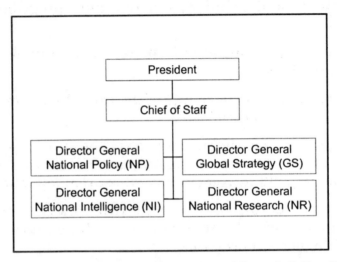

**Figure 2. Top-Level Presidential Staff
Leadership Positions.**

The most basic aspect of a new approach to presidential leadership must be reflected in the integration of national policymaking between national security and national competitiveness together with the simultaneous elevation of global strategy (more properly "grand strategy" but the pundits would take unfair advantage), national intelligence, and national research to the top table. We will discuss each of these blocks in turn.

National Policy.

Figure 3 illustrates an approach to national policymaking that provides balance between three major tracks in national policy: security, competitiveness, and treasury, while also providing for directed attention to each of the four threat types. Perhaps most importantly, each threat type has its policy counterpart in each of the three tracks.

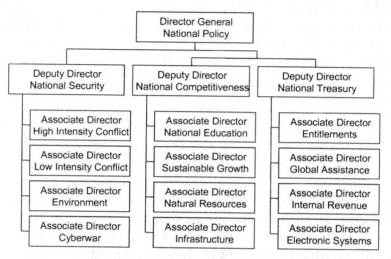

Figure 3. Balanced Approach to National Policymaking Staff.

Ideally, what will emerge out of such a staffing approach is a matrixed policy, planning, and programming process that specifically charts national treasury, national competitiveness, and national security investments in relation to one another.

A situation like Kosovo, for example, would have inspired, several years before-hand, a deliberate calculation of the costs of substantial foreign assistance to include resettlement funding intended to avoid the genocide that has occurred, versus the costs of an after-the-fact aerial bombing campaign seeking to limit the genocide and the consolidation of Serbian power.

Such a staff approach would place a very high value on understanding and utilizing non-military sources of power while also appreciating the degree to which others can use non-military sources of power to affect U.S. national security and U.S. competitiveness.

Global Strategy.

David Abshire has written an entire book on what a strategic element might look like if placed within the National Security Council.[8] His thoughts on the need for an autonomous oversight body for strategic thinking run counter to the popular misconception among policymakers that they can handle strategic thinking *en passant*.

Figure 4 suggests a distinction between broad and independent global strategizing and integrated response management. The global strategy arm is provided with international strategic council as well as a global reserve for providing recurring independent looks at long-range issues. The global strategy arm should have the flexibility to undertake special projects while also being responsible for recurring leadership retreats at which a mix of executive, legislative, and private sector leaders would review a given strategic question.

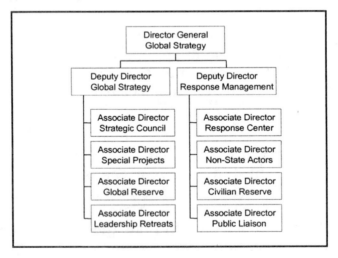

Figure 4. Enhancing Presidential Capabilities for Strategic Action.

On the response side, we move away from the popular term "crisis management" and provide for a more balanced and integrated response capability. The Response Center will interact with several nodes including the national intelligence community, Net Assessments, National Security Operations staff and others. The Response Center will be supported by subordinate elements that are trained, equipped, and organized to leverage people—a civilian reserve of experts, the mass media, and large non-state groups.

National Intelligence.

The national intelligence community, traditionally defined as those government agencies that do **secrets**, is no longer effective in supporting presidential policymaking in relation to either national security—its focus during the Cold War—or national competitiveness and electronic security, its necessary focus in the 21st century.

There is nothing wrong with the very good people or the very good process embodied in national intelligence. Where we are failing today is in our concepts, doctrine, organization, resource trade-offs, and outreach to both the U.S. private sector and to other international intelligence organizations.

In the absence of any internal reform responsive to the Aspin-Brown Commission, we must return to legislatively mandated reform, and we must engage the president in leading the charge for a complete makeover of our national intelligence community.[9]

The fundamental proposition in the Figure 5 is that our existing classified intelligence community is good and should be retained at its present funding level, but that it is not good enough to fully satisfy presidential requirements for what joint doctrine calls Relevant Information.[10] The president needs a Director General for National Intelligence who is able to leverage existing classified and routine staff capabilities while overseeing the following substantive enhancements.

259

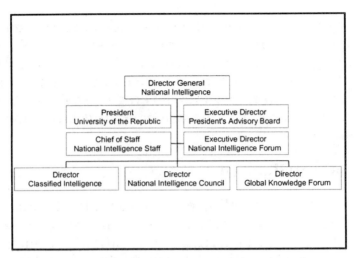

Figure 5. Enhancing National Intelligence Support to the President.

1. Elevation of the National Intelligence Council to a role co-equal to that of the entire classified intelligence community. This larger body of perhaps 60 experts would provide direct support to the president, the Cabinet, and congressional leaders.

2. Creation of a 60-person Global Knowledge Forum with a budget of between $1.2 and $1.5 billion a year with which to acquire open source intelligence on behalf of the president and the executive departments as well as the classified intelligence community.

3. Establishment of a 15-person administrative faculty for a University of the Republic charged with bringing together leadership "cohorts" across government and private sector lines.[11]

National Research.

Both national security and national competitiveness depend heavily on national research. The problems with duplicative waste (government not knowing what private sector has already mastered) have gotten out of hand, especially in the high-profile Critical Technologies arena.

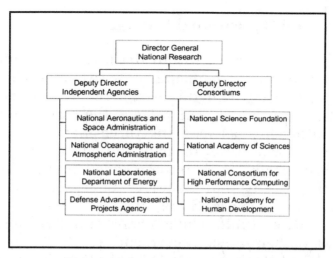

**Figure 6. Establishing Presidential Leadership
Over Research.**

Figure 6 proposes one response to this challenge. This staff element will provide for presidential leadership over research, with one half of the staff serving to better coordinate government investments in directed research, while the other half of the staff will improve the ability of government to work jointly with selected private sector partners in a variety of consortiums exempted from anti-trust actions by the Department of Commerce.

A National Academy for Human Development is suggested because the United States is spending too much money on technology and not nearly enough on human factors.

By placing this staff at the presidential level instead of the departmental level, opportunities for presidential leadership will be enhanced in other ways. The other staff elements (national security, national competitiveness, national treasury) will be better able to matrix their requirements away from the parochialism of the departments.

Cabinet and Operational Changes.

Apart from changes within the president's immediate staff, this chapter recommends only two other changes of significance. First, and this would require congressional legislation, we should acknowledge the complexity of the inter-relationship between the three major departments responsible for national security and put a "human in the loop." Specifically, it is recommended that a Secretary General for National Security be placed above the Secretaries of Defense, State, and the Attorney General. The latter three would remain members of the Cabinet and retain all of their previous prerogatives.

We must mention General Colin Powell here. Regardless of who wins the presidential election in November 2000, it would make sense to appoint Colin Powell as Secretary of State and also as the first Secretary General for National Security, with the South-Central campus, adjacent to State, as the shared national security staff facility. His stature and good will would comfort both the public and the international community as we experiment with this new system. The prestige of State would be elevated, Defense would be under control, and Law Enforcement would receive attention from a leader of great *gravitas*.

Secretary General for National Security.

The Secretary General would serve as a presidential surrogate in addressing the constant day-to-day decisions that require guidance in order to rapidly resolve issues of policy, planning, and programming within the larger context of the budget submitted to Congress by the president and appropriated by Congress for operations. No more than 10 percent of any one department's budget need be subject to administrative reallocation.

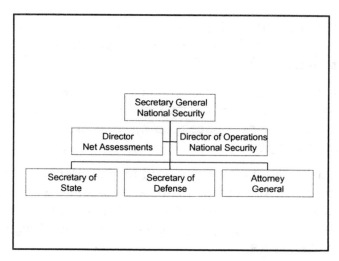

Figure 7. Enhancing Presidential Leadership for National Security.

The Secretary General would focus primarily on the larger policy issues where the secretaries themselves have not been able to come to rapid resolution, and would serve as a means of integrating national security policy making across departmental boundaries.[12]

Integrated Net Assessments and Operational Direction.

Second, the Secretary General would require both an integrated Net Assessments staff, and an integrated Operations staff. Both could be built around a very modest cadre of the "best and the brightest" drawn from each of the three departments to create truly inter-agency capabilities.

The Net Assessments staff, to be elevated above the three departments and given a substantial budget for conducting net assessments in relation to each of the four threat types (to include relative homefront vulnerabilities) would be the primary means by which the Secretary General would examine alternative options for proposing to the president new capabilities and realignments of resources between the three departments.

263

1. The existing DoD Net Assessments staff would continue to focus on conventional threats and the Revolution in Military Affairs.

2. A new element would focus exclusively on Special Operations and Low Intensity Conflict and would include a mix of paramilitary, peacekeeping, and transnational law enforcement experts.

3. Another new element would bring together experts on major religious and ethnic groups as well as environmental issues, and focus on assessments of alternative timelines and costs for precluding major clashes between large groups of non-state actors.

4. Finally, a new element would be added, which would focus upon a mix of trade and technology competition, economic espionage and information warfare.

Although the Secretary General should have the authority to realign up to 10 percent of any Department's resources in any single fiscal year, multi-year initiatives and major realignments would have to be submitted through the president's budget process and approved by Congress.

At the same time that the Secretary General would require a Net Assessments process, there would also be required a joint Operations staff. A portion of the existing Joint Staff could be assigned as the cadre for this element. Modest in size, its role would be to serve as an operational interface to the three departments, the national intelligence community, the Net Assessments staff, and the presidential staff.

This staff, also, would be organized by threat type, and help bring together inter-departmental resources applicable specifically to each threat type. A significant mission for this operational staff would be to recommend "on the fly" adjustments to departmental programs.

Budget Realignments.

Depending on who is counting what, the DoD budget ranges from $250 billion to $270 billion per year (with new construction) to over $300 billion a year (with DoD-controlled national intelligence elements). Regardless of whether or not the United States gets the additional procurement funds that many concerned leaders have advocated, some form of interim adjustment of DoD priorities must be made, to allow us to develop minimal mandatory capabilities against emerging threats.

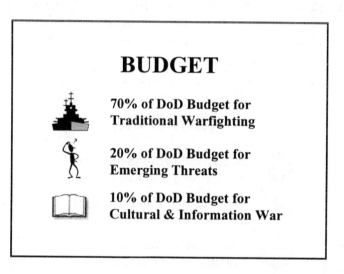

Figure 8. Leveraging the DoD Budget.

While remaining under the oversight of the armed services and national security committees, it is essential that additional funds be earmarked for emerging threats (for which a new sub-committee has fortuitously been formed this year on the Senate side) and for cultural and information war. The Emerging Threats oversight authorities in Congress will require some form of cross-over authorization authority with their counterparts on the Judiciary committees (to address special operations and transnational crime) and on the Foreign Affairs committees (to address realignments toward information peacekeeping and assistance).

Reserve and Guard Implications.

The Reserve and National Guard forces that exist today are a vestige of the past, when **generic** manpower was the critical weak link in mobilization. Utilizing the Reserve and the National Guard was primarily about **bodies**—about **manpower** and being able to supplement the active duty forces. While that aspect remains, what has really become important about the Reserve and the Guard, at least conceptually, is their ability to "bank" special skills that need not be on active duty until they are actually needed—this is about **brainpower**.

RESERVE

 Double the size of the Reserve and National Guard

 Place emphasis on foreign area knowledge and global travel

 Dramatically increase exploitation of civilian skills

Figure 9. Leveraging Private Sector Through Reserve and Guard.

Instead of fruitlessly attempting to train active duty personnel in specific foreign languages they are allowed to use for only one operational tour before returning to the normal career pattern, the United States should use the Reserve. We should create entire regiments dedicated to specific language groups (e.g., Arabic, Chinese, Russian), with each regiment having a battalion of intelligence specialists, a battalion of military police, a battalion of engineers, and a battalion of judge advocates and public affairs specialists.

With such a regiment, it would be a simple matter to rotate each company within the battalion in sequence, and in this way provide for very high quality foreign language and foreign area support. Such a regimental organization could be "virtual" in that members could be located anywhere in the world, training together just once a year, but familiar with one another through collaboration tools and online exercises, and intimately familiar with their area of interest because of their civilian employment.

The National Guard could fruitfully consider a complete make-over in which it becomes the heart of Homeland Defense, with separate battalions or even brigades trained to support law enforcement, to carry out disaster relief, and to provide for electronic security and counterintelligence. The legal restrictions on the use of the military to carry out law enforcement duties within our borders are sound, but represent an old paradigm. Those elements of the National Guard assigned to law enforcement duties should in fact be a law enforcement reserve, not a military reserve, and should have all of the training, certification, and authority of a normal law enforcement officer.

The Reserve and the National Guard would also be excellent environments within which to test new roles and relationships, as well as new legal parameters, without interfering with our active duty readiness, and without detriment to the effectiveness of our active duty forces.

Private Sector Roles and Responsibilities.

The 21st century will see a transformation in the relationship between government and the private sector, between the military and commercial providers, between law enforcement and private security companies.

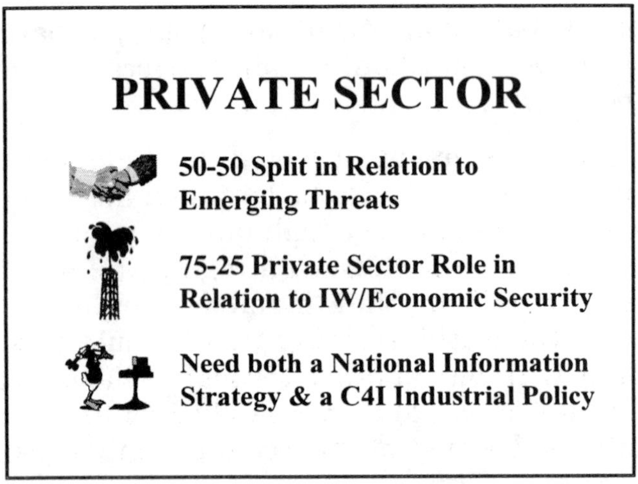

PRIVATE SECTOR

50-50 Split in Relation to Emerging Threats

75-25 Private Sector Role in Relation to IW/Economic Security

Need both a National Information Strategy & a C4I Industrial Policy

Figure 10. New Roles and Responsibilities for the Private Sector.

"Overt action" will replace "covert action" as the primary means of influencing emerging threat groups.[13] In combination with legislative incentives and insurance risk premiums as well as employee demands, multinational corporations will finally find that their best interests are served if they plan jointly with government for the achievement of selected national security objectives of mutual interest. A major task for the Emerging Threats Subcommittee in the Senate will be that of leading the discussion and definition of what these new roles and responsibilities for the private sector must be.

In relation to information warfare and economic security, it will be incumbent on Congress to pass "due diligence" legislation that places the major responsibility for self-protection on the private sector, while also requiring the communications and computing industries to live up to tough real-world standards for "safe computing."

Finally, both Congress and the Administration will have to come together to establish in carefully selected areas where consensus is achievable, both a national information strategy and a Command, Control, Communications, Computers, and Intelligence (C4I) industrial policy. We

268

have neither a national information strategy today, nor an industrial policy. The National Information Infrastructure is primarily focused on connectivity and was originally a plan to provide five selected research centers with very high bandwidth—the plan was hijacked by the civil libertarians and became a popular initiative to wire schools and businesses into the Internet. At the same time, the U.S. Government historically eschews an "industrial policy" for fear of being tarred with the brush of government interference with business. In fact, the vulnerability of America to both electronic attack and global economic instability are so great that nothing less than a coherent collaborative effort between the government (both Federal and State) and the private sector (with the knowledge and the resources) will permit us to establish a national information strategy as it pertains to homeland defense and home-based aspects of both national security and national competitiveness.

Information Strategy.

Today's decisionmaker, from the president and the Secretary of Defense down to the most junior commander, lacks both a focused collection capability for obtaining all Relevant Information, and a reliable "all-source" analysis system able to fuse secret and non-secret sources into distilled, reliable and timely "intelligence."[14] The current staff process for any decisionmaker relies almost completely on a stream of "free" inputs received from counterpart bureaucracies, international organizations, and private sector parties pursuing their own agendas. At the same time, the narrowly focused secret or restricted steam of information is often afforded direct access to the decisionmaker without being subject to in-depth staff scrutiny and proper integration with unclassified official and external information. Functionally, today's staff process lacks the organization, knowledge, and funding necessary to methodically obtain information from specific international and other non-governmental organizations or

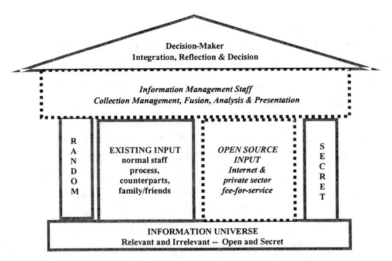

**Figure 11. Enhancing Internal Capabilities
Through Relevant Information.**

to manage the collection of original information from
external sources. Over-arching both these limitations, there
is no top-level Relevant Information analysis staff
organization that is able to provide the decisionmaker with
filtered, fused and analyzed "all-source" decision-support.
The major initiative in the early 21st century within defense
must be the restoration of command responsibility for being
properly informed, to include major procurement actions
pertaining to open sources of information.

Changing Rules of the Game.

The United States has spent decades—a half-century—
refining an information management system which
assumes that

1. secret sources and methods are the heart of our
national-level decision-support process;

2. leaders will decide and the people will follow; and

3. our most important decisions are "time-sensitive"
with relatively obvious detail.

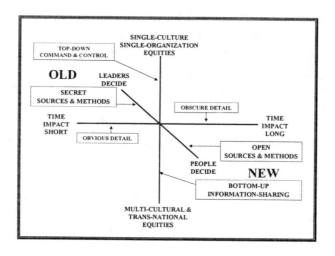

Figure 12. From "Control" to Consensus.

Our traditional construct is still applicable to many issues, but both our political environment and the information environment have turned many of our basic premises upside down. We are entering a century when the ability to master open sources—the vast flood of open sources in many languages, many mediums, many levels of detail—will be vital to public decisionmaking about very complex issues including the survival of several generations across several continents. Unfortunately, we have constrained our ability to confront the challenges of the day.

As Senator David L. Boren notes in his foreword to my book, *On Intelligence*, presidential policymaking in the future must pay much greater heed to cultural and psychological factors. Our decisions in the future must be made in partnership with non-governmental organizations, as they control the majority of the needed information and also have superior networks for achieving consensus within their chosen issue areas.[15]

What this really boils down to is a need to both think, and produce, intelligence in forms that can be shared with

271

domestic as well as international constituencies. We must, in other words, turn our own intelligence community on its head, and focus on creating a new and much enhanced community that embraces the private sector's mastery of open sources of intelligence, while refocusing our secret capabilities much more narrowly.

Building Blocks for Creating a "Smart Nation."

In the age of information, "warfare" and "national security" are at root about how a nation manages its intellectual resources. A nation's ability to discover, discriminate, distill, and digest "intelligence" is the core competency in the age of information.

Policy intelligence cannot and should not exist in isolation. To be truly effective in a networked world where the "butterfly effect" can have significant unanticipated consequences, policy intelligence needs to have four pillars: international intelligence that draws on military, coalition, law enforcement, and business as well as media sources; domestic intelligence that draws on legally and ethically available domestic sources of all kinds; strategic intelligence that deliberately draws out alternative scenarios and thinks unconventionally about both domestic and international issues; and integrative intelligence that makes sense of the other three in relation to both external threats and domestic imperatives.

The foundation for a "smart nation" is an educated citizenry. Indeed, a wise man once said that "a nation's best defense is an educated citizenry." A major aspect of any national information and intelligence strategy must be the development of architectures and protocols, including oversight standards, that nurture civic duty, educate citizens as to both the threats and opportunities facing America, and provide a means for individual citizens to contribute vital indications and warnings at every level of government.

Elements of a National Information Strategy.

Three specific elements of a national information strategy are recommended. None exists today, nor is any one of these three elements being seriously discussed at any level of government.

First, it is essential that a national strategy be devised for the digitization and preservation of content. Although our leaders have long understood that vast stores of knowledge were going to waste for lack of connectivity, the vaunted National Information Infrastructure (NII) does little to encourage the organization and enhancement of web-based knowledge. A wide variety of standards, as well as financial incentives, are required if we are to rapidly move dissertations, conference proceedings, and other mainstream publications to a web-based architecture that is properly indexed and also properly protected in terms of electronic copyright and electronic payment.

Second, it is essential that the process for developing standards for software be accelerated and also stabilized. A minimal standard for compound documents (integrated text and images) is required by law if we are to leverage the power of the Internet and the power of desktop capabilities across organizational lines. Security and inter-change standards are also required and they must be understandable by anyone with access to a computer. The current debate over Microsoft illustrates this problem perfectly—Microsoft's continued unwillingness to make its Application Program Interfaces (API) transparent and stable could be said—has been said by some—to have seriously undermined U.S. national security and national competitiveness.

Finally, we need a digital Marshall Plan as well as a digital New Deal. America lives in a glass house and is terribly vulnerable, not only to asymmetric attacks on its electronic infrastructure, but to self-generated crises caused by ignorance and a lack of global understanding. We

Figure 13. Recommended National Information Strategy.

must bring Africa, the Middle East, Asia, the Balkans, and Latin America into the 21st century, and do so in the grand manner that we evinced when saving Europe in the aftermath of World War II. At home, we must exert special efforts to empower every individual, whether schoolchild or adult with reading difficulties, so as to make our entire population, within a single generation, Internet-capable.

Elements of a DoD Information Strategy.

I have written elsewhere[16] about information peacekeeping as the purest form of war and about the central role that intelligence must play in the 21st century. It is vital for all of us to understand that in the Information Age, bytes are bullets, we are in a state of constant chaos and competition, and we require the total mobilization of all of the brain-power, all of the intellectual property, all of the information, that is in any way available for harnessing to the common good. In this era, the heart of national security and national defense lie in the domains of information and intelligence and not in the traditional domains of armed forces. DoD, however, must still take the lead.

274

This chapter suggests that DoD ask not what the president can do for DoD but rather ask what DoD can do for the president. The bottom line here is that only DoD has the resources—if managed wisely—to provide the president with the flexibility to create new methods for managing national security, and for funding new priorities that are unconventional in nature and span traditional departmental boundaries.

DoD must choose to pay the bill for this larger national construct—it must help pay the bill for a restructuring of the National Security Council; for the creation of a position of Secretary General for National Security; for the creation of four separate net assessment centers; and for the funding of modest but very valuable initiatives including a digital Marshall Plan and a digital New Deal.

DoD can set the example for how policy and operations will be managed in the 21st century by going virtual on its task forces and devising means for rapidly and readily including private sector experts—from all walks of life, all nations, with and without clearances, into its decisionmaking process.

DoD STRATEGY

$$$ Pay the bill, leverage information

 Go virtual on task forces including private sector experts, coordination, archives

 Migrate from existing C4ISR toward web-based commercial network, release best encryption to public

---

Figure 14. Recommended DoD Strategy.

At the same time, because this kind of global virtual architecture must of necessity be web-based, it is essential that DoD plan now for quickly migrating away from its existing Command, Control, Communications, Computers, Intelligence, Surveillance, and Reconnaissance (C^4ISR) infrastructure. DoD must become the champion for permitting presidential-level encryption—the best that the National Security Agency is capable of devising—into the public domain, for the simple reason that in the 21st century, the president's most important counselors and sources of insight are going to be in the private sector, not within the U.S. Government. Only DoD can lead this radical migration.

Elsewhere, in the rapid expansion of NATO with its constantly increasing number of bi-lateral Partners for Peace (PfP), we see opportunities for new forms of regional intelligence concepts, doctrine, and architectures. The PfP can be best served by having NATO move away from the U.S.-dominated C4I infrastructure that is very secret and very expensive, and adopt instead an Internet-based architecture that anyone can join at whatever their level of computer and communications sophistication.

Also in Europe we see the forthcoming demise of the Western European Union (WEU) actually sparking a very robust discussion about the need for a European intelligence policy and regional European intelligence architectures. The WEU Satellite Centre at Torrejon, having proven its value, is likely to become the centerpiece of the first-ever regional intelligence community, where selected national and even U.S. capabilities are connected "virtually" to produce regional intelligence. The United Kingdom Open Source Information Centre; the Joint Analysis Center at Molesworth, and the German pilot project to mix civilian, military, and law enforcement intelligence specialists are all candidates for virtual integration to serve both Europe and NATO.

Virtual Reach.

Figure 15 describes this new approach to information sharing. Instead of relying on a single *President's Daily Brief* as the top-level intelligence document for each day, instead of relying on a tiny cadre of grossly over-worked members of the National Security Council staff, the president, and his principals in government, will have achieved a "virtual reach" that embraces and leverages all knowledge available throughout the government (and down to the state and local governments), all knowledge available throughout the nation, including the richest possible sources of knowledge in academia, the media, and the business community, and all knowledge available globally.

We have a long way to go before we can move within this virtual intelligence community with ease. New standards and understandings will have to be developed encompassing how we share information, how we compensate one another for shared information, how we pay for selected services, and how we authenticate individuals and organizations as sources of information. This is nothing short of a major global campaign to "make sense" across national, ethnic, class, and educational boundaries. Just as the world once had to devise fuel, rail, and highway standards to facilitate global commerce, so now must the world establish information exchange and information compensation standards.

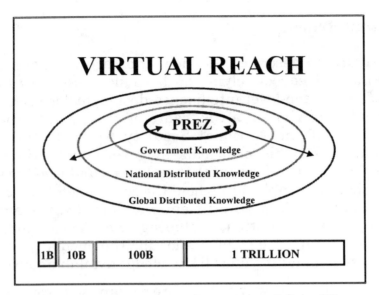

Figure 15. Creating the Virtual Intelligence Community.

Conclusion.

The conclusions to this study are straight-forward.

1. DoD leadership must empower the president—it will not work the other way around. DoD leadership, working in concert with its authorization and appropriations counterparts in the Senate and the House of .Representatives, must come to a deliberate understanding of the world, of the need, and of the means by which to empower the president and restore coherence to U.S. national security policy making and operations.

2. DoD has the funds to enable full cooperation from both the Department of State and the Department of Justice. This entire program will cost no more than $3 billion a year—$1.5 billion for a national intelligence make-over that fully integrates open sources of intelligence into Federal decisionmaking—and $1.5 billion a year for a global digital Marshall Plan that has digital New Deal elements here at home.

3. There is no need to physically restructure the government. Speaking in very practical terms, the Secretary General for National Security and all of the new elements proposed for the National Security Council can be housed in the South Central campus near the Department of State and recently vacated by the Central Intelligence Agency.

4. There will need to be a Presidential Decision Memorandum and consensus on the Hill in order to achieve legislation with the necessary statutory authority for both the new Secretary General for National Security, and several of the president's principal staff including the Director General for National Policy, Director General for National Intelligence, the Director General for Global Strategy, and the Director General for National Research.

The United States is at a juncture where the president can neither direct nor persuade. Presidential leadership in national security policymaking requires a startling leap forward, a leap that can only be financed and bureaucratically enabled by the Department of Defense. It will take a small group of like-minded leaders, but if such a group can be put into place, the rest of the department, and hence the rest of the government, will follow. Only in this way can cohesion and continuity be restored to presidential leadership and national security policymaking.

ENDNOTES – CHAPTER 12

1. The original version of this paper is at *www.oss.net/Papers/white/S99Paper.doc.* A published version is at *www.defensdaily.com/reports/securpolicy1099.htm.*

2. "TAKEDOWN: The Asymmetric Threat to the Nation," *Defense Daily Network,* December 1998, at *www.defensedaily.com/reports/takedown.htm.*

3. Dr. James Schlesinger said this to the Senate Committee on the Budget, February 24, 1999. The complete text of his remarks is reprinted in *Colloquy,* April 1999.

4. The political science literature makes reference to a 6-year period as the norm for change in organizations that desire change. Senator Daniel Patrick Moynihan (D-NY), writing in *Miles to Go: A Personal History of Social Policy*, Cambridge, MA: Harvard University Press, 1997, writes of how it takes 25 years to effect significant change in U.S. policies and the organizations and spending patterns that reflect those policies.

5. Mich E. Kabay, *The NCSA Guide to Enterprise Security: Protecting Information Assets*, New York: McGraw-Hill, 1996, Chapter 1, Figure 1, p. 11. The figure in the book is superseded by this information, provided by Dr. Kabay in personal communications to Robert Steele, OSS CEO, March 12, 1998.

6. The Clinton administration National Security Council has the following elements, in this order of priority:

Office of the National Security Advisor
Executive Secretary
African Affairs
Asian Affairs
Central and Eastern Europe
Defense Policy and Arms Control
Democracy, Human Rights and Humanitarian Affairs
Environmental Affairs
European Affairs
Global Issues and Multilateral Affairs
Intelligence Programs
Inter-American Affairs

This is actually a pretty good organization for dealing with the spectrum of defense and diplomatic issues. It can be functionally improved, especially in relation to transnational criminal and financial issues, cultural, migration and health issues, and science & technology issues. One alternative treatment of how best to improve national security policymaking in relation to home defense, finance and trade, and science and technology is provided in Stephen A. Cambone, *A New Structure for National Security Policy Planning*, Washington, DC: Center for Strategic and International Studies, 1998.

7. Richard E. Neustadt and Ernest R. May, *Thinking in Time: The Uses of History for Decision Makers* New York: Free Press, 1988, provide a valuable study of how different times provide different measures and different perspectives from which to address the same facts. They suggest these measures and perspectives should be operationalized for the White House within the global strategy unit. This same unit should also be conscious of the full range of works on clashing civilizations, cultural imperialism, religious filters, and so on. If the National Intelligence Council is the integrator of "real world" information, then

the global strategy unit must be the integrator of the intangible factors and the "wild card" aspects that tend to be set aside by the day-to-day analysts and their managers.

8. David M. Abshire, *Preventing World War III: A Realistic Grand Strategy*, New York: Harper & Row, 1988.

9. For a complete critique of our existing intelligence community and detailed recommendations on where we need to go, see *On Intelligence: Spies and Secrecy in an Open World*, AFCEA International Press, May 2000. With a foreword by Senator David L. Boren (former Chairman of the Senate Select Committee on Intelligence) and supporting blurbs from The Honorable Dick Kerr, former Deputy Director of Central Intelligence as well as several European flag officers, the book includes detailed recommendations for dramatically enlarging the scope and substantially changing the nature of the U.S. Intelligence Community. With a 50-page annotated bibliography that integrates Silicon Valley, Internet, management, and hacking books with the more traditional literature; a 62-page index; and 30 pages of proposed legislation, the National Security Act of 2001, this is a basic reference work on intelligence. Available directly from *www.amazon.com*.

10. *On Intelligence*, endnote 11, Chapter 8.

11. *Ibid.*, endnote 11, Chapter 12. Harlan Cleveland, *The Knowledge Executive: Leadership in an Information Society*, New York: E.P. Dutton, 1985, makes a compelling case for precisely this kind of "higher education" for policymakers.

12. OODA Loop: Devised by Col John Boyd, "Orient, Observe, Decide, Act." As Bill Gates has noted in his latest book, *Business @ The Speed of Thought*, New York: Time Warner, 1999, the chief characteristic of the 21st century is going to be "velocity." This point was made in the 1980s by Brigadier Simpkin in his book, *Race to the Swift: Thoughts on 21st Century Warfare*, Washington, DC: Brassey's, 1985.

13. In the early 1990s David Ignatius, then editor of the Outlook section of *The Washington Post*, wrote a very provocative piece on how overt groups were proving much more effective than covert campaigns to foster democracy and achieve other worthy goals.

14. The conventional understanding of "intelligence" as information that is inherently classified is incorrect. Data is the raw print, signal, or image. Information is data that has been collated into a

generically useful product that is generally broadcast. Both the *New York Times* and most of what is now called "intelligence" are actually unclassified or classified *information*. **Intelligence** is information that has been deliberately discovered, discriminated, distilled, and delivered to a decisionmaker in order to answer a specific question. Most intelligence is **not** classified.

15. Jessica Matthews makes this argument in "Power Shift," *Foreign Affairs,* January-February 1997.

16. *On Intelligence*, endnote 11, Chapter 10.

CHAPTER 13

CONCLUSION

Douglas T. Stuart

As this volume goes to the printer, the American people are once again engaged in the quadrennial process of selecting a new president. Whichever candidate is elected, the new commander in chief will confront daunting national security problems, many of which have been discussed in this volume. He may also have to make substantial changes in the national security bureaucracy in order to cope with these problems.

The incoming president will be able to draw on many sources of information and advice as the new administration begins to consider reconstructing the machinery for national security planning and execution. One particularly valuable resource will be the Commission on National Security/21st century, which will be submitting its Stage Three report to the Secretary of Defense in the spring of 2001. Their report will offer specific recommendations for reform of the national security bureaucracy.

The incoming president (or, more realistically, his policy advisers) will also benefit from reading this volume. If members of the next administration do pick up this book, they will find several interesting and, we believe, important points of consensus among the contributors. Three bear special mention.

First, most of the authors in this volume have either asserted or implied that 21st century threats to U.S. national security will be more complex, multifaceted, and variable than at any time in our history. These threats will provide both challenges and opportunities for a new

Administration seeking to reform national security institutions. Furthermore, to a much greater extent than in the past, these threats will be composed of both domestic and international elements. Transnational crime, which Senator John Kerry has described as the "new war," epitomizes the problem of "intermestic" threats to our national security. Arguing that the "new war" against transnational crime demands both coordinated international action and American leadership, Kerry concludes that:

> While none of us is willing—nor should we be—to give up any sovereignty; we must reexamine and, if necessary, change some laws to harmonize with a new, effective system of international law.[1]

As the president's incoming team develops plans and procedures for confronting intermestic threats to U.S. national security, they would be well advised to heed Senator Kerry's argument. But they would also be well advised to err in favor of caution as they review proposals for the application of the machinery of international war fighting to issues which have traditionally been within the purview of domestic law enforcement. Such proposals will founder on three realities:

- Public opposition to perceived infringements on the constitutionally-protected civil liberties of U.S. citizens.

- Congressional resistance to the expansion of executive authority.

- The exacerbation of existing tensions in civil-military relations.

The second point of consensus among most of the contributors to this volume is that a national security bureaucracy that was created in 1947 cannot adequately address the 21st century global security environment. Even allowing for the changes which have taken place in the national security system over the last 5 decades(successive revisions of the National Security Act, passage of the Goldwater-Nichols Act, etc.) the system is simply too slow moving and unresponsive in its processes, too "stove piped" in its structure and too narrow in its focus. Defending the national security of the United States in the age of globalization and information will require dramatic reforms to the U.S. Government's industrial age organizations and planning processes.

Several contributors to this volume have responded to these defects by recommending some form of Goldwater Nichols Act for the interagency process. To the extent that such a reform would require omnibus legislation, the incoming president may be well advised to steer clear of this kind of ambitious structural reform at the beginning of his administration. The need is certainly great, but the timing and the circumstances may not be conducive to success.

Determining the scope and timing of defense reform will be a major issue for the next administration. Harry Truman was able to work with the "damned 80th Congress" to pass the 1947 National Security Act because all parties shared a sense of emergency derived from their common experiences with Pearl Harbor and World War II. No comparable "burning platform" (to borrow William Navas' phrase) exists today.

This having been said, the incoming president should waste no time in reaching out to key members of Congress to establish new, informal procedures for dialogue on issues of national security and defense reform. As Harold Koh has observed in *The National Security Constitution*, "When Congress enacted the National Security Act of 1947, its greatest error was its failure to address its own role in the national security system."[2] The transformation of the relationship between the president and Congress in the area of national security is one of the least appreciated and most problematic aspects of the history of the 1947 Act.

Congressional punishment, or micromanagement, of the executive branch, by means of such devices as appropriations and oversight, is no substitute for productive executive-legislative consultation on issues of national security. It will not be easy for the incoming president to establish new procedures for working with members of the House and Senate, in particular because of generational and demographic changes in the makeup of Congress. But new procedures and attitudes are essential for the efficient handling of America's national security challenges. They are also a necessary first step toward fundamental reform of the national security bureaucracy for the 21st century.

The third point of agreement is that any reform of the national security bureaucracy must be guided by a coherent and compelling national security strategy. This will be an extraordinarily difficult task, due to the aforementioned complexity and fluidity of the threat environment. The problem will be exacerbated by the fact that no major power poses a near-term threat to American survival. This combination of multiple, abstruse, and asymmetric threats, and an overall environment of relative security, are not conducive to the articulation of a coherent and compelling national security strategy. But difficulty will not exempt the incoming president from the responsibility to develop such a strategy.

As the only branch of the government that has a large and well-established infrastructure dedicated to strategic planning, the Department of Defense (DoD) is in a unique position to assist the president in formulating such a strategy.

One important instrument which is available to the Secretary of Defense to help shape future discussions about national security is the congressionally mandated Quadrennial Defense Review (QDR). The 2001 QDR is currently under construction within the defense community. The primary QDR authors would be well advised to begin by accepting one of the conclusions of the Phase Two report of the U.S. Commission on National Security/21st Century: ". . . American national security strategy must find its anchor in U.S. national interests."[3] The concept of national interest is a notoriously soft and unreliable guide for foreign and defense planners, but it is also an unavoidable and indispensable precondition for thinking about national security.

The Phase Two Commission report made a very modest attempt to stimulate thinking about America's interests. So did the 1997 QDR, which sought to distinguish between vital, important, and humanitarian interests.[4] The QDR 2001 authors should consider being much more ambitious—and accord a high priority to the articulation of a coherent and compelling vision of U.S. national interests. Ideally, this vision will be specific enough to guide policy but also general enough to obtain the support of a wide cross-section of the Washington policy community and the American people.

Formulating such a list of interests will be a demanding exercise but it will also be beneficial, in three ways. First and most importantly, a well-constructed list of national interests will provide the logical basis for the QDR's proposed national security strategy. Second, a listing of U.S. national interests will stimulate national debate about America's role in the post-Cold War international system. Third, in order to develop a list of U.S. national interests, DoD will have to work closely with other executive branch agencies, including the Department of State and the National Security Council (NSC). Ideally, this exercise will result in the establishment of new procedures for, and habits of, interagency consultation and policy coordination. Until the American people, Congress, and the president are ready to pass a new National Security Act, these types of modest improvements in interagency cooperation may be the best that we can hope for.

ENDNOTES – CHAPTER 13

1. John Kerry, *The New War: The Web of Crime that Threatens America's Security*, New York: Simon and Schuster, 1997, p.187.

2. Harold Koh, *The National Security Constitution: Sharing Power After the Iran-Contra Affair*, New Haven: Yale University Press, 1990, p. 166.

3. *Seeking a National Strategy: A Concert for Preserving Security and Promoting Freedom,* April 15, 2000. The report is available on line at *www.nssg.gov/PhaseII.pdf.*

4. According to the 1997 QDR, "Decisions about whether and when to use military forces should be guided, first and foremost, by the U.S. interests at stake. . . ." The QDR is available on line at *www.defenselink.mil/pubs/qdr/sec3.html.*

GLOSSARY

ABDA	Australia, British, Dutch, American
AIDS	Auto Immune Deficiency Syndrome
API	Application Program Interfaces
BIA	Beirut International Airport
BRAC	Base Realignment and Closure
BUR	Bottom-Up Review
C^4I	Command, Control, Communications, Computers, and Intelligence
C^4ISR	Command, Control, Communications, Computers, Intelligence, Surveillance, and Reconnaissance
CCS	Combined Chiefs of Staff
CIA	Central Intelligence Agency
CIG	Central Intelligence Group
CINCFE	Commander in Chief, Far East
CINCs	Commanders-in-Chief
CJCS	Chairman of the Joint Chiefs of Staff
CPG	Contingency Planning Guidance
CSAF	Chief of Staff Air Force
DIA	Defense Intelligence Agency
DMC	Defense Management Council
DOD	Department of Defense
DPG	Defense Planning Guidance
ETO	European Theater of Operations
FBI	Federal Bureau of Investigation
FEMA	Federal Emergency Management Agency
GM	General Motors

GNA	Goldwater-Nichols Act
GNP	Gross National Product
IWGs	Interagency Working Groups
JAAF	Joint Action Armed Forces
JAAN	Joint Action of the Army and Navy
JCS	Joint Chiefs of Staff
JPC	Joint Planning Committee
JROC	Joint Resource Operations Command
JSCP	Joint Strategic Capabilities Plan
JSOs	Joint Specialty Officers
JSSC	Joint Strategic Survey Committee
LIC	Low-Intensity Conflict
MAAG	Military Assistance Advisory Group
NATO	North Atlantic Treaty Organization
NCA	National Command Authorities
NCOs	Non-Commissioned Officers
NEO	Noncombatant Evacuation Operations
NIA	National Intelligence Authority
NII	National Information Infrastructure
NME	National Military Establishment
NPD	National Defense Panel
NPR	National Performance Review
NRO	National Reconnaissance Office
NSA	National Security Agency
NSC	National Security Council
NSRB	National Security Resources Board
NSS	National Security Strategy
JCS	Organization of the Joint Chiefs of Staff

OMB	Office of Management and Budget
OODA	Observation-Orientation-Decision-Action
OPD	Operations Division
OSD	Office of the Secretary of Defense
OSRD	Office of Scientific Research and Development
OSS	Office of Strategic Services
PfP	Partners for Peace
POA	Pacific Ocean Area
POM	Project Objective Memorandum
PPB	Planning-Programming-Budgeting
PPBS	Planning, Programming, and Budgeting System
QDR	Quadrennial Defense Review
RDB	Research and Development Board
RMA	Revolution in Military Affairs
SAC	Strategic Air Command
SHAEF	Supreme Headquarters, Allied Expeditionary Force
SOLIC	Special Operations and Low Intensity Conflict
SWNCC	State-War-Navy-Coordinating Committee
SWPA	Southwest Pacific Area
UN	United Nations
WEU	Western European Union
WPD	War Plans Division

ABOUT THE CONTRIBUTORS

JOSEPH R. CERAMI, a U.S. Army colonel, is Chairman of the Department of National Security and Strategy at the U.S. Army War College, Carlisle Barracks, Pennsylvania. From 1993 to 1998, he served as Director of International Security Studies and taught the core strategy course and advanced courses on Vietnam and Congress in the Advanced Warfighting Studies Program. Colonel Cerami has held command and staff positions in the Field Artillery and as an operations and plans officer in the United States, Germany and Korea. From 1980 to 1983, he was Assistant Professor of Political Science at the U.S. Military Academy. Colonel Cerami has published articles in *Parameters, Military Review,* and *Field Artillery.* He has a B.S. in Engineering from West Point, an M.A. in Government from the University of Texas at Austin, and an M.M.A.S. in Theater Operations from the School of Advanced Military Studies, at Fort Leavenworth, KS. He is currently a Ph.D. candidate in the Pennsylvania State University School of Public Affairs.

GRANT T. HAMMOND is Director of the Center for Strategy and Technology and Professor of International Relations at the Air War College, Maxwell AFB, AL. He now teaches in the Department of Strategy, Doctrine and Airpower but was the first civilian Chair of the Department of National Security Studies at the Air War College from 1992-94 and was the first Chair of National Security Strategy, 1994-96. Dr. Hammond holds an A.B. from Harvard in Modern European History and an M.A. and Ph.D. in International Relations from the Paul H. Nitze School of Advanced International Studies of The Johns Hopkins University. He was commisioned in the U.S. Army in 1966 and served in the U.S. Army Reserve until 1977. Dr. Hammond has held fellowships from the U.S. Government (NDEA), the Woodrow Wilson Foundation, the American Council on Education, the Mellon Foundation, and the Pew

Foundation. He was elected to membership in the Cosmos Club, Washington, DC, in 1994. In addition to teaching, Dr. Hammond has held a variety of administrative posts, having served three times as a department chair, been an Associate Dean and Dean at Lenoir-Rhyne College, and also Executive Officer of the Center for International Affairs at Harvard University. He is a recognized expert in case study teaching and learning, has worked as a consultant on Capitol Hill and for SRI Incorporated, and has also been a featured speaker on creativity and leadership at conferences for American business and industry. He was a major participant in two Chief of Staff of the Air Force (CSAF) commissioned year-long studies—SPACECAST 2020 in 1993-94 and AF 2025 in 1995-96 for which he was twice awarded the Meritorious Civilian Service Award. Since joining the Air War College in 1989, Dr. Hammond has received annual awards for his lecturing, teaching, research, and writing, including the Air University Commander's Outstanding Faculty Achievement Award, 1991 and the Air War College's Outstanding Teacher, 1998-99. Dr. Hammond is a frequent guest lecturer at home and abroad on defense issues, future conflict, creative thinking, strategy, airpower and peace keeping. His first book was *Countertrade, Offsets and Barter in International Political Economy* (London: Pinter Publishers, 1990). His second book, *Plowshares Into Swords: Arms Races in International Politics, 1840-1991* (University of South Carolina Press, 1993) was reviewed by Colin Gray in *Survival* "as the book for which generations of scholars have been waiting." He has published articles in a number of journals including *Air Power Journal, Defense Analysis, Joint Force Quarterly, The Journal of Conflict Studies, Washington Quarterly, Small Wars and Insurgencies, Naval War College Review*, and the *Journal of Innovation and Management*, and contributed numerous book chapters as well. He has completed another—*The Mind of War: John Boyd and American Security*—and is working on two more, *The Cosmology of War* and *Plumber, Soldier, Statesman, Sheik: The Crises of October 1973.*

JOHN HILLEN is the Chief Operating Officer at Island ECN, Inc., an alternative trading system on Wall Street that functions as an electronic stock exchange. When he wrote this chapter, Dr. Hillen was Senior Fellow for Political-Military Studies and Special Assistant to the President and CEO at the Center for Strategic and International Studies (CSIS). Prior to coming to CSIS, he was the Olin Fellow for National Security Studies at the Council on Foreign Relations. Dr. Hillen is a former U.S. Army officer and decorated veteran of close combat in the Persian Gulf War. An Army paratrooper, he continues to serve as a reserve officer in the U.S. Special Operations Command. He received his education at Duke University, King's College London, and Oxford, where he earned his doctorate in international relations. A contributing editor at *National Review*, Dr. Hillen has published widely in many other journals and newspapers including *Foreign Affairs*, *Orbis*, *The International Herald Tribune*, *The Washington Post*, *The Wall Street Journal*, and *The Christian Science Monitor*. He has contributed to many books and is the author of *Blue Helmets: The Strategy of UN Military Operations* (Brassey's Inc) and editor of *Future Visions for U.S. Defense Policy* (CFR Press). In 1999 Dr. Hillen was appointed a member of the Congressionally mandated National Security Study Group chaired by former Senators David Boren and Warren Rudman.

DAVID JABLONSKY, a retired U.S. Army Colonel, is the Professor of National Security Affairs, Department of National Security and Strategy, U.S. Army War College. He has a B.A. from Dartmouth College in European history; an M.A. in international relations from Boston University; and an M.A. and Ph.D. in European history from Kansas University. He is the author of five books, eight monographs, and numerous book chapters and articles. Dr. Jablonsky has held the Elihu Root Chair of Strategy and the George C. Marshall Chair of Military Studies at the War College.

LAWRENCE J. KORB is Vice President and Director of Studies and holder of the Maurice Greenberg Chair at the Council on Foreign Relations. Prior to joining the Council, he served as Director of the Center for Public Policy Education and Senior Fellow in the Foreign Policy Studies Program at the Brookings Institution, Dean of the Graduate School of Public and International Affairs at the University of Pittsburgh, and Vice President, Corporate Operations at the Raytheon Company. Mr. Korb served as Assistant Secretary of Defense (Manpower, Reserve Affairs, Installations and Logistics) from 1981 through 1985. In that position, he administered about 70 percent of the defense budget. Mr. Korb is Chairman of the Board for the Committee of National Security, and a Board Member of the Washington Center, the Procurement Round Table, and the National Military Family Association. He is also a member of the International Institute of Strategic Studies, the National Academy of Public Administration, and the Aspen Strategy Group. He was a member of the Defense Advisory Committee for President-Elect Reagan (1980) and a member of the Defense Issues Group for President-Elect Bush (1988). Mr. Korb received his M.A. from St. John's University in 1962 and his Ph.D. in 1969 from the State University of New York at Albany. He has held several academic positions, among them: Assistant Professor of Political Science, the University of Dayton, 1969-71; Associate Professor of Government, U.S. Coast Guard Academy, 1971-75; Professor of Management, U.S. Naval War College, 1975-1980; and Adjunct Professor in National Security Studies, Georgetown University, 1981-93. Mr. Korb served on active duty for 4 years as Naval Flight Officer and retired from the Naval Reserve with the rank of Captain. Mr. Korb's 15 books and 150 articles on national security issues include *The Joint Chiefs of Staff. The First Twenty-five Years*; *The Fall and Rise of the Pentagon*; and *American National Security: Policy and Process*. His articles have appeared in such journals as *Foreign Affairs, Public Administration Review, The New York Times Sunday Magazine, Naval Institute Proceedings*, and

International Security. Over the past decade Mr. Korb has made over 500 appearances as a commentator on such shows as the Today Show, Good Morning America, Face the Nation, This Week with David Brinkley, the MacNeil-Lehrer News Hour, The News Hour with Jim Lehrer, Nightline, 60 Minutes, Larry King Live, and Crossfire. His op-ed pieces have appeared in such major newspapers as *The Washington Post, The New York Times, The Wall Street Journal, The Los Angeles Times, The Philadelphia Inquirer,* and *The Christian Science Monitor.*

DOUGLAS C. LOVELACE, JR., became the Director of the Strategic Studies Institute in May 2000. He holds the Douglas MacArthur Professor of Research Chair at the U.S. Army War College. His army career included a combat tour in Vietnam and a number of command and staff assignments. While serving in the Plans, Concepts and Assessments Division and the War Plans Division of the Joint Staff, he collaborated in the development of documents such as the National Military Strategy, the Joint Strategic Capabilities Plan, the Joint Military Net Assessment, national security directives, and presidential decision directives. He also was Director of Military Requirements and Capabilities Management at the U.S. Army War College. He is a graduate of the U.S. Army Command and General Staff College and the National War College. He holds an MBA from Embry Riddle Aeronautical University and a J.D. from Widener University School of Law. He is a member of the Pennsylvania and New Jersey bars. He has published extensively in the areas of national security and military strategy formulation, future military requirements, and strategic planning.

GABRIEL MARCELLA is Professor of Third World Studies with the Department of National Security and Strategy, U.S. Army War College. He served as International Affairs Advisor to the Commander-in-Chief, U.S. Southern Command, Panama, 1987-89. Dr. Marcella has written extensively on strategy, low-intensity conflict, and Latin American policy. His writings have appeared in the *Journal* of Inter-American Studies and World Affairs, Estudios Internacionales, Inter-American Economic Affairs, North-South, Analysis, Seguridad Estrategica Regional, Military Review, Parameters, Air University Review, and in various edited volumes. His most recent works include Warriors in Peacetime: The Military and Democracy in Latin America; Reconciling the Irreconcilable: The Troubled Outlook for US Policy Toward Haiti; Haiti Strategy: Control, Legitimacy, Sovereignty, Rule of Law, Handoffs, and Exit; War and Peace in the Amazon: Strategic Implications for the United States and Latin America of the 1995 Ecuador-Peru War; and The Presidential Advisory System and the Making of Latin American Policy. He is co-author/co-editor of the forthcoming book, Security Cooperation in the Western Hemisphere: Resolving the Ecuador-Peru Conflict. In addition, he has served on policy study commissions dealing with Caribbean security, Central American recovery and development, international terrorism, and U.S. interests in Latin America. His current research focuses on civil-military integration in national security decisionmaking.

CONSTANTINE MENGES, is currently a Senior Fellow with the Hudson Institute; from 1990 to 2000 he was a Professor and Director of the Program on Transitions to Democracy at the George Washington University. Having received his Ph.D. in International Relations and Comparative Politics (Soviet Union, Germany) from Columbia University, Dr. Menges has worked on Soviet, European, and other geopolitical issues as well as transitions to democracy in key world regions as a scholar, author, and senior government official. He has worked at the policy level for three U.S. presidents, most recently from 1981-86, including 3 years in the White House as Special Assistant to the President for National Security Affairs where transitions to democracy were among his responsibilities. During the 1970s, his public service responsibilities included international economic diplomacy, and he also served at the Department of Health, Education,

298

and Welfare as Assistant Director for Civil Rights and as Deputy Assistant Secretary for Education. Dr. Menges has published a large number of articles and books on foreign policy: *Spain: The Struggle for Democracy* (1978); *Inside the National Security Council* (Simon and Schuster, 1988, paperback 1989), on the President and the making of foreign policy; *The Twilight Struggle* (1990) on the foreign policies from 1979-89 of the U.S. and the Soviet Union in five regional conflicts; *The Future of Germany and the Atlantic Alliance* (1991), which explains the process of communist unraveling in Europe and conceptualizes the stages of transition to democracy; and as editor and contributor to *Transitions from Communism in Russia and Eastern Europe* (1994) and *Partnerships for Peace, Democracy and Prosperity* (1997). Articles by Dr. Menges have appeared in the *New York Times, The Washington Post, The New Republic, National Review and Commentary*; he has also appeared frequently on the national media to discuss international trends and issues. He is founding editor of the journal, *Problems of Post-Communism*. His work on foreign policy has also involved extensive experience abroad including research travel to Eastern Europe since 1961 and to the former Soviet Union since the 1970s. Dr. Menges has been a witness to a number of transforming events including: the building of the Berlin Wall in 1961 where he worked to help individuals escape; the 1968 Soviet-led invasion to suppress reform in Czechoslovakia where he worked with the non-violent resistance; and the U.S. civil rights movement where he served as a volunteer in Mississippi during the summer of 1963.

WILLIAM A. NAVAS, JR., a retired U.S. Army major general, was the Director, Army National Guard, National Guard Bureau, Washington, DC. As Director, he formulated, developed, and coordinated all programs, policies and plans affecting the Army National Guard and its more than 362,000 citizen-soldiers. Prior to this assignment, General Navas served since 1987 in a variety of senior level positions in the Department of Defense, as the

Deputy Director Army National Guard, Vice Chief of the National Guard Bureau, Military Executive of the Reserve Forces Policy Board and most recently as the Deputy Assistant Secretary of Defense/Chief of Staff for Reserve Affairs. General Navas was commissioned as a Regular Army officer in 1965 through Army ROTC from the University of Puerto Rico in Mayaguez, and first served with U.S. forces in the Federal Republic of Germany. He later commanded a Combat Engineer company in Vietnam. Captain Navas left active duty in 1970 and joined the Puerto Rico Army National Guard. Like many Guardsmen, General Navas has served in more than one branch. In the Guard he commanded Engineers at the company level and a battalion each of Military Police and Infantry. He has been an operations and training officer at battalion, brigade and State headquarters levels. As a Colonel, he commanded the first Engineer Training Exercise in Central America. His last State assignment before going to the National Guard Bureau was as Director of Plans, Operations, Training and Military Support, (G3) Puerto Rico Army National Guard. In addition to an undergraduate degree in civil engineering, General Navas holds a Master of Science in Management Engineering from the University of Bridgeport in Connecticut. He has attended numerous military schools, including the Command and General Staff College, of which he is a Distinguished Graduate (1976), and the Inter-American Defense College.

ROBERT D. STEELE is a retired Marine Corps infantry and intelligence officer. He is the founder and president of Open Source Solutions, Inc. and is an acknowledged expert on computer and information vulnerabilities. Mr. Steele holds graduate degrees in International Relations and Public Administration from Leigh University and the University of Oklahoma. He has also earned certificates in intelligence policy from Harvard University and in defense studies from the Naval War College.

DOUGLAS T. STUART holds the Robert Blaine Weaver Chair in Political Science and is Director of the Clarke

Center for the Interdisciplinary Study of Contemporary Issues at Dickinson College. He is also an adjunct professor at the U.S. Army War College. He received his Ph.D. in International Relations from the University of Southern California in 1979. Dr. Stuart is the author or editor of five books, four monographs, and over 25 published articles dealing with international affairs. His areas of research specialization include U.S. European security relations, and Asian security and arms control. He is a member of the editorial board of Westview Press ("Dilemmas in World Politics" series), a Councilor with the Atlantic Council (Washington, DC), and a member of the International Institute for Strategic Studies (IISS, London) and the Italian Institute for International Affairs (IAI, Rome). Dr. Stuart is a former NATO Fellow, and a regular lecturer at the U.S. Army War College. During the 1989-90 academic year, he was a visiting scholar at the Brookings Institution in Washington, DC. In 1994, Dr Stuart completed a 2-year research project on the future of European security (sponsored by the Ford Foundation) and began an 18-month project under the auspices of the IISS to establish guidelines for American military policy in post-Cold War Asia. This research resulted in an Adelphi Paper in early 1996. In the summer of 1996, Professor Stuart began work on an ongoing project relating to the 1947 National Security Act and its ramifications for U.S. foreign and security policy making. During his 1997-98 sabbatical, he undertook research relating to this topic while serving as a visiting scholar at the Elliott School of International Affairs, George Washington University, Washington, DC. Dr. Stuart received Dickinson's Ganoe Award for Inspirational Teaching in 1992, and its Distinguished Teaching Prize in 1996.